P9-CFI-023

## THE AUTHORS

LEONARD L. BAIRD is senior research psychologist at the Educational Testing Service in Princeton, New Jersey.

RODNEY T. HARTNETT is senior research psychologist in the Higher Education Research Group at the Educational Testing Service.

The other authors are identified in the front of the book.

# Understanding Student and Faculty Life

*Using Campus Surveys to Improve Academic Decision Making*

# Leonard L. Baird
# Rodney T. Hartnett
# and Associates

# Understanding Student and Faculty Life

Jossey-Bass Publishers

San Francisco • Washington • London • 1980

UNDERSTANDING STUDENT AND FACULTY LIFE
*Using Campus Surveys to Improve Academic Decision Making*
> by Leonard L. Baird, Rodney T. Hartnett, and Associates

Copyright © 1980 by: Jossey-Bass Inc., Publishers
433 California Street
San Francisco, California 94104
&
Jossey-Bass Limited
28 Banner Street
London EC1Y 8QE

**Library of Congress Cataloging in Publication Data**

Baird, Leonard.
  Understanding student and faculty life.

  Bibliography: p. 269
  Includes index.
  1. Universities and colleges—United States—
Evaluation. 2. College environment—Evaluation.
3. College students—United States—Psychology—
Evaluation. 4. College teachers—United States—
Psychology—Evaluation. I. Hartnett, Rodney T.,
joint author. II. Title.
LB2328.B27          378.78                    79-24863
ISBN 0-87589-443-7

Manufactured in the United States of America

JACKET DESIGN BY WILLI BAUM

FIRST EDITION

*Code 8003*

*The Jossey-Bass Series
in Higher Education*

# Preface

————————•·❦·•————————

This book is about a relatively new kind of information that can help administrators, professors, and students make better choices, act more effectively, and evaluate the success of their activities more accurately.

*Understanding Student and Faculty Life* shows how environmental assessments can assist academic decision makers by providing facts about many critical aspects of their institution, including the extent and quality of the communication among its members, their sense of community, their emphasis on academic rigor, and the power of the campus bureaucracy. Some of these assessments ask students, teachers, or administrators to describe the people in their college or its environment in relatively neutral ways to provide as objective a view of the institution as possible. Other assessments ask people to evaluate their college's environment judgmentally and to offer opinions about possible changes in it. Still others assess specific campus characteristics such as student-faculty interaction by means other than collecting individual perceptions and opinions. This book, for the first time, brings together comparative information about these several types of assessments and discusses their relative strengths and weaknesses for practical action and institutional improvement.

In Chapter One, Leonard Baird describes the history, uses, and importance of campus surveys. These techniques can provide a student-generated information base for administrative decision making, which Alexander Astin advocates in Chapter Two. They can also be adapted to analyze various campus groups and thus shape the parts of colleges and universities, as Robert Pace notes in Chapter Three. In Chapter Four, Rodney Hartnett shows how extensively faculty environments for research and teaching vary and how these variations can be assessed. Environmental assessments that supply social and economic information can also help colleges set their long-range goals and achieve their objectives, as Norman Uhl explains in Chapter Five. Richard Anderson in Chapter Six shows how interinstitutional data can be used to evaluate major policy decisions, such as whether to maintain or drop the institution's religious affiliation and whether to remain a single-sex institution or go coeducational. In Chapter Seven, Francis Wuest and Robert Jones show how studies of college environments can become embroiled in campus politics, and they offer first-hand advice about how to avoid such imbroglios. Baird offers guidelines for choosing the best assessments and procedures in Chapter Eight, and Baird and Hartnett present a compendium of basic information about available assessment measures in the final chapter.

All in all, the contributors to this book show the present and potential uses of environmental information in a variety of academic contexts. They demonstrate that the thirty-five years of research on campus environments have increased our understanding of how colleges operate and educate—and how they could be more effective. Comparable efforts to measure the characteristics of individuals have a history at least twice as long: at the minimum seventy-five years, if we ignore the 2,000 years of Chinese Imperial examinations. It is not unreasonable to expect that we can improve the measurement of college environments and that our understanding of environments will soon equal our understanding of individuals.

*Princeton, New Jersey*                              LEONARD L. BAIRD
*September 1979*                                       RODNEY T. HARTNETT

# Contents

———•⌒∞⌒•———

xiii

# The Authors

---···‹∞›···---

LEONARD L. BAIRD is senior research psychologist at the Educational Testing Service in Princeton, New Jersey. For the past fourteen years he has conducted studies of educational environments, the prediction of academic success, testing, the entrance of students into higher education, and graduate and professional education.

RODNEY T. HARTNETT is senior research psychologist in the Higher Education Research Group at Educational Testing Service, Princeton. His research and writing during the past several years have been in the areas of program evaluation in higher education, educational environments, student development, and graduate education.

RICHARD E. ANDERSON is assistant professor of higher education at Teacher's College, Columbia University, and coordinator of the Joint Degree Program in Higher Education Administration at Columbia University.

ALEXANDER W. ASTIN is professor of higher education at the University of California, Los Angeles; president of the Higher Education Research Institute; and director of the Cooperative Institutional Research Program.

ROBERT G. JONES, formerly professor of sociology at the University of Virginia, is now a practicing attorney in Virginia Beach, Virginia.

C. ROBERT PACE is professor of higher education in the Graduate School of Education at the University of California, Los Angeles.

NORMAN P. UHL is associate vice-chancellor for Academic Affairs, for Research, Evaluation, and Planning, and professor of education and psychology at North Carolina Central University in Durham, North Carolina.

FRANCIS J. WUEST is program director, Center for Professional Development, Kansas City Regional Council for Higher Education.

1      *Leonard L. Baird*

# Importance of Surveying Student and Faculty Views

————————•⟨∞⟩•————————

- A college president who has achieved many reforms at her college wants to know if these reforms have changed the social and intellectual atmosphere.
- A high school senior choosing colleges wants to know what they are really like.
- A university provost wants to know how students and faculty feel about the university's programs and facilities so that needed changes can be made.
- A dean of students who has organized an experimental living group program in the dormitories wants to know if the academic

experiences of the students in the group are different from those of other students.
- A counselor working with potential dropouts wants to know why these students feel turned off by the college.

Each of these people needs information to make decisions. They need information about the complexities of an institution's *environment*—that is, the interplay among its people, processes, and things. Important aspects of a college's environment are the perceptions, expectations, satisfactions, and dissatisfactions of the people who make up the college community. Information about the college environment is a critical addition to the knowledge of most decision makers about their institution, which is often limited to their personal experience and intuition and those of the relatively few members of the college community with whom they meet or communicate. An understanding of how their college works, how it differs from other colleges, how the members perceive its realities, and how they react to their perceptions is important so that decision makers can avoid actions that would be detrimental to their college. Administrators and faculty members can use environmental information to compare their institution with similar colleges in order to identify areas where changes are needed, to make suggestions about how to improve the environment, and to measure the effectiveness of these changes. Also, this information can be used to identify areas of agreement and disagreement among an institution's significant subgroups and subenvironments about policies, goals, facilities, and priorities.

Students can use environmental information in deciding which college to attend and to learn what to expect from their college experience so that they can adapt to the college more easily. And institutional researchers and scholars of education can use environmental information to help understand the influence of college on postadolescent socialization and personal development, to assess interpersonal relations on the campus, to measure the conditions surrounding learning, and to analyze the relations among students, professors, and administrators.

This volume shows how these various functions can be carried out by using a variety of complementary approaches and techniques for assessing the environment. The purpose of this first chapter is to describe and illustrate the variety of approaches that has developed over the years. Recognition of the need to assess college environments has grown throughout this century. Early attempts to assess basic institutional data eventually led to extensive survey research in the 1950s and 1960s that was designed to gather student and faculty observations and opinions about college characteristics. That work, continued to the present, has resulted in at least five different approaches or techniques discussed here, including interpretive, reputational, perceptual, and stimulus methods.

## Simple Institutional Data

The first recognition of the need for better information about colleges stemmed from the problems faced by students choosing among colleges in the early decades of this century, when most students had to rely on folklore, informal opinions of acquaintances, and propaganda from the colleges.

As colleges and enrollments grew in the 1920s, 1930s, and 1940s, teachers and counselors as well as students and parents realized the complexity of choosing a college and sought systematic information about colleges. As a result, the first comparative guides were published, which attempted to provide systematically information about a large variety of colleges. The first truly comprehensive guide, *American Universities and Colleges* (published by the American Council on Education in 1928), summarized basic facts about 400 accredited institutions. Now in its tenth edition, the guide includes a brief description of each college's general features, history, governance, calendar, admissions requirements, degree requirements, teaching staff, special programs, fees, financial aid, enrollment, student life, library, finances, and buildings and grounds, as well as, in some cases, the academic ability of freshmen. More than 1,250 institutions are described.

*The College Handbook,* published much later by the College Entrance Examination Board, includes similar information plus detailed data about the academic ability of incoming freshmen. These and other guides provide a great deal of information that students can use to choose a college. But the information in such guides remains unanalyzed and uninterpreted. There is no easy way for a student or a counselor to know what information is critical and what the college is really like, particularly from the colleges' descriptions of themselves. Moreover, the guides do not compare colleges on any common dimensions other than academic selectivity. Thus, while immensely better than the opinions of high school friends and teachers, the guides do not allow students to compare colleges on clearly defined and measured dimensions.

The inadequacies of guidebook data can be made clearer with an example. Consider a high school student in California who has an excellent chance of being admitted to one of the nine campuses of the University of California and who has narrowed the choice to two campuses—the University of California at Irvine and the University of California at Los Angeles—because of their programs related to ecology. Here is how *The College Handbook* describes the undergraduate programs and student life for each (College Entrance Examination Board, 1977, pp. 123–124):

### University of California at Irvine

Curriculum. Undergraduate degrees offered: Bachelor's. Major fields of study: Area studies (comparative culture), biological sciences (biology), computer and information sciences (general), engineering (general), fine and applied arts (general fine arts, art, art history and appreciation, music-performing/composition/theory, dramatic arts, dance), foreign languages (French, German, Spanish, Russian), health services and paramedical technologies (nursing-practical), letters (general English, comparative literature, classics, linguistics, philosophy), mathematics (general), physical sciences (general physics, general chemistry), public affairs and services (social ecology), social sciences (general, history).
Special academic programs: Work-study, study abroad, cross-registration with University of Southern California in ROTC program. Special remedial services: Preadmission summer program, reduced course load, remedial instruction, tutoring, special counselor. Military training: Air Force ROTC. Tests used for counseling, placement, or credit: Placement, credit, or both will generally be given for

grades of 3 and higher in AP Examinations. Credit will generally be given on basis of CLEP General and Subject Examinations. English Composition ACH used for freshman English placement. Academic regulations: Freshmen must earn minimum grade-point average of 2.0 to continue in good academic standing.

Student Life. 1976 freshman class: 1,157 men, 997 women. 96 percent from in state, 41 percent live in college housing, 46 percent live with family, 13 percent live in private housing, 22 percent have minority backgrounds. Programs undergraduates choose: Arts and science 85 percent, engineering 7 percent, fine and performing arts 8 percent. Student activities: Student government, student newspaper, radio, film, drama, choral groups, opera, musical theater, dance, symphony orchestra, concert band, pep band, Black Student Union, Chinese Association, Kababayan, Moviemiento, Estudiantil Chicano de Aztlan, Women's Center, fraternities, sororities. Athletics: Baseball, basketball, cross-country, football, golf, handball, ice hockey, rowing, rugby, sailing, softball, swimming and diving, tennis, track and field, volleyball, water polo. Student services: Counseling, health services, employment service for undergraduates, placement service for graduates, learning skills center, cross-cultural center, office of veterans affairs, international student adviser.

### University of California at Los Angeles

Curriculum. Undergraduate degrees offered: Bachelor's. Major fields of study: Area studies (East Asian, Russian and Slavic, Latin American, Middle Eastern, general European, West European, ancient Near Eastern civilizations, Jewish studies), biological sciences (biology, bacteriology, biochemistry, kinesiology), business and management (business economics), communications (general), engineering (general, geological), fine and applied arts (art, art history and appreciation, music-liberal arts, dramatic arts, dance, applied design, cinematography), foreign languages (French, German, Italian, Spanish, Chinese, Japanese, Latin, classical Greek, Hebrew, Arabic, Scandinavian languages, Slavic languages, African languages, Portuguese), health professions (nursing, public health), interdisciplinary studies (general liberal arts and science, folklore and mythology, ethnic arts, cybernetics), letters (general English, classics, linguistics, philosophy, religious studies), mathematics (general), physical sciences (general physics, general chemistry, astronomy, atmospheric sciences and meteorology, geology, geophysics and seismology, geography-ecosystems), psychology (general, psychometrics, psychobiology), social sciences (anthropology, economics, history, geography, political science and government, sociology, Afro-American studies, Mexican American cultural studies, Asian-American).

Special academic programs: Honors program, independent study, work-study, study abroad. Special remedial services: Remedial instruction, tutoring, special counselor. Military training: Air Force ROTC, Army ROTC, Navy ROTC. Tests used for counseling, placement, or credit: Placement, credit, or both will generally be given for grades of 3 and higher in AP Examinations. Credit will generally be given on basis of CLEP General and Subject Examinations. Maximum of 15 quarter hours of credit by examination may be counted toward degree. Academic regulations: Freshmen must earn minimum grade-point average of 2.0 to continue in good academic standing. 80 percent of freshmen complete year in good academic standing.

Student Life. 1976 freshman class: 3,783 men and women. 96 percent from in state, 23 percent live in college housing, 32 percent live with family, 45 percent live in private housing, 30 percent have minority backgrounds. Enrolled freshmen have average SAT-verbal score of 489 and average mathematical score of 550. Programs undergraduates choose: Arts and science 22 percent, engineering 8 percent, fine and performing arts 6 percent, health services 1 percent, humanities 9 percent, life sciences 19 percent, physical sciences 9 percent, social sciences 26 percent. Student activities: Student government, student newspaper, magazine, yearbook, radio, television, film, drama, choral groups, opera, musical theater, dance, symphony orchestra, marching band, concert band, fraternities, sororities. Athletics: Archery, badminton, baseball, basketball, bowling, cross-country, fencing, football, golf, gymnastics, handball, racquet ball, rifle, rowing, rugby, soccer, softball, squash, swimming and diving, table tennis, tennis, track and field, volleyball, water polo, wrestling. Student services: Counseling, health services, employment service for undergraduates, placement service for graduates.

From these descriptions the student can see that UCLA has more students and more programs and that more Irvine freshmen live in college housing. But not all related information is presented in comparable ways. For example, although the percentages of students enrolled in arts and sciences fields at both institutions are actually the same, the UCLA description breaks this percentage into more specific categories. Thus, a student might draw an inaccurate conclusion about UCLA's arts and science emphasis. But more important, the student would have to work hard to find information on other important factors in his or her decision, such as student and faculty concerns and activities that make up the ethos, culture, or "life" of the campus.

Furthermore, while such guides can sometimes help a student choose a college, the information they contain is irrelevant to the decisions faced by people within the college. Administrators cannot use it to make the institution more efficient or effective, nor could counselors use it to study their college's influence on students' values, vocational choices, or intellectual growth. For these purposes, other approaches to environmental information are needed.

### Factual Measures

One system analyzes factual information about college environments in terms of various theoretical or empirical ideas. For example, Astin and Holland (1961) developed the Environmental Assessment Technique (EAT), which is based on the assumption that a college's environment depends on the personal characteristics of its students, faculty, administration, and staff. Thus, as Astin explains (1972a, p. 1):

> Since the undergraduate's personal contacts are chiefly with fellow students, it is further assumed that the major portion of the student's environment is determined by the characteristics of his fellow students. Accordingly the environment was defined in terms of eight characteristics of the student body: average intelligence, size, and six personal orientations based on the proportions of the students in six broad areas of study.

The six personal "orientations" of students were based on Holland's theory of vocational choice (1973) and were estimated by using the percentages of students majoring in "realistic" (technical) fields, scientific fields, social fields, "conventional" (clerical) fields, "enterprising" (business and sales) fields, and artistic fields.

This relatively simple system of comparing facts about colleges led to a number of correlational studies. For example, Astin and Holland (1961) found that their EAT variables correlated with the perceptions of students about their institutions, with the average intelligence of students strongly related to "understanding" as measured by the College Characteristics Index, and enrollments in technical fields related highly negatively with its Humanism scale. And Astin (1963a) showed that an institution's size correlated with seniors' ratings of faculty contacts, with students at large colleges tending to report that they seldom saw professors. Most of these correlations were both sizable and plausible. Altogether, Astin and Holland marshaled substantial evidence that these several characteristics of the student body have a considerable influence on student life. Other scholars used these characteristics in a wide variety of other studies, such as that by Rock, Baird, and Linn (1972) regarding the influence of the environment on student achievement and knowledge. (For a review of these studies and findings, see Holland, 1973.)

More recently, Richards, Seligman, and Jones (1970) modified the EAT strategy to derive measurements of school environments by counting the number of courses and the number of faculty members rather than using the proportions of students in the six types of fields derived from Holland's theory. In the same study, Richards, Seligman, and Jones derived similar measures for graduate school environments—graduate faculty, graduate curriculum, and graduate degrees classified into the six types.

Another factual strategy, originally used by Astin (1962), is to employ the statistical technique of factor analysis to examine and summarize institutional information found in college directories and fact books, such as tuition and the number of books in the library per student. Astin compared some thirty-three characteristics of four-year colleges and obtained six dimensions that accounted for many of the differences (technically, 80 percent of the variance) among the colleges: affluence or wealth, size, private versus public control, proportion of males in the student body, technical emphasis, and homogeneity of curriculum and EAT scores. He then used these six measures to show, for instance, that very bright students were less likely to aspire to the Ph.D. degree in large colleges, predominantly male colleges, and colleges emphasizing clerical curricula (Astin, 1963b).

Astin's factor analytic strategy was used by Richards, Rand, and Rand (1966) on junior colleges to identify six somewhat similar factors: cultural affluence, technological specialization, size, age, transfer emphasis, and business orientation; Richards and Braskamp (1969) showed that these factors were related to a wide variety of student characteristics. Subsequently, Richards, Rand, and Rand (1968) used the same strategy with medical schools and found four factors that accounted for most of the differences in their characteristics: affluence, Canadian versus United States admissions practices, size, and hospital-training emphasis.

More recently, Astin (1977) studied the influence of different types of colleges on students' development, using a typology of fifteen types of institutions, such as very selective, private, nonsectarian, four-year colleges; nonselective, Protestant, four-year colleges; public, two-year colleges; and predominantly black colleges. The results showed that different types of colleges had quite different impacts on students. For example, contrary to educational folklore, the academic self-confidence of students in very selective colleges is not depressed even though these students do become more self-critical, presumably because of the high intellectual standards of these colleges.

These factual measures of environmental characteristics have clearly been useful in research studies. They are inexpensive to use, since they do not require the administration of survey instruments; they describe colleges in parsimonious terms; they can be obtained for all colleges, as Astin (1965) has done; they show relations to environmental measures based on other approaches; and they can be used to test theoretical predictions (Holland, 1968; Astin, 1972b). Studying the influence of the "fit" between students

and their college with respect to their vocational choices and satisfactions, these researchers obtained findings that supported Holland's theory of career development.

In addition, factual measures can help students choose appropriate colleges, as Astin's 1965 book *Who Goes Where to College?*
sought to do by providing students with comparative scores for all
four-year colleges. However, student use is limited by the varying
accuracy of the scores. And as useful as factual measures are in
showing how colleges differ, they offer little help to administrators
who would like to assess or improve their campuses, because factual
measures alone offer little to aid our understanding of influential
differences between colleges. We must understand as well the conditions that factual characteristics create, as Feldman and Newcomb (1969) have emphasized, and we must account for these conditions so that we can know what will make our colleges reach their
goals more effectively. Thus, research has shown that large colleges
tend to be impersonal and bureaucratic but to offer more facilities
and options compared with small colleges, but what programs will
best allow a large institution to become more personal while retaining the quality and variety of its offerings?

## Interpretive Approaches

Another approach that has been used in many books written
about colleges in the last two decades is based on the observations
and interpretations of expert investigators who describe the main
features and characteristics. Like anthropological observers, the
investigators attempt to apply their general knowledge of social,
educational, and organizational structures to a particular situation.
Thus observers of higher education like James Cass and Max
Birnbaum began to write guides containing capsule descriptions of
colleges based on institutional information, such as that presented
in the American Council on Education or College Board guides,
but supplemented by ideas gleaned from the catalogues, the student newspapers, and campus visits. These interpretations occasionally described very unusual college environments quite accurately, but they were and are at best only a rough guide to most
colleges. To illustrate one such guide, "written by students, for

students," the descriptions are provided of UCLA and Irvine in the 1976–77 edition of *The Insiders' Guide to the Colleges,* compiled and edited by the staff of the *Yale Daily News* (1975, pp. 71, 75–77).

*University of California at Irvine*

The campus at *Irvine* is located in Orange County—which says a lot. For Orange County, one of the most conservative counties outside the Deep South, is the home of Disneyland, San Clemente, and the John Birch Society. Although Irvine does not fit in in any way, shape, or form, between the poles of Walt Disney and Richard Nixon, it is also a long way intellectually and ideologically from Berkeley. Irvine's superficial liberalism is one reason why Irvine students are not exactly *persona grata* in the surrounding community.

Academically, Irvine is an interesting and exciting place with a host of young professors who are often more innovative than their students. The anthro and social science departments attempted a unique experiment—they set off a little plot from the rest of the campus (called "the farm") and imported a Colombian family to live on it in their natural habitat.

Most of Irvine's academic alternatives are far less offbeat. By building up outstanding biology and psychobiology (neurochemistry, neuroanatomy, and neurophysiology departments) faculties, the school has become a gathering place for premed types of late. The schools of social science and social ecology have also maintained "progressive and innovative" reputations.

Undeniably, Irvine has its disadvantages. A whopping 87 percent of its students commute. Little organized community social life exists, and a car is a must to escape Irvine on the weekends. For entertainment, many go to Balboa Island which is far from being a peanuts-and-crackerjack sort of place. Of course, some of the best surfing beaches in the southland are only miles and minutes away.

*University of California at Los Angeles*

Don't expect to meet the next Bill Walton in any of your UCLA classes. Don't expect to meet anyone, for that matter. UCLA may be the only school in the country with more parking structures than classroom buildings.

An exaggeration, of course, but you get the idea. UCLA is huge, and was probably the original inspiration for the notion that large universities are impersonal. Most undergraduates are from Los Angeles (with the exception, of course, of the football and basketball teams). Those who still live at home, and a great many do, tend to remain faithful to their high school cliques with very little wandering afield. Some, in desperation, move on campus; into dorms or fraternities, just so they can meet some new people.

Most students here find that they meet no one in class. For one thing, many classes are huge. There are exceptions, certainly, particularly in more relaxed areas such as art, foreign languages, theater arts, or women's classes. But for the most, lecture courses, with grad students leading discussion sections of erratic quality, are the rule. A popular psychology class draws 800, with hundreds of others unable to register. Naturally, sitting in a different seat every day, and feeling more like strangers than fellow travelers, the UCLA student meets no more people than he might at a movie or other well-attended public function.

As if size wasn't enough of a disadvantage, the atmosphere itself is highly impersonal. Some students, knowing what they are in for, apply just so they will never have to come face-to-face with a professor. That anonymity will not be challenged for the simple reason that it is impossible with such volume. Many students feel scared to consult a professor who has just lectured to 800 students. Partly as a result of this attitude, the professors are not nearly as busy seeing students personally as they should be, and as many assume they are.

If the undergraduate feels lost amidst a maze of activity and purpose that seems not to concern him, it is probably because he is. UCLA is remarkably active in the community. Far more goes on there than mere undergraduate education. The graduate schools, particularly law and medicine, are well respected. University Extension offers many highly worthwhile and innovative courses open to the entire community. The theater arts department may be the best in the nation; excellent film festivals and dramatic presentations are the result. Well-attended top name concert series, the justly famous athletic teams (which need no further mention), an excellent hospital, extensive science facilities, an experimental elementary school, and community-related projects in the social sciences serve far more than the student community.

These are all available to the undergraduate, as is the city of Los Angeles, which receives more criticism than it deserves from almost everyone, including its residents.

Academic overstimulation is not a feature of UCLA. Science majors have been known to work hard, some very hard indeed, in the quest of a med school acceptance. Over all, UCLA education is about average.

Some of the dorms are fairly decent, offering a wide variety of possibilities, particularly in the high-rise apartment life-style. Westwood rent is notoriously high, and the immediate campus community is somewhat frat-jock-LA-freak-oriented. Many prefer to make a new life for themselves within driving distance of campus, but out of its sphere of influence, thus ignoring the University as much as possible, while taking advantage of the city itself. At UCLA, that's not all that bad an idea.

The poorest examples of this interpretive approach include other "inside colleges" books; the best examples are the insightful analyses of some social scientists whose realistic descriptions point out the complex interactions among the multitude of personal and social variables of a college. However, this interpretive approach cannot readily be quantified, seldom leads to consistent judgments, and is costly and time consuming (since a thorough study requires living in the environment for some time). Finally, the results greatly depend on the knowledge and awareness of the investigator, which can vary greatly, not only from person to person but from college to college and occasion to occasion.

For example, even such astute observers as Riesman and Jencks can misinterpret an environment. In 1962 they described San Francisco State as a quiet, docile, unstimulating commuters' campus (p. 163):

> Faced with an idea, only a few students will pursue it with excitement, but neither will they reject or resent it. Rarely are they interested in brooding on their studies, but are at least willing to assimilate the subject-matter put before them. . . . Intellectual indolence inevitably thrives among physically exhausted students who simply look blank if they are asked what they do with their leisure time.

As Pace (1968) has pointed out, their description of the campus environment was inaccurate: measures of students' perceptions of the campus at the time showed that students found the campus a stimulating and activist environment, as the turbulent events on the campus in subsequent years revealed. In brief, the method of using the observer's impressions seems unreliable as well as impracticable on a large scale.

## Reputational Approaches

One of the oldest approaches to assessing colleges has been the effort to rank them according to prestige or quality. Lists of the "best" institutions have been produced for many years. Usually these have been the work of a single person or a few individuals who have gathered together institutional information, personal impressions, and academic scuttlebutt, although they have sometimes examined such criteria as the academic qualifications of the faculty and the nature of the facilities. This approach is still being used by Gourman (1977), who purports to rate not only the overall quality of American and foreign institutions but also their quality in specialized fields, ranging from aerospace engineering to music, to speech pathology and audiology, to zoology. In addition, he rates the quality of premedical and prelaw curricula, scholarship programs, trustees, administration, student services, and even the balance between academic and athletic programs.

Obviously, no individual or small group of individuals has the knowledge or ability to make these kinds of ratings accurately. No one can know the quality of programs in every field well enough to judge them all or even to provide a very good estimate of the overall quality of an institution. Perhaps most important, such judgments tend to be unidimensional—concentrating almost entirely on the academic reputation of the institution or its selectivity in terms of admissions. Colleges with famous instructors or high average SAT scores among their students can nonetheless be dismal places for many students—places where many students do not grow personally, socially, or even intellectually. In short, there is no direct correspondence between prestige ranking and educational excellence.

A more systematic use of a reputational approach has been developed to assess quality in graduate and professional education. It involves asking a sample of professors in each field to rate the programs in their own field—for example, to rate the quality of the graduate faculty and the attractiveness of their program to prospective graduate students—and then averaging the ratings. (Clark, 1976, reviews the procedures used in these studies and their drawbacks.) Such studies were conducted by Cartter (1966) and by Roose and Andersen (1970). These were followed by ratings of professional schools (Blau and Margulies, 1974) and by ratings of departments and professional schools (Cartter and Porter, 1977).

As an illustration of these ratings, Table 1 lists the ten top-rated American graduate departments in three fields, based on ratings of the quality of the faculty. The raters in each field were department chairpersons, senior scholars, and young scholars in graduate departments in the respective field at 130 universities. (Departments at the University of California at Irvine were not eligible for ranking because it was so new—only four years old at the time.)

Such ratings have been criticized on many grounds. (For a

**Table 1. Graduate Departments Rated Among
the Top Ten, in Three Fields, 1969**

| *Psychology* | *Chemistry* | *Linguistics* |
|---|---|---|
| 1. Stanford | 1. Harvard | 1. MIT |
| 2. Michigan | 2. Cal Tech | 2. UCLA |
| 3. Cal., Berkeley | 3. Cal., Berkeley | 3. Texas |
| 4. Harvard | 4. Stanford | 4. Cal., Berkeley |
| 5. Illinois | 5. MIT | 5. Chicago |
| 6. Pennsylvania | 6. Illinois | 6. Pennsylvania |
| 7. Minnesota | 7. UCLA | 7. Yale |
| 8. Wisconsin | 8. Chicago | 8. Harvard |
| 9. Yale | 9. Columbia | 9. Michigan |
| 10. UCLA | 10. Cornell | 10. Cornell |

*Source:* Roose and Anderson, 1970.

review of their procedures and drawbacks, see Clark, 1976.) Some critics feel that they are like basketball polls, with misplaced emphasis on "who's number one" or in "the top ten." Others (such as Elton and Rose, 1972) have examined the technical adequacy and meaning of the ratings, suggesting that the raters are chiefly rating the research production of a graduate department's faculty. Thus, departments that emphasize the education of teachers or practitioners or that serve purposes other than research tend to be rated low, even when they have excellent programs. Still other critics, such as Hagstrom (1971), have examined the ways prestige itself, or the "halo effect," of certain institutions can alter ratings. In some studies, "departments" were rated high even when the universities in question did not have such departments. Finally, such ratings do not seem to have many uses, since they are too global and unidimensional to provide a department with much direction.

For these reasons, a recent study (Clark, Hartnett, and Baird, 1976) compared the prestige ratings of selected departments with student, faculty, and alumni descriptions of the departments as well as with factual information about the departments. The results indicated that wealthy, large departments with much research activity are well regarded by peers and students, suggesting that a department's curriculum or program may be unduly credited for its reputation. Peer ratings of the quality of the department were found to be related to such traditional measures as the publication rates of instructors and faculty research activity but were not related to students' reports of the quality of teaching or the excellence of the environment for learning. This result suggests that peers should be used as judges of programs with caution; they may judge a program chiefly on the research efforts of its faculty and ignore or misinterpret its educational quality. Perhaps the most important finding about the character of education in highly rated departments was that actual publication rates of alumni were not related to peer ratings of the departments, the research activity of faculty, or the quality of the environment. However, where alumni were working was correlated with peer ratings, suggesting that committees hiring new Ph.D.'s are as impressed with the prestige of the department as with the qualifications of the applicant.

In sum, reputational ratings have tended to be based on only one type of information about departments and are poor guides to the educational excellence of the departments. As Hartnett, Clark, and Baird put it (1978, p. 1,314):

> Peers' judgments of the quality of the department's faculty [are] based largely on scholarly publications. They say little or nothing about the quality of instruction, the degree of civility or humaneness, the degree to which scholarly excitement is nurtured by student-faculty interactions, and so on. In brief, the peer ratings are not ratings of overall doctoral program quality but, rather, ratings of the faculty employed in those programs, reflecting primarily their research records. No claim has ever been made that the ratings are more than this, but they have often been interpreted as being more by those who used them.

Clearly, reputational measures provide inadequate assessments of institutional characteristics.

## Perceptual Measures

The next systematic attempts to gain an understanding of college environments were based on personality theory and clinical psychology. At Syracuse University, Pace and Stern began to work with the idea that a student's behavior depends not only on personality but also on the demands of the college and the interaction between the student's personality and the college. For example, a rigid student may do well in a structured college class but poorly in an unstructured one. Specifically, Pace and Stern attempted to implement the ideas of Harvard psychologist Henry Murray about the personality "needs" of an individual and the "presses" of the environment that influence the individual's behavior. To measure individual needs, they used Stern's personality test, the Activities Index (AI). To assess environmental presses—the rewards, constraints, and emphases of the environment as perceived by the individual—they designed the College Characteristics Index (CCI). (For detailed information about the CCI and other perceptual measures, see Chapter Nine.) Murray's theories did not require that needs and presses be conceived as parallel, but for the purpose of exploring the potential value of the CCI, Pace and

Stern included scales to parallel those of the AI. They addressed their original research to the practical problem of improving the prediction of college academic performance by studying student-college fit (Pace and Stern, 1958b). For example, a student with a high need for friendship supposedly would make better grades in a warm, friendly college than in an impersonal, unfriendly one because individual needs and environmental press would match.

The basic idea behind the CCI as well as later perceptual measures is that of an opinion poll of the campus, whereby students, faculty, or administrators are asked to report their opinions of what the college is like. This idea worked, but the length and complexity of the original version of the CCI limited its utility. It contained 300 true-false items about the college environment, which formed 30 ten-item scales. Some of the items and many of the scales, such as those for "harm-avoidance" and "narcissism," seemed more appropriate to a personality test than to environmental descriptions. Furthermore, the 30 scales made it difficult to describe a college's environment parsimoniously. And finally, the unit used in the statistical analyses of the CCI was individual students' responses rather than the average response at the colleges, which meant that the CCI showed how individuals' perceptions differed rather than how colleges differed according to the perceptions of their students.

Stern (1965, 1970) further analyzed the CCI; developed versions for use in high schools, evening colleges, and other organizations; and, by factor analyzing it and his AI together, attempted to describe the "culture" of colleges in joint terms of the personal characteristics of their students and their students' perceptions of their environments. But the need-press system did not seem to hold up, at least as originally conceived (Pace, 1969; Saunders, 1962; Stern, 1970): Studies showed that people's personalities differed independently of differences in college environments.

Because of these difficulties, Pace abandoned the need-press parallelism and focused on the college environment itself by using the average scores of colleges as the unit of analysis, selecting items that seemed directly relevant to the college experience, and using the statistical techniques of cluster analysis and factor analysis to reduce the number of scales so as to reflect only the major differences between colleges. The outcome was his College and University Environment Scales (CUES). CUES originally consisted of 150 items drawn from the CCI, with thirty item scales on five dimensions: Practicality, reflecting the college's emphasis on practicality, status, and college fun; Community, reflecting the friendliness and warmth of the campus; Awareness, reflecting an active cultural and intellectual life; Propriety, reflecting properness and conventionality; and Scholarship, reflecting the academic rigor of the college. Representative items from each scale are shown in Table 2. To establish their validity, Pace (1969) related these scales to other information about colleges. For example, colleges scoring high on Scholarship had a greater proportion of doctorates among their faculties than did those scoring low, while small colleges were more likely than large colleges to score high on Community. (For facts about the current second edition of CUES, see Chapter Nine.)

Both the CCI and CUES have frequently been used to study differences not only among colleges but also among major fields; among fraternities, sororities, and other living groups; and among different classes (such as freshmen and seniors). One of their most interesting applications has been for comparing the expectations of college by incoming freshmen with perceptions of the college held by upperclassmen. These studies, summarized by Feldman and Newcomb (1969), indicate that most new students—regardless of the college they are entering—expect their college to be intellectually stimulating, scholastically demanding, and friendly.

The importance of this gap may not be realized. Other studies have shown that the wider the gap between students' expectations and the realities of the college, the more likely students are to have problems in adjusting to the institution. Pace, in his report "The Use of CUES in the College Admissions Process" (1966b), has suggested how CUES could be used to give high school students a better idea of what the colleges in which they are interested are really like. For example, at some colleges fewer than 10 percent of the students answer items from CUES, such as those in Table 1, in the scored direction, while at others more than 90 percent answer in the scored direction. Such data would be helpful.

Sasajima, Davis, and Peterson (1968) found that colleges with high scores on the CUES Awareness scale were more likely to

## Table 2. Items from the College and University Environment Scales (CUES)

| Item | Average Percentage Agreeing Across 100 Colleges (1969) |
|---|---|
| *From the Community Scale* | |
| The school helps everyone get acquainted. | 52 |
| This school has a reputation for being very friendly. | 65 |
| Faculty members rarely or never call students by their first names.[a] | 55 |
| There is a lot of group spirit. | 44 |
| *From the Scholarship Scale* | |
| The professors really push the students' capacities to the limit. | 35 |
| Students are very serious and purposeful about their work. | 58 |
| Class discussions are typically vigorous and intense. | 30 |
| The school is outstanding for the emphasis and support it gives to pure scholarship and basic research. | 49 |
| *From the Practicality Scale* | |
| Student pep rallies, parades, dances, carnivals, or demonstrations occur very rarely.[a] | 42 |
| The big college events draw a lot of student enthusiasm and support. | 57 |
| The college offers many really practical courses such as typing, report writing, and so on. | 37 |
| Anyone who knows the right people in the faculty or administration can get a better break here. | 41 |
| *From the Awareness Scale* | |
| Many students here develop a strong sense of responsibility about their role in contemporary social and political life. | 56 |
| Students are encouraged to take an active part in social reforms or political programs. | 47 |
| There is a lot of interest here in poetry, music, painting, sculpture, architecture, and so on. | 48 |
| Special museums or collections are important possessions of the college. | 47 |
| *From the Propriety Scale* | |
| Drinking and late parties are generally tolerated, despite regulations.[a] | 45 |
| Bermuda shorts, pin-up pictures, and so on, are common on this campus.[a] | 32 |

[a]Scored direction is "false."
*Source:* Pace, 1969.

have had student protests for civil rights and against U.S. militarism during the 1960s. Similar relationships between measures of institutional characteristics and the incidence of various forms of protest have been reported by Bayer and Astin (1969), Astin (1971), and Peterson and Bilorusky (1971). And in a major study with CUES, Pace (1974) compared the activities of upperclassmen and alumni of 100 institutions of eight types with the CUES scores of these institutions. Pace found that these eight types of institutions, selected to reflect the diversity of American higher education, had quite different patterns on CUES, as shown in Figure 1. The bars show the range of scores within each type, and the heavy lines show the average scores within each type. For example, selective universities, engineering schools, and selective liberal arts colleges had similar high scores on the Scholarship dimension, but engineering schools had very low Awareness scores, while the other two had very high scores; selective liberal arts colleges had very high scores on the Community scale, while the other two had low scores. General (less selective) liberal arts colleges had Community scores as high as those of selective liberal arts colleges, but had lower Scholarship and Awareness scores. The other types of colleges—general comprehensive universities, state colleges and other less comprehensive universities, strongly denominational colleges, and teacher's colleges—also showed distinctive patterns on CUES. However, the most important results of Pace's study were the correlations between CUES scores and the activities and attitudes of students and alumni. For example, one of his activity scales concerned art—whether students and alumni read about it, talk about it, go to galleries and museums to see it, buy it, and express themselves through it. Pace found this scale correlated .67 among upperclassmen and .62 among alumni with their college's score on the CUES Awareness scale. A college scoring high on this scale would have "an environment that encourages concern about social and political problems, individuality and expressiveness through the arts, and tolerance of criticism" (Pace, 1974). To some extent, this result may seem unsurprising; people who experience an environment that encourages expressiveness through the arts should be expected to be active in art. But colleges that score high

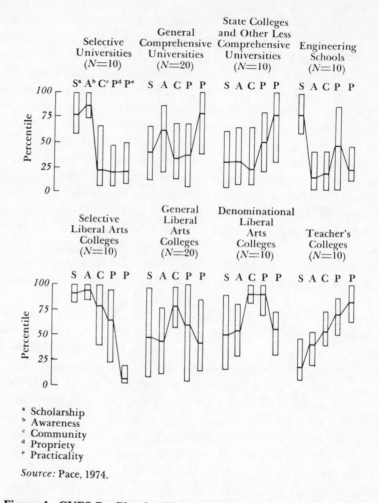

* Scholarship
* Awareness
* Community
* Propriety
* Practicality

*Source:* Pace, 1974.

**Figure 1. CUES Profiles for Eight Different Types of Institutions**

on the CUES Awareness scale are seldom art schools; usually they are private liberal arts colleges, many of which do not consider themselves to place an extraordinary emphasis on art education. And they are not necessarily highly selective, so the high scores on art activity received by these schools' upperclassmen and alumni cannot be explained simply by the caliber of students that the college attracts. Thus the art activity of these students and alumni is largely an outcome of the lively intellectual atmospheres of their colleges.

This study illustrates how the outcomes of college education can be related to particular characteristics of colleges. In recent years a great deal of attention has been paid to defining and assessing outcomes. However, even when adequate outcome measures are available, we must assess the important characteristics of colleges in order to say anything meaningful about how college affects these outcomes. Without such information we are unable to know what aspects of a college lead to what outcomes or why certain outcomes occur.

The work of Pace and Stern led a number of investigators to develop a variety of perceptual assessments of colleges based on the views of people who study and work in the colleges. For example, Thistlethwaite (1960, 1966) developed scales from CCI items to help distinguish between colleges that had graduated a large number of students who went on to obtain doctorates and those that had not. He and Wheeler (1966) subsequently examined the influence of college environments on the plans of students to attend graduate or professional school. By statistically controlling for students' characteristics when they entered college, including their ability, sex, family standing, and initial degree aspirations, the researchers found that students' senior educational goals tended to be more ambitious than expected in those colleges whose faculties were friendly, supportive, enthusiastic, and competent as teachers; encouraged the aspirations of their students by their interactions with students and by their own examples; and downplayed the vocational relevance of their fields. In these colleges, the faculties were joined by the students' peers in supporting student esthetic and intellectual activity—a good example of how faculty and student attitudes and behaviors affect students' aspirations.

Other perceptual measures, sometimes combined with factual information, have been developed for general institutional use rather than for solving particular research problems. For example, Peterson developed the College Student Questionnaire (CSQ), a two-part instrument designed to assess student characteristics as freshmen and then their characteristics and their satisfaction with college later in their college careers (see Chapter Nine). CSQ information can often be quite illuminating, as Table 3 shows. It lists the responses of juniors and seniors at thirty-eight colleges to representative items from four CSQ satisfaction scales. The Satisfaction with Faculty items suggest that students at these colleges were not very impressed with their professors. Overall, over two-thirds of the students said that only a minority of their professors could be called superior, and a majority of the students felt that their professors had not really challenged their intellectual and creative capacities. Although students were split in their views of the interest that their professors had in them, there were large differences among types of institutions, with less than half of the university students feeling that the majority of their teachers were interested in them and nearly two-thirds of the students in Protestant colleges feeling this way.

In the area of satisfaction with the administration, the views of students in different types of institutions differed regarding rules and regulations, the assistance received from their college, and the administrations' treatment of students. But few sizable differences among types of colleges emerged on the two scales regarding satisfaction with majors and with students. Thus, the majority of students in all types of colleges did not feel that their classmates were too intellectual, and the majority were satisfied with their competitiveness. However, the students' views were split regarding the concern of their fellow students for political and social issues.

The CSQ has been used in many studies, particularly of residence groups (see the review by Longino and Kart, 1974) and of subgroups. In one section, students read four paragraphs describing four "orientations," which correspond to the well-known Clark and Trow (1966) typology of student subcultures—academic, nonconformist, vocational, and collegiate.* The students then rank the

---

*The academic subculture is described as intellectually curious, valuing academic achievement, and identifying with the faculty and the college. The nonconformist subculture is described as intellectual, but detached from the college, and involved in the cultural and political life of society. The vocational subculture is described as emphasizing career training and vocational preparation for the purpose of economic mobility; the collegiate subculture is described as valuing the social life, interpersonal relations and activities college provides.

**Table 3. Percentage of True Responses by Juniors and Seniors on Selected Items from Four Scales of the College Student Questionnaire (CSQ)**

| | All Institutions (N=38) | Universities (N=6) | Public Colleges (N=8) | Independent Colleges (N=10) | Protestant Colleges (N=6) | Catholic Colleges (N=8) |
|---|---|---|---|---|---|---|
| *From the Satisfaction with Faculty Scale* | | | | | | |
| What proportion of the faculty members who have taught you during the past year would you say are superior teachers? | | | | | | |
| 1. Very few | 37 | 38 | 39 | 38 | 30 | 30 |
| 2. Less than half | 33 | 35 | 31 | 28 | 29 | 32 |
| 3. More than half | 23 | 21 | 24 | 23 | 27 | 25 |
| 4. Almost all | 8 | 6 | 6 | 10 | 13 | 12 |
| So far this year how successful would you say your instructors at this college have been in challenging you to produce to the limit of your intellectual and creative capacities? | | | | | | |
| 1. They have been wholly unsuccessful. | 15 | 16 | 15 | 15 | 13 | 10 |
| 2. Several have been somewhat successful. | 48 | 49 | 48 | 43 | 48 | 46 |
| 3. Several have been quite successful. | 30 | 29 | 31 | 30 | 31 | 29 |
| 4. Almost all have succeeded in continuously challenging my intellectual capacities. | 7 | 5 | 6 | 9 | 8 | 15 |

## Table 3. Percentage of True Responses by Juniors and Seniors on Selected Items from Four Scales of the College Student Questionnaire (CSQ) (Continued)

| | All Institutions (N=38) | Universities (N=6) | Public Colleges (N=8) | Independent Colleges (N=10) | Protestant Colleges (N=6) | Catholic Colleges (N=8) |
|---|---|---|---|---|---|---|
| What proportion of the faculty members you have observed at this college would you say are genuinely interested in students and their problems? | | | | | | |
| 1. Very few | 16 | 17 | 18 | 9 | 10 | 7 |
| 2. Less than half | 35 | 39 | 35 | 28 | 24 | 28 |
| 3. Over half | 37 | 35 | 38 | 39 | 39 | 37 |
| 4. Almost all | 12 | 8 | 9 | 21 | 26 | 27 |
| *From the Satisfaction with Administration Scale* | | | | | | |
| Would you agree that most of the existing rules and regulations on this campus are logical and necessary? | | | | | | |
| 1. Strongly disagree | 15 | 13 | 15 | 17 | 28 | 8 |
| 2. Disagree, but not strongly | 29 | 29 | 27 | 32 | 32 | 25 |
| 3. Agree, but not strongly | 45 | 47 | 48 | 41 | 30 | 49 |
| 4. Strongly agree | 10 | 10 | 9 | 11 | 9 | 17 |
| How do you feel about the assistance (or lack of assistance) in thinking through your educational and vocational plans which you have received at this college (from teachers, counselors, deans, and so on)? | | | | | | |

| 1. Very dissatisfied | 14 | 11 | 16 | 16 | 17 | 10 |
| 2. Somewhat dissatisfied | 36 | 37 | 40 | 28 | 27 | 24 |
| 3. Fairly satisfied | 39 | 39 | 34 | 39 | 36 | 49 |
| 4. Very satisfied | 9 | 9 | 8 | 14 | 11 | 15 |

Would you agree that the college administration here generally treats students more like children than like adults?

| 1. Strongly agree | 22 | 19 | 29 | 14 | 31 | 12 |
| 2. Agree, but not strongly | 30 | 30 | 30 | 26 | 28 | 29 |
| 3. Disagree, but not strongly | 30 | 33 | 26 | 31 | 23 | 32 |
| 4. Strongly disagree | 17 | 17 | 14 | 23 | 13 | 25 |

*From the Satisfaction with Major Scale*

Would you say there is anything approaching a "group spirit" or a feeling of common identity among the students in your department?

| 1. No, practically none. | 22 | 27 | 20 | 22 | 17 | 14 |
| 2. Yes, but it is rather weak. | 24 | 24 | 27 | 24 | 23 | 20 |
| 3. Yes, to a moderate degree. | 28 | 27 | 29 | 25 | 29 | 39 |
| 4. Yes, it is quite strong. | 17 | 16 | 18 | 14 | 11 | 21 |

Would you agree that the department or division in which you are doing your major work tends to reward conformity and punish individualism?

| 1. Strongly agree | 12 | 14 | 13 | 5 | 6 | 11 |
| 2. Agree, but not strongly | 19 | 19 | 19 | 19 | 14 | 21 |
| 3. Disagree, but not strongly | 33 | 35 | 34 | 26 | 26 | 32 |
| 4. Strongly disagree | 28 | 25 | 28 | 32 | 32 | 26 |

## Table 3. Percentage of True Responses by Juniors and Seniors on Selected Items from Four Scales of the College Student Questionnaire (CSQ) (Continued)

| | All Institutions (N=38) | Universities (N=6) | Public Colleges (N=8) | Independent Colleges (N=10) | Protestant Colleges (N=6) | Catholic Colleges (N=8) |
|---|---|---|---|---|---|---|
| **So far this term how interesting have you found the course work in your major field?** | | | | | | |
| 1. Rather dull for the most part. | 12 | 16 | 10 | 7 | 9 | 10 |
| 2. So-so | 19 | 18 | 22 | 20 | 14 | 20 |
| 3. Fairly interesting | 36 | 38 | 38 | 36 | 34 | 33 |
| 4. Very interesting | 24 | 22 | 24 | 21 | 23 | 28 |
| *From the Satisfaction with Students Scale* | | | | | | |
| **How satisfied are you with the amount of competitiveness for grades you have found among your classmates since you have been at this college?** | | | | | | |
| 1. Very dissatisfied (that is, they are either much too competitive or much too noncompetitive) | 13 | 12 | 13 | 15 | 14 | 11 |
| 2. Somewhat dissatisfied | 22 | 21 | 22 | 21 | 19 | 24 |
| 3. Fairly satisfied | 47 | 48 | 49 | 38 | 40 | 37 |
| 4. Very satisfied (that is, they are as competitive as I would like them to be) | 17 | 18 | 15 | 16 | 18 | 26 |

Speaking generally, how satisfied are you with the degree of concern about political, economic, and social issues shown by most students at this college?

|  |  |  |  |  |  |  |
|---|---|---|---|---|---|---|
| 1. Very dissatisfied | 16 | 15 | 18 | 12 | 16 | 13 |
| 2. Somewhat dissatisfied | 33 | 31 | 34 | 29 | 30 | 29 |
| 3. Fairly satisfied | 41 | 43 | 38 | 42 | 38 | 46 |
| 4. Very satisfied | 9 | 9 | 8 | 8 | 7 | 11 |

Would you agree that there are *too many* students on this campus who are so wrapped up in their intellectual development that they are close to failures as social persons?

|  |  |  |  |  |  |  |
|---|---|---|---|---|---|---|
| 1. Strongly agree | 9 | 12 | 6 | 8 | 13 | 10 |
| 2. Agree, but not strongly | 23 | 27 | 20 | 23 | 24 | 24 |
| 3. Disagree, but not strongly | 34 | 35 | 35 | 27 | 30 | 27 |
| 4. Strongly disagree | 30 | 24 | 35 | 33 | 25 | 37 |

*Source:* Educational Testing Service, 1972.

paragraphs according to "the accuracy with which each portrays your own point of view." Using this basic information, investigators have found differences in the attitudes, values, personalities, and behaviors of students holding the various viewpoints, thus lending support to the validity of the typology and its value in helping a college to understand the dynamics of its student subcultures and the reactions of its students to the college. (See lists of recent studies in Doucet, 1977, and Terenzini and Pascarella, 1977.)

To meet the needs of colleges for information about their students' attitudes, the American College Testing Program developed *The Institutional Self-Study Service Manual* (1970), which provides data about students' educational and occupational plans, backgrounds, college goals, college activities, college accomplishments, sense of progress toward attaining their college goals, and satisfaction with college policies, practices, facilities, and student personnel services. Similarly, to help colleges obtain staff and student opinions about the extent to which they were functioning optimally in various areas, Educational Testing Service developed the Institutional Functioning Inventory (IFI) (Peterson and others, 1970). Table 4 shows how data from one IFI scale, Democratic Governance, can reveal major differences in attitudes of important campus groups. For example, many faculty members at the twenty-two institutions studied report that they have some opportunities to influence decisions; however, they also indicate that they do not have any real authority, since actual governance is in the hands of the administration. In contrast, administrators at these institutions sense that the institution is governed democratically with the faculty heavily involved. As can be imagined, such IFI responses vary greatly among colleges. For example, at one institution faculty members on the average answered over eleven of these twelve questions in the scored direction, whereas at another institution they answered fewer than three in this direction. This kind of information can be vital to administrators in showing what their faculty members think about conditions at their college and how their views compare with those of faculties at other colleges.

Following up the IFI, Peterson and Uhl (1977) developed the Institutional Goals Inventory (IGI) to help colleges determine the degree of consensus among their members about various institutional goals and to help colleges order their priorities in obtaining these goals. Using a strategy developed by the sociologists Gross and Grambsch (1974), they designed the IGI so that respondents can rate each of ninety statements of goals both according to how those goals are currently emphasized at the college and according to how they should be emphasized. The differences between these ratings show how closely present campus goals match the goals that people prefer and identify areas where changes may be needed; furthermore, differences among groups of respondents on their preferred goals show how much agreement exists about institutional purposes and objectives. Most of the goal statements form scales that refer to the following thirteen outcomes, or substantive objectives, that a college may seek to achieve:

1. Academic Development (acquisition of knowledge; preparation for advanced study; high intellectual standards)
2. Intellectual Orientation (attitudes about learning and development of intellectual abilities)
3. Individual Personal Development (personal goals; sense of self-worth; self-confidence)
4. Humanism/Altruism (respect for diverse cultures; concern for peace, moral issues, and the welfare of man)
5. Cultural/Esthetic Awareness (appreciation of art forms and humanities; student participation in such activities)
6. Traditional Religiousness (dedication to orthodox, often fundamental religion)
7. Vocational Preparation (specific occupational curriculums; career fields; career planning)
8. Advanced Training (maintenance of advanced graduate education and research)
9. Research (extension of the frontiers of knowledge through research)
10. Meeting Local Needs (continuing education for adults; serving as a cultural and resource center)
11. Public Service (commitment of institutional resources to solving social and environmental problems)

**Table 4. Responses of Faculty Members and Administrators at Twenty-Two Institutions to Items on the Democratic Governance Scale of the Institutional Functioning Inventory (IFI), 1971-1976**

| Item | Percentage of Faculty (N=3,444) | | Percentage of Administrators (N=691) | |
|---|---|---|---|---|
| | Agreeing | Disagreeing | Agreeing | Disagreeing |
| In general, decision making is decentralized whenever feasible or workable. | 56 | 43 | 72 | 26 |
| Meaningful arrangements exist for expression of student opinion regarding institutional policies. | 75 | 24 | 85 | 14 |
| In dealing with institutional problems, attempts are generally made to involve interested people without regard to their formal position or hierarchical status. | 43 | 55 | 58 | 41 |
| This institution tends to be dominated by a single "official" point of view. | 48 | 49 | 34 | 64 |
| Power here tends to be widely dispersed rather than tightly held. | 30 | 68 | 42 | 56 |
| Serious consideration is given to student opinion when policy decisions affecting students are made. | 69 | 31 | 83 | 15 |
| In reality, a small group of individuals tends to pretty much run this institution. | 67 | 31 | 60 | 40 |
| Governance of this institution is clearly in the hands of the administration. | 73 | 26 | 58 | 40 |

| | | | | |
|---|---|---|---|---|
| In arriving at institutional policies, attempts are generally made to involve all the individuals who will be directly affected. | *49* | 49 | *67* | 32 |
| There is wide faculty involvement in important decisions about how the institution is run. | *38* | 60 | *54* | 44 |
| Students, faculty, and administrators all have opportunities for meaningful involvement in campus governance. | *54* | 44 | *73* | 26 |
| A concept of "shared authority" (by which the faculty and administration arrive at decisions jointly) describes fairly well the system of governance on this campus. | *39* | 58 | *56* | 42 |

*Note:* The direction of the scored response is in italics.
*Source:* Educational Testing Service.

12. Social Egalitarianism (open admissions; educational experiences relevant to the evolving interests of women; attention to the needs of minority groups)

13. Social Criticism/Activism (criticisms of prevailing American values; educating for basic changes in American society)

The remaining statements form seven scales relating to educational or institutional process goals:

14. Freedom (academic freedom; openness to controversy; freedom for faculty and students to choose their own life-styles)

15. Democratic Governance (decentralized decision making; responsive and participative government)

16. Community (commitment to the welfare of the institution; interaction and mutual respect among students, faculty, and administrators)

17. Intellectual/Esthetic Environment (intellectually exciting campus rich in experiences)

18. Innovation (continuous educational innovation and experimentation)

19. Off-Campus Learning (travel; work-study; credit by examination)

20. Accountability/Efficiency (concern for program efficiency; accountability and evidence for program effectiveness)

Use of the IGI in 105 California institutions (Peterson, 1973) showed that different groups associated with each institution held very different views about the existing goals of the institution as well as about desired goals. For example, Table 5 rank-orders the responses of each of seven groups connected with the University of California (including the UCLA and Irvine campuses). It shows, for example, that the faculty respondents ranked academic development seventh among the twenty as a desired goal for the university and fourth as an existing goal of the institution.

Figures 2 and 3 illustrate the possible differences among different types of institutions in their perceived and desired goals. The data were obtained from faculty members of the University of California, the California State University and Colleges, Califor-

**Table 5. Desired and Existing Rank Orders of Twenty Goals for Groups Associated with the University of California, 1972**

| Goal | Faculty (N=551) | Upper Division Students (N=478) | Graduate Students (N=335) | Administrators (N=131) | Chancellors (N=7) | Regents (N=7) | Community Residents (N=249) |
|---|---|---|---|---|---|---|---|
| 1. Academic Development | | | | | | | |
| Desired | 7 | 14 | 10 | 6 | 9 | 5 | 7 |
| Existing | 4 | 3 | 3 | 3 | 5 | 5 | 2 |
| 2. Intellectual Orientation | | | | | | | |
| Desired | 1 | 3 | 1 | 2 | 2 | 4 | 2 |
| Existing | 7 | 7 | 7 | 5 | 6 | 8 | 6 |
| 3. Individual Personal Development | | | | | | | |
| Desired | 10 | 4 | 8 | 8 | 10 | 8 | 4 |
| Existing | 14 | 18 | 18 | 13 | 10 | 11 | 17 |
| 4. Humanism/Altruism | | | | | | | |
| Desired | 12 | 9 | 12 | 15 | 12 | 13 | 9 |
| Existing | 16 | 16 | 15 | 15 | 16 | 14 | 10 |
| 5. Cultural/Esthetic Awareness | | | | | | | |
| Desired | 13 | 16 | 16 | 16 | 16 | 16 | 16 |
| Existing | 15 | 12 | 14 | 14 | 17 | 17 | 14 |
| 6. Traditional Religiousness | | | | | | | |
| Desired | 20 | 20 | 20 | 20 | 20 | 20 | 20 |
| Existing | 20 | 20 | 20 | 20 | 20 | 20 | 20 |

Table 5. Desired and Existing Rank Orders of Twenty Goals for Groups Associated with the University of California, 1972 (Continued)

| Goal | Faculty (N=551) | Upper Studes Division (N=478) | Graduate Students (N=335) | Administrators (N=131) | Chancellors (N=7) | Regents (N=7) | Community Residents (N=249) |
|---|---|---|---|---|---|---|---|
| 7. Vocational Preparation | | | | | | | |
| Desired | 15 | 11 | 13 | 13 | 15 | 10 | 6 |
| Existing | 13 | 14 | 12 | 16 | 13 | 15 | 16 |
| 8. Advanced Training | | | | | | | |
| Desired | 5 | 8 | 5 | 3 | 7 | 1 | 5 |
| Existing | 2 | 2 | 2 | 2 | 2 | 1 | 3 |
| 9. Research | | | | | | | |
| Desired | 6 | 12 | 9 | 4 | 3 | 3 | 8 |
| Existing | 1 | 1 | 1 | 1 | 1 | 2 | 1 |
| 10. Meeting Local Needs | | | | | | | |
| Desired | 14 | 15 | 15 | 14 | 11 | 11 | 12 |
| Existing | 12 | 9 | 8 | 12 | 12 | 10 | 11 |
| 11. Public Service | | | | | | | |
| Desired | 11 | 10 | 11 | 11 | 13 | 15 | 14 |
| Existing | 11 | 11 | 10 | 11 | 14 | 13 | 12 |
| 12. Social Egalitarianism | | | | | | | |
| Desired | 19 | 19 | 19 | 19 | 19 | 18 | 19 |
| Existing | 18 | 17 | 16 | 18 | 18 | 18 | 19 |

| | 1 | 2 | 3 | 4 | 5 | 6 | 7 |
|---|---|---|---|---|---|---|---|
| **13. Social Criticism/Activism** | | | | | | | |
| Desired | 17 | 13 | 14 | 17 | 18 | 19 | 17 |
| Existing | 17 | 15 | 17 | 17 | 15 | 19 | 13 |
| **14. Freedom** | | | | | | | |
| Desired | 4 | 2 | 3 | 7 | 8 | 9 | 15 |
| Existing | 3 | 5 | 5 | 4 | 3 | 6 | 4 |
| **15. Democratic Governance** | | | | | | | |
| Desired | 9 | 6 | 6 | 10 | 14 | 14 | 13 |
| Existing | 10 | 13 | 13 | 10 | 11 | 12 | 8 |
| **16. Community** | | | | | | | |
| Desired | 2 | 1 | 2 | 1 | 1 | 2 | 1 |
| Existing | 8 | 8 | 9 | 7 | 4 | 3 | 15 |
| **17. Intellectual/Esthetic Environment** | | | | | | | |
| Desired | 3 | 5 | 4 | 5 | 4 | 7 | 3 |
| Existing | 6 | 6 | 6 | 6 | 7 | 4 | 5 |
| **18. Innovation** | | | | | | | |
| Desired | 8 | 7 | 7 | 9 | 5 | 12 | 10 |
| Existing | 9 | 10 | 11 | 9 | 9 | 9 | 7 |
| **19. Off-Campus Learning** | | | | | | | |
| Desired | 18 | 17 | 18 | 18 | 17 | 17 | 18 |
| Existing | 19 | 19 | 19 | 19 | 19 | 16 | 18 |
| **20. Accountability/Efficiency** | | | | | | | |
| Desired | 16 | 18 | 17 | 12 | 6 | 6 | 11 |
| Existing | 5 | 4 | 4 | 8 | 8 | 7 | 9 |

*Source:* Peterson, 1973.

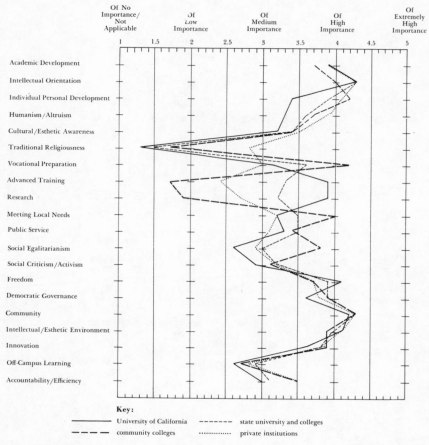

Figure 2.  Faculty Ratings of Existing Goals
for Four Types of California Institutions, 1972

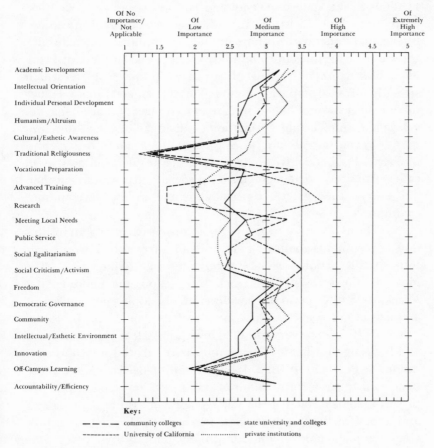

Figure 3. Faculty Ratings of Desired Goals
for Four Types of California Institutions, 1972

nia's community colleges, and its private colleges and universities. As Figure 2 shows, in 1972 faculty members of the University of California perceived less emphasis on individual personal development on their campuses than did faculty members of private four-year colleges or of the state's community colleges. Similarly, faculties in the state university and college system perceived less emphasis than faculties in other colleges on innovation, intellectual/esthetic environment, and community. And naturally, the views of faculties in community colleges and in the University of California on the goals of advanced training and research strongly differ. Comparing Figures 2 and 3 suggests that faculties in all colleges would like to see greater emphasis on academic development, intellectual orientation, individual personal development, freedom, democratic governance, community, and intellectual/esthetic environment. In other results, students in all colleges desired greater emphasis on social criticism/activism than did every other group, especially people in the surrounding communities.

The IGI cannot by itself create consensus among an institution's constituents about its goals nor can it translate desired goals into specific actions, as Uhl notes later in Chapter Five. (For ideas on the translation of goals into action, see Lenning and Micek, 1976.) But periodic consideration of people's perceptions of an institution's goals (and not merely of its claimed purposes) by using the IGI can be very useful to institutional leaders in clarifying and focusing on what is relevant to its particular approach to education. As Peterson (1970, p. 4) has written, "Goals may serve as the basic element in a formulation of the institution's policy, philosophy, or ideology. Stated goals help tie together assumptions, values, and hopes for the institution into a coherent policy that then provides standards and guides for present and future . . . decisions and actions."

A more recent effort involving perceptual measures has been the design of survey instruments for use at particular types of colleges. For example, Warren and Roelfs (1972) developed the Student Reactions to College questionnaire for two-year colleges to use in identifying institutional strengths and weaknesses according to the students. To maximize the instrument's usefulness to staff members and relevance to students, Warren and Roelfs did not simply develop their own questions; instead, they interviewed community college students, faculty members, and administrators about what they thought was important to know about two-year colleges. And on a pretest version of the form, students were asked to write in issues of importance to them that were not covered in the questionnaire. The final instrument has 150 items and covers instruction, studying, faculty and staff contact with students, student goals and planning, registration and class scheduling, other administrative problems, student activities, financial problems, housing, food services, and transportation. In addition, it includes nine background questions about the student and space for twenty questions that the college can develop itself. Warren and Roelfs' approach to instrument development provides a model for future work in obtaining information for colleges that would help in decision making.

### Perceptual Measures of Subenvironments

After working with perceptual measures for several years, some researchers realized that although they assessed the overall environments of colleges well, they did not reflect the many parts of the institutions. Even small colleges contain several distinctive subcultures or subgroups, while large universities and multipurpose institutions often seem to be heterogeneous collections of self-contained subenvironments. For instance, students in a university school of engineering tend to form groups with other engineering students and their instructors, while students in business, nursing, or arts and sciences schools form similar association networks. Researchers hypothesized that the impact of an institution would be different among these different subgroups because the institution's goals would be implemented by people who have different goals and characteristics.

The environments of students can differ along many other lines, also. For example, commuters and residential students differ in numerous ways (for example, see Chickering, 1974), as do residence hall students and fraternity or sorority students (for example, see Baird, 1969) and as do even such presumably homogeneous groupings as sororities (for example, see Selvin and Hagstrom, 1966). Student environments can also vary according to the educational values that students bring to college and the subcultures that they form, such as academically oriented groups, rebellious nonconformist groups, "fun" groups, and groups that value college for its vocational payoff (Clark and Trow, 1966). Newcomb, for example, showed that students form friendships on the basis of similarity of attitudes and values. Since the environments that students experience are largely formed by the people with whom they associate, the environments that are the target of change must be carefully defined.

One example of such definition is provided by Pace and Baird (1966), who report results for the College Characteristics Analysis (CCA), which is designed to assess the subenvironments of colleges. The CCA measures four environmental emphases: (1) an intellectual, humanistic, esthetic emphasis; (2) a friendly, group welfare emphasis; (3) a scientific, independent emphasis; and (4) a practical, status-oriented emphasis. The CCA was unique in its specification of the parts of the college or university to which the student's replies should refer. In this way, the CCA assessed the overall college environment, the academic subcultures, and the peer subcultures. Pace and Baird found that the subgroups influenced most specific attitudes and behavior, although the total environment influenced students' general evaluations of their progress and development during college. Compared with the student's entire college experience, a specific peer group or membership group is a relatively small stimulus, the impact of which is perhaps best seen on attitudes and behavior that are correspondingly limited and pertinent to that stimulus. More global criteria require more global influences (Pace and Baird, 1966, p. 242).

Using a somewhat different approach, Centra (1968) compared conventional residence halls with living-learning units at Michigan State University by using sixty-five CUES items that were reworded slightly to apply to residence halls rather than to the university in general. Living-learning units were intended to enhance the cultural and intellectual life of the students and to establish a more personal, less hotel-like environment. To achieve this end, the halls included faculty offices, classrooms, libraries, and auditoriums. Centra found that on a dimension reflecting scholarship, awareness, and propriety, conventional halls scored both highest and lowest. Furthermore, despite their larger size, the living-learning units had community scores that were very similar to those of the smaller conventional units. The significance of this study is that an instrument can be developed for the specific purpose of comparing groups within an institution.

Moos and Gerst (1974) developed a more generalized instrument, the University Residence Environment Scale (URES), in order to assess the social climate of university student living groups, such as dormitories, fraternities, and sororities. (The details of the development of this instrument are given in Gerst and Moos, 1972.) The 100 items yield ten scores: involvement, emotional support, independence, traditional social orientation, competition, academic achievement, intellectuality, order and organization, student influence, and innovation. The URES has been related to students' anxiety, depression, and hostility; friendship patterns; satisfaction with the residence group; and personal development. These studies show that the residence group plays an important role in students' progress and satisfaction with their college careers. They also show how environmental information about the subenvironments of colleges can be used to improve the college experience for students. More information about these scales is provided in Chapter Nine.

### Perceptual Assessments of Graduate and Professional School Environments

As the previous pages have shown, many instruments have been designed to assess important features of the total college environment and its segments. Most recently, a number of studies, such as those by Creager (1971) and Hartnett and Katz (1977), have investigated the environments of one of the most important elements in higher education—graduate and professional schools. These studies and studies of specific fields, such as medicine and law, have suggested that the varieties of advanced education differ in important ways that have a number of possible consequences for students. For instance, these investigations indicate that graduate and professional schools differ significantly in their environments for teaching and learning, even across fields of comparable difficulty. These differences are found in almost every area, including the teaching styles of professors, formal degree requirements, views of the administration, and views of the academic program. Although the largest differences seemed to be in the nonpersonal areas of requirements, program structure, and administrative policies, the highly individual area of professor-student relationships—both academic and personal—also varied greatly among the fields.

For example, Table 6, showing selected responses to a survey of the views of first-year students in graduate and professional schools (Baird, 1974), suggests some of the differences among the different fields. The rather impersonal academic rigor of law school is suggested, for example, as is the liberalism of the social sciences and the relatively relaxed pace of graduate schools of education.

The results concerning the overall environments for learning in these fields suggest that specific features of the academic program must be evaluated in their general context, including such factors as the nature of the demands of the field, the goals of the institutions, the academic structure, and the characteristics of the people who are attracted to the field.

Interfield comparisons can also provide insights into the nature of the demands of graduate and professional education. For example, it is striking that fields which appear to be equally demanding, such as law and medicine, seem to have very different effects on their students' sense of satisfaction and level of tension. Many students in law felt that they were in a stressful and competitive situation, in part probably because of the low grades awarded in many law schools. Medical students reported that they worked hard but did not appear to feel competitive stress, in part probably because of the pass/fail and similar grading systems used in the majority of medical schools. These findings suggest that nontraditional grading systems can be used in graduate and professional schools with little loss of academic rigor and "quality" with the benefit of reducing unnecessary student tension.

Perhaps the most intriguing possibility suggested by these results is that academic programs can be designed to meet the

**Table 6. Graduate and Professional School Students' Descriptions of Their Reactions to Their Academic Programs**

| Item | Graduate Arts and Humanities (N=274) | Graduate Biological Sciences (N=158) | Graduate Physical Sciences, English (N=606) | Graduate Social Sciences (N=360) | School of Education (N=442) | Law School (N=461) | Medical School (N=435) | Average Percentages |
|---|---|---|---|---|---|---|---|---|
| Curriculum[a] | | | | | | | | |
| I do not like the course work, but it is required for the career I have chosen. | 34 | 38 | 39 | 41 | 47 | 53 | 37 | 42 |
| Requires much more studying than undergraduate college. | 71 | 56 | 67 | 73 | 48 | 93 | 86 | 71 |
| Requires a much different kind of studying than undergraduate college. | 79 | 75 | 72 | 81 | 69 | 94 | 81 | 79 |

**Table 6. Graduate and Professional School Students' Descriptions of Their Reactions to Their Academic Programs (Continued)**

| Item | Graduate Arts and Humanities (N=274) | Graduate Biological Sciences (N=158) | Graduate Physical Sciences, English (N=606) | Graduate Social Sciences (N=360) | School of Education (N=442) | Law School (N=461) | Medical School (N=435) | Average Percentages |
|---|---|---|---|---|---|---|---|---|
| The curriculum allows sufficient time for thoughtful consideration of the content. | 39 | 53 | 52 | 49 | 53 | 38 | 30 | 45 |
| Students[a] | | | | | | | | |
| There are lots of student cliques. | 55 | 50 | 47 | 54 | 49 | 68 | 77 | 57 |
| Students work hard at their studies. | 81 | 85 | 89 | 83 | 70 | 96 | 97 | 87 |
| Professors[b] | | | | | | | | |
| Professors expect students to be prepared at every class session. | 79 | 64 | 68 | 72 | 68 | 93 | 50 | 72 |

| | | | | | | | | |
|---|---|---|---|---|---|---|---|---|
| Professors have liberal political views. | 39 | 37 | 25 | 59 | 36 | 55 | 22 | 37 |
| Professors take strong positions on controversial issues. | 29 | 23 | 15 | 33 | 36 | 37 | 17 | 28 |
| Professors give each student a clear idea of how well he is doing. | 43 | 43 | 51 | 44 | 50 | 10 | 41 | 43 |
| Professors are more concerned with research than teaching. | 18 | 42 | 35 | 36 | 17 | 9 | 34 | 24 |
| Professors exercise a good deal of discipline in the classroom. | 23 | 25 | 30 | 19 | 5 | 49 | 23 | 29 |

[a]Figures show percentage of each group responding that the statement is "somewhat" or "very" descriptive of their department or school.
[b]Figures show percentage of each group responding that the statement was true of 50 percent or more of their professors.
[c]Includes students in some other fields.
Source: Baird, 1974.

needs of the fields more efficiently and more humanely. By examining the effects of programs on students as described by appropriate environmental studies, the fields could at least eliminate features of their environments that are irrelevant to their pursuit of excellence or that even interfere with that pursuit, as Hartnett and Katz (1977) have suggested.

Related research has concentrated on the differences among departments or schools *within* fields. Although conducted for a variety of reasons, these studies make one important point: Environments for learning within fields can vary almost as much as environments among fields. For example, Table 7 shows selected responses of 547 students from seven medical schools, selected as being representative, high-quality institutions with different program goals. The study from which these data were taken (Baird, 1976a) was looking for (1) aspects common to most schools, (2) aspects that differed, and (3) the overall profile of each school, showing the relation between teaching and learning. This study did find the schools much alike in some respects—most students said that their professors seldom gave them helpful feedback on their tests and papers, seldom gave them an idea of how well they were doing, seldom voiced political views, seldom took strong positions on controversial issues, and seldom were helpful advisers. Thus, the most common characteristic of teaching in the first year of medical school seems to be a lack of communication between students and professors about the students' performance.

However, the teaching staffs varied considerably in their accessibility and treatment of students, as shown in Table 7.

Although students in every school seemed reconciled to their school's formal requirements, their views of three areas differed considerably: the clarity of requirements, the relevance of the requirements to the actual work of the profession, and opportunities for independent study. Also, the medical schools differed considerably in the quality of their library collections, laboratory facilities, and classroom equipment, according to students' reports.

Students in every school thought their peers friendly, bright, and hardworking, but their views of their peers' intellectual independence, political involvement, honesty, and altruism were not consistent. The schools also varied considerably in the degree

of competition, program flexibility, and opportunities for individual programs and creative work, as well as in conventionality,
liberalism, and informality.

These results suggest that the climates for learning and
socialization to professional roles may differ from school to school
within many fields. Studies of the methods and goals of socialization in graduate and professional education should thus consider
school environment. By systematically including information about
variations in environments, research may provide a better understanding of institutional effects on student development. Also, if
this kind of information was systematically collected and widely
available, it could help students select schools suited to their needs
and also help schools evaluate and improve themselves. Thus, for
schools to assess and describe themselves periodically might be
quite useful. With a better knowledge of their own demands and
characteristics, schools would be able to study the consequences of
their current policies and programs, consider new alternatives, and
evaluate the success of their curriculums and policy innovations.

Perhaps the most important implication of the differences
within types of graduate schools is that several different kinds of
excellence within graduate and professional education are possible,
as the results reported by Clark, Hartnett, and Baird (1976)
suggest. The reasons for these varieties of quality need to be
analyzed in other research, as do the personal and professional
consequences of each model for students and faculty. Of particular
value would be studies relating differences in schools to differences
in their rates of attrition and, eventually, to the professional skill
and contributions of their graduates.

### Perceptual Measures for Other Purposes

Besides assessing subenvironments, a number of researchers
have developed assessments for particular purposes. For example,
Pfeifer and Schneider (1974) developed an instrument for assessing university life whose items were based on essays written by
black and white students. The final instrument had 115 items, answered on a five-point scale, and was administered to samples of
black and white students. The responses were factor analyzed sepa-

**Table 7. Percentage of Students Agreeing with Various Statements About Their Medical Schools**

| Item | School A | School B | School C | School D | School E | School F | School G |
|---|---|---|---|---|---|---|---|
| Professors are friendly and accessible to students. | 83 | 66 | 67 | 82 | 44 | 50 | 42 |
| Professors clearly explain the subject matter. | 63 | 45 | 55 | 62 | 27 | 27 | 47 |
| Professors encourage out-of-class contact about academic work. | 54 | 43 | 49 | 58 | 52 | 27 | 14 |
| Professors encourage classroom discussion. | 49 | 18 | 26 | 50 | 27 | 15 | 33 |
| Professors give helpful feedback on tests, papers, and reports. | 18 | 3 | 26 | 32 | 11 | 11 | 7 |
| Professors are excellent teachers. | 43 | 34 | 35 | 20 | 23 | 9 | 28 |
| Professors are so divided into factions that they harm students' academic progress. | 1 | 15 | 4 | 8 | 49 | 32 | 19 |
| Professors are top-notch researchers. | 72 | 66 | 24 | 28 | 30 | 22 | 37 |
| Professors complement each other in providing coherent and comprehensive instruction. | 49 | 38 | 45 | 30 | 27 | 10 | 21 |
| Professors stimulate student learning. | 55 | 43 | 42 | 36 | 23 | 5 | 21 |
| There is poor communication between administrators and students. | 29 | 74 | 51 | 72 | 77 | 84 | 74 |
| The administration is responsive to the needs of the school and students. | 89 | 80 | 87 | 82 | 41 | 51 | 57 |
| Students are friendly. | 88 | 94 | 91 | 94 | 83 | 77 | 87 |
| Students are very bright. | 91 | 86 | 91 | 88 | 83 | 81 | 85 |
| Academic cheating is fairly common. | 3 | 0 | 1 | 8 | 24 | 50 | 3 |
| Students value the money they will make in their careers more than the opportunities for helping people. | 37 | 29 | 36 | 46 | 39 | 61 | 39 |

| | | | | | | |
|---|---|---|---|---|---|---|
| There is keen competition for grades. | 17 | 60 | 45 | 62 | 79 | 67 | 46 |
| The course work is dull. | 36 | 37 | 45 | 36 | 38 | 70 | 51 |
| Provides many opportunities for research and creative work. | 79 | 60 | 47 | 62 | 41 | 33 | 41 |
| Allows considerable choice in courses students may take. | 80 | 22 | 6 | 8 | 18 | 5 | 2 |
| Primarily teaches skills and practical training. | 63 | 40 | 52 | 46 | 36 | 37 | 46 |
| Provides opportunity for innovative programs on an individual basis. | 77 | 52 | 34 | 52 | 24 | 23 | 13 |
| The department has an informal environment. | 72 | 49 | 64 | 56 | 35 | 49 | 44 |
| There is a strong esprit de corps among students and faculty. | 55 | 51 | 41 | 36 | 20 | 13 | 27 |

*Source:* Baird, 1976a.

rately for the two groups. The results showed that the dimensions of university climate differed for black and white students and that blacks viewed the university more negatively. The white dimensions were impersonal academic atmosphere, administrative neglect, social interaction, racism, and racial separatism. The black dimensions were institutional racism, nonacademic atmosphere, social isolation, personal racism, non-classroom-related activities, and attempts at communication. These results suggest that blacks and whites approach their college experience with quite different perspectives, which must be considered to make lasting progress toward mutual understanding of black and white students.

An example of an instrument designed for a particular school is the forty-one-item, four-scale questionnaire about the Purdue University environment developed by Noeth and Dye (1973). According to their Personnel Services scale, students did not believe that the student personnel service was doing a good job, although the staff personnel thought they were. Specific items indicated particular areas in which students felt improvements were needed.

## Perceptual Information for Students as Consumers

During the 1970s, numerous individuals, agencies, and national commissions began to analyze postsecondary education from the perspective of the student as a consumer. Their basic idea was that students, as potential "buyers" of competing products or services, were entitled to as much information about their purchase as were buyers of automobiles, homes, appliances, and other consumer goods. From this vantage point, accurate and detailed information about colleges was not merely desirable but essential for informed student choices. Such information had not previously been viewed as a student right, however. As a result, these groups concluded that the lack of good information was one of the basic problems confronting prospective college students (National Commission on the Financing of Postsecondary Education, 1973; *Second Newman Report*, 1973; *Consumer Protection in Postsecondary Education*, 1975).

These various concerns led to the creation in 1975 of a National Task Force for Better Information for Student Choice. The several reports that stemmed from its efforts (El-Khawas, 1978; Stark, 1977, 1978) identified three essential areas for improved information: costs and financial aid, academic offerings and requirements, and the results of attendance. With respect to costs and financial aid, the task force recommended detailed explanations of how aid packaging works, the actual calculation of a student expense budget, charts allowing students to estimate their own likely financial needs, full explanations of financial aid eligibility restrictions, and the like. In terms of academic offerings and requirements, they suggested that institutions provide information about the academic experiences of current students, detailed explanations of policies governing credit by examination, information on the professional interests of faculty members, descriptions of typical modes of instruction, and other aspects of the educational experience at the college. Finally, the task force urged institutions to provide students with information about related employment fields, attrition and retention data (including patterns of interrupting studies and returning), details on two-year college graduates who attempt to transfer to four-year institutions, and student ratings of faculties, academic programs, and support services.

Much of this recommended information can be assembled from basic operational statistics. For example, the University of Illinois at Urbana-Champaign has reported to prospective undergraduates that graduate assistants teach as many as 62 percent of the introductory courses in some programs while full professors teach only 4 percent (Stark, 1978, p. 90). But some of the recommended information concerns student and faculty attitudes, for which perceptual measures are needed. Thus, in conjunction with the task force's efforts, both UCLA and Irvine have sampled campus opinion regarding academic atmosphere and student life. Here is what UCLA reported about its academic environment (Stark, 1978, p. 88):

> **Question:** What do students say about teaching and about faculty-student relationships? Some people say that professors at UCLA are more interested in research than in teaching undergraduates and that you don't have much chance to see the professors except in class. Is that true?

**Answer:** Most of the faculty members are interested and involved in research. If they weren't, they probably wouldn't be at UCLA—research is part of their job. Not many faculty members spend all of their time teaching undergraduates.

Student opinion about undergraduate teaching is divided. Half the students in our sample (50 percent) said they thought it was generally true that many faculty members have a genuine interest in undergraduate teaching. Other students in our sample disagreed (30 percent), and the rest were undecided. On faculty-student relationships, nearly everyone agreed that if students make the effort, faculty members are accessible (80 percent). Most students also said that students who are having difficulty in a course are encouraged to talk with the professor about it (70 percent). Although many students (63 percent) said they felt intimidated by some faculty members in their major field, they also said the faculty are very helpful if you go to see them (60 percent).

**Question:** What about classroom teaching? Do students think their professors are interesting or dull?

**Answer:** We asked students whether they thought most faculty members tried to stimulate student interest and enthusiasm in their courses. A majority of the students said they thought that was true (62 percent). We also asked whether they thought professors in their major field were often colorful and vivid in presenting their knowledge and viewpoints. A great many students in the fine arts (74 percent) and humanities (66 percent) said they thought their professors were often colorful and vivid in presenting their subject matter. In other major fields, there was less agreement with that statement (generally around 40 percent).

And here is what Irvine (UCI) reported about its academic environment on the basis of using the College Student Questionnaire (CSQ) and the College and University Environment Scales (CUES), Institutional Functioning Inventory (IFI), and Institutional Goals Inventory (IGI) (Stark, 1978, pp. 90, 136):

Faculty and students strongly agree that UCI offers a high level of academic development.
UCI's faculty concern for advancing knowledge was rated 9.7 (10 point scale) while the national norm on faculty concern for research was 4.5 (IFI).

The top three items which were chosen to describe UCI's goals were academically related (IGI).

Students and faculty believe that the UCI faculty conduct excellent quality research which significantly contributes to the advancement of knowledge, and that faculty are highly creative and innovative in the classroom (IGI).

85 percent of the students compared to 80 percent nationally perceived the faculty as dedicated scholars (CUES).

Adjusting to the academic environment of the University turned out to be less of a problem than anticipated (CSQ):

31 percent of entering students expected problems handling course content but only 15 percent of juniors and seniors actually had problems (student attrition not accounted for).

8 percent of the entering students anticipated problems choosing a major, while only 4 percent of juniors and seniors reported that they experienced difficulty in making the choice (student attrition not accounted for).

CUES reflects the heavy emphasis on studying at UCI. 73 percent of the students indicate there is much studying over weekends as compared to 58 percent nationally.

CSQ finds that juniors and seniors feel there is not adequate study space on the campus (38 percent UCI as compared to 13 percent nationally).

UCI students compare equally to other university students in the nation in quality of study habits and satisfaction with major (CSQ).

Here is a description of student life at UCLA (Stark, 1978, p. 102):

> **Question:** As you've said, in a place as big as UCLA people are bound to have some different impressions about it. I guess what I'd like to know is whether there is anything they all agree on—regardless of who they are, what field they are in, or whether they live on campus or don't?
>
> **Answer:** Yes, indeed there are. Here are some of the things that just about everyone (95 percent or so) agrees are characteristic of UCLA.
>
> • They agree that the University has many facilities related to student activities and campus life—athletic facilities, the recreation center, eating places, and patios, bookstore, student union and meeting rooms.

- They agree that the University provides many services for students—health services, study skills center, counseling center, the placement and housing services.
- They agree that the University has excellent library facilities.
- They agree that a lot of distinguished public figures come to the campus for special events.
- They agree that there are a great many concerts and cultural events on the campus.
- They agree that the campus setting, its landscaping, and architecture are attractive and distinctive.

Moreover, a very large majority of the students (from two-thirds to three-fourths or more) also say that they use and appreciate the facilities; that the student services are a real benefit; that the public speakers, concerts, and cultural events are a stimulating and satisfying part of the University environment; and that they genuinely appreciate the esthetic quality of the campus.

Question: A lot of us who are still in high school wonder about the social life and student activities in a place as big as UCLA. Is it hard to meet people and to get involved in extracurricular activities?

Answer: Just about everyone in our sample of upperclassmen agreed that there are so many activities and events at UCLA that students can always find interesting things to do (85 percent). Most of them also agreed that there are many opportunities for students to get together in extracurricular activities (71 percent). Despite opportunities, not everyone makes an effort to get involved, and perhaps many don't want to. Quite a few of them described student activities and social life as highly competitive (43 percent). Also, quite a few of them (41 percent) thought that students are generally apathetic about getting into extracurricular activities. Those who live at home were more likely to think so (47 percent). On the other hand, students who said that most of their friends live in the dormitories, fraternities, or sororities did not describe the students as apathetic about getting into activities (only 25 percent thought they were).

A majority of students (56 percent) said that it's hard to meet people in class. But a majority (52 percent) also said that students develop friendships with many people outside their major field. On that score, there's a big difference between students who have lived on the campus and those who live at home. Two-thirds of the students who have lived on campus (67 percent) said that they developed friendships with many people outside their major field, but less than half (43 percent) of the students who live at home said this.

And here is a briefer description of the social life at Irvine (Stark, 1978, p. 101):

> *Student attitudes (CUES)*
> Positive:
> • Students feel free to do things on the spur of the moment.
> • There is a great deal of acceptance of others.
> • Students receive due process consideration when accused of violation of college rules.
> • Overall student experiences are enriching and stimulating.
> • It's a place where students do not exert pressures on one another.
>   Negative:
> • UCI exhibits a relatively low degree of student awareness of politics, society, and the arts.
> • UCI does not facilitate everyone getting acquainted.
> • Upper-division students do not assist new students in adjusting to campus life.
> • There is not a lot of group spirit at UCI.
> • Practical courses are unavailable.

Although these descriptions are not completely comparable, they provide a much better idea of the academic and social life at UCLA and Irvine than the guidebook descriptions quoted earlier. A student may conclude, for instance, that Irvine appears to its students to be more strictly academic than UCLA, that UCLA offers more stimulating activities, and that some effort may be needed at either institution to develop friendships with other students.

Such descriptions are likely to meet with resistance in some quarters—particularly at those institutions that have good reason to be concerned about the effects that more accurate information might have on their ability to attract students. Thus even a voluntary free program sponsored by the College Entrance Examination

Board, which encouraged institutions to report student opinions about themselves based on Centra's Questionnaire on Student and College Characteristics (QSCC), had to be abandoned because so few colleges made use of the results in the board's *College Handbook* (see Centra, 1968, 1970). Understandably anxious about declining enrollments and rising costs, college administrators may realistically fear the loss of students if less-than-positive opinions about their institutions are published; however, such information will become increasingly important as student consumerism grows in influence during the 1980s.

## Limitations and Strengths of
## Perceptual Measures

One might think that one could use the variety of perceptual measures of college environments to help solve many problems that colleges face. However, the instruments have two major limitations that must be considered before they are used.

Most fundamental is the ambiguity of the meaning of an aggregate perception of an environment. A person's perceptions of a social situation depend on many things, as Feldman (1972) has pointed out. For example, students select subgroups, major fields, courses, and activities consistent with their interests and characteristics. Professors and administrators likewise have different experiences that affect how they perceive the environment. However, we should note that Pace (1966a) and Hartnett and Centra (1974) have provided evidence that personal characteristics have little influence on environment scores and that environmental scores for subgroups seldom differ from the scores of the majority (this result may be due to the global nature of the instruments, a point we shall return to later).

Another problem is that the accuracy of perceptions depends on the knowledge of the respondent. For example, most students know very little about some aspects of faculty life, and commuting students have little to say about life in the dormitories.

Because of their generality and ambiguity, perceptual measures may not be very useful in evaluating or changing colleges. For example, what can an administrator do if his college scored at the

50th percentile on a scale of Friendliness? The score offers no guide to action, he doesn't know if the score is good or bad, and he is not sure what the Friendliness scale really measures. However, a student choosing a college may find perceptual scores more useful. The student's problem is that the colleges in which she is interested may not have used the perceptual measure or made it publicly available, particularly if they didn't like the results.

What, then, are the strengths of perceptual measures? First, even if they do not deal with details, perceptual measures can serve a general monitoring function, alerting the administration when things may be going wrong. If the sense of community or the degree of academic rigor seems to be dropping or is below expectations, current policies and programs should be examined to find the cause. Astin, in Chapter Two, explains how such information could be used as part of a student-generated information base.

Second, the research surrounding the measures can help a college to recognize and deal with some of its problems, such as unusually high dropout rates. For example, Astin (1972c) reported that colleges that are low in the cohesiveness of student peer environment and that demonstrate relatively little concern for the individual student have dropout rates above average. (In a later publication, Astin, 1975, suggests some ways to increase the cohesiveness and the demonstrated concern for individuals.)

Third, these measures can be useful tools in evaluating programs and innovations by providing information about their consequences. For example, Dugmore and Grant (1970) evaluated the effectiveness of a clustering program for freshmen at the University of Utah. Concerned about the impersonality that some students complained about, the university arranged to have freshmen grouped into as many of the same classes as possible so they could share similar experiences and form acquaintances and friendships. CUES was used as part of the evaluation. Counter to all expectations, the CUES community scores were lower for these students than for students who were not clustered, which indicated less friendliness and concern. The university decided to abandon this program despite the considerable effort invested in establishing it.

Another example of the use of perceptual information in evaluating programs was reported by Donahue (1971). He found that when residence halls at Michigan State University were made coeducational, the CUES Campus Morale score increased and the Scholarship score declined, especially among the men. However, the overall grade point average did not decline.

A third example was reported by Doman and Christensen (1976), who evaluated the effectiveness of "Group Life Seminars" at Kansas State University. These seminars were designed to discuss, in an informal setting, freshmen's reactions to the college and their personal, social, and academic problems. The freshmen participating in the seminars had higher scores on the CUES scales of Scholarship, Awareness, Practicality, and Campus Morale than nonparticipating freshmen had.

A fourth use of this information is to help decision makers understand the subtle and complex culture of their campuses. This subtlety may be difficult to see and thus may lead us to assume that we know more about the actual functioning of the college than we really do. Perceptual measures provide a method to identify and understand the subtleties of the college, including the intellectual and social climate and the interplay among people, processes, policies, and facilities. These measures can also show how some groups know little about other groups' perceptions and problems. For example, according to Pascarella (1974), administrators thought that students would rate their university's environment much higher on CUES scales than they did. Similarly, other studies indicate that administrators have a considerably more positive view of their colleges than do students, providing evidence that these groups clearly have very different perspectives. The results of assessments could be used to form a basis for discussions to help these groups understand each other's assumptions and viewpoints.

Finally, perceptual measures can help colleges understand the consequences of their emphases. For example, Bayer and Astin (1969), using the Concern for Individual Students scale of the Inventory of College Activities, found that students in institutions scoring high on this scale felt that faculty, administrators, and fellow students were friendly and helpful. They felt part of the college and participated in its activities. Students in low-scoring colleges tended to feel alone and alienated from the faculty and the institution. The lack of concern for individual students is a common student complaint, especially at large institutions, and a cause of concern for faculty and administrators who hope to create a collegial climate. Bayer and Astin found that various measures of faculty quality—degrees, publications, and research—were negatively correlated with Concern for Individual Students scores across 225 colleges.

Thus, upgrading the quality of an institution's faculty may unintentionally reduce the quality of the college experience for students (similar findings were reported for graduate schools in Clark, Hartnett, and Baird, 1976). Hopefully, this inverse relationship is not unavoidable. Some colleges are able to have both humane environments and high-caliber faculty (conversely, some manage to have neither). By employing environmental measures, institutions can see some of the consequences of their decisions and develop alternative courses of action to reach their goals.

In short, environmental measures can provide information unavailable from other sources and thereby help decision makers understand and evaluate their institutions, plan and assess the success of programs, and improve the quality of college life for students and faculty.

### The Stimulus Approach

Astin (1972a) has developed an approach to environmental assessment that he calls a "stimulus" approach. His idea was that the actual behaviors of students and faculty and specific features of the college represent stimuli that affect each student's perceptions of the college as well as each student's own behavior. Astin expressed this idea as follows:

> The "college environment" was considered to include anything about the institution that could be regarded as a potential "stimulus" for the student. A "stimulus" was defined as follows: *Any behavior, event, or other observable characteristic of the institution capable of changing the student's sensory input, the existence or occurrence of which can be confirmed by independent observation.*

He provides the following as examples of possible stimuli:

A. Peer Environment
   1. Average number of hours per week spent in various activities (bull sessions, studying)
   2. Frequency of dates of different types
   3. Roommate's behavior ("messy," "liked to talk")
   4. Typical mode of dress (for class, for dinner)
   5. Membership in campus organizations
B. Classroom Environment
   1. Observations of instructor's behavior (frequency of lectures versus discussion, types of assignments)
   2. Observations of behavior of self and other students in class (asked questions, took notes)
   3. *Modus operandi* of class (seating assigned, smoking permitted, roll taken)
C. Administrative Environment
   1. Disciplinary consequences of potential violations (drinking, cheating, demonstrations, and so on).
   2. Frequency of actual violations of regulations

Astin used this approach to develop the Inventory of College Activities (ICA), mentioned above, in the following manner. Astin asked students to respond to 275 relatively specific items concerning their own behaviors and the characteristics of their peers, classrooms, college rules, and so on. In addition, students responded to 75 items that were similar to CUES items so that their "image" of their college could be determined, the idea being that a college's image may also act as a stimulus. By analyzing separately the items referring to peer, classroom, administrative, and physical environments, Astin found twenty-seven dimensions by which colleges differed. Analysis of the image items produced 8 additional dimensions. The content of the dimensions clearly depended on the particular items that Astin used. For example, the peer environment dimensions ranged from the general factor "competitiveness vs. cooperativeness" to "regularity of sleeping habits."

When Astin and Panos (1969) studied the influence of college environments on the vocational and educational plans and achievements of college students, the stimulus and image measures had a considerable influence that was independent of and sometimes larger than such factual variables as size and type of control (for example, public or Catholic). In predicting twenty-eight criteria after controlling for input, factual environmental variables appeared in the equations eighty-eight times, while stimulus and image factors appeared sixty-eight times, thus appearing to reflect something unique in college environments that influence students' development. Thus, while the facts about a college may tell us a good deal, we still need to know more to understand its environment fully.

A related idea is that of "unobtrusive" measures (Webb and others, 1966). These have been classified as physical traces (for example, consumption of writing pads), archival (for example, average numbers of books checked out of the library per student or number of dropouts), and observations (for example, observing professors' teaching practices). Although this approach appears promising, it has rarely been applied to the college environment, partly because much of the information would be prohibitively expensive to obtain for a large number of colleges. Furthermore, measures related to unobtrusive measures (for example, student/faculty ratio and number of books in the library per student), have been less meaningful and certainly less informative than anticipated. However, many of the institutional data approaches could be considered as "unobtrusive measures." (The advantages and limitations of these approaches were discussed earlier.)

## A Combined Approach

In an effort similar to Astin's ICA work, Centra (1972) analyzed data on fifty-three variables for 103 colleges that were generated by three methods of assessing college environments—student perceptions, students' self-reports of their behavior, and objective institutional data. Centra used multimethod factor analysis, which removes the variance in results due to different assessment methods by focusing on correlations between rather than within assessment methods. Altogether, ten factors resulted, including four that were similar in each method and had also appeared in a traditional factor analysis of the data, and that should reflect valid differences among institutions. These were female cultural emphasis versus athletic emphasis, large size versus faculty-student interaction, academic stimulation, and activism. However, as Centra points out:

> There were, nevertheless, a number of variables for which convergent-discriminant validity was not found, and to the extent that the classification scheme used in this study was reasonable in categorizing variables that measure the same domain, then each method would seem to tap *some* information not predictably obtained by other methods. In general, therefore, there are certain kinds of information that can be obtained by only one method, even when it appears that two or more methods assess the same domain.

Furthermore, as the contributors to this book demonstrate, different methods of assessment are appropriate for different purposes. For example, officials in a large institution *know* that its size makes good faculty-student interaction difficult. Therefore, they look to perceptual measures for clues about how to improve these relations on their campus.

## Conclusion

It is obviously difficult to assess a college's environment. Various approaches can be used, each with a different purpose. How are we to find the most useful approach? To answer this question is the purpose of this book. Several of the contributors have been involved in the development of perceptual and factual measures, and others have wide experience in the use of the instruments. However, the contributors have not written about their particular instruments or experiences; rather, they have discussed general issues involved in the use of the instruments and reported the latest thinking and research. They present a rich diversity of ideas and information concerning the use of the instruments that can improve the effectiveness of decision making.

To see this more clearly, it may be useful to categorize the approaches outlined in this chapter as follows: (1) measures based on the average characteristics of the people in the environment (for example, Astin and Holland, 1961; Richards, Seligman, and Jones, 1970) and those based on the characteristics of the environment considered separately from the people in it (Baird, 1971); (2) measures of between-college differences, such as size (for example, Pace, 1969), and within-college differences, such as fraternity characteristics; and, (3) measures useful for understanding the environment and for decision making (Cain and Watts, 1970).

To illustrate the functions of environmental measures in these three groupings, the contributions to this volume are listed below by author with the appropriate cell number corresponding to Figure 4, which shows a classification of college environmental measures.

*Decision-Oriented Purposes of Between-College Measures*
- Guiding students to appropriate colleges and helping students learn what to expect from their college experience so that they can adapt to college more easily (Cell 4; Baird)
- Allowing a college to compare its environment with environments of similar colleges, which could help identify areas where changes are needed (Cell 2; Wuest and Jones)

*Decision-Oriented Purposes of Within-College Measures*
- Providing data that will help identify areas where changes are needed and areas of agreement and disagreement about policies, goals, facilities, and priorities for the institution (Cells 5, 6, 8; Uhl)
- Providing data that will suggest ways to improve the environment and measuring the effectiveness of changes (Cell 6; Astin)

|  | Purpose | |
| --- | --- | --- |
| Information Distinguishing | General Knowledge | Decision Making |
| Among Institutions<br>In terms of characteristics | 1 | 2 |
| In terms of the people in them | 3 | 4 |
| Within Institutions<br>In terms of characteristics | 5 | 6 |
| In terms of the people in them | 7 | 8 |

**Figure 4. Types of College Environment Measures**

- Identifying significant subgroups and subenvironments at the college and describing their characteristics (Cell 8; Pace)

*Purposes of Environmental Measures for Understanding Colleges*
- Gaining an understanding of the influence of colleges on post-adolescent socialization and personal development (Cell 1; Baird)
- Measuring the conditions surrounding learning (Cell 5; Anderson)
- Assessing the significant aspects of interpersonal relations on the campus among students, professors, and administrators on different campuses (Cells 3, 7; Hartnett).

Clearly, no one instrument would fulfill all these purposes. In fact, several approaches would probably be needed for any one purpose. Several of the contributors to this book suggest that future research work should develop instruments designed to measure those elements of the college environment that have been found to be significant in previous work and that various psychological and sociological theories would indicate are important.

On the practical side, the use of instruments should lead to action; thus, they should refer to specific aspects of the environment that can be changed by the administration. Also, instruments should be developed that include the expert opinion of students about matters affecting them, of faculty about matters affecting them, and so on. As this chapter suggests, the measures should also provide evidence about the effectiveness of administrative decisions. Furthermore, the results obtained through assessments should be easy to communicate to everyone who will be involved in any change. These ideas are discussed at greater length in Chapter Eight.

When decision makers can understand and assess (1) the characteristics of the people in their colleges; (2) the workings of the programs, policies, and processes of their colleges; and (3) the interactions among the programs, policies, and processes, they can consider options and make decisions that will create better intellectual and social environments on their campuses:

- The college president mentioned at the beginning of this chapter, who wished to examine the changes brought about by reforms, could compare faculty responses to the Institutional Functioning Inventory several years ago with current reactions. If, for instance, the Undergraduate Learning and Concern for Advancing Knowledge scores have decreased, one price of the reform may have been a reduction in traditional academic values. The president could thus begin to investigate revisions of the reforms that will retain positive features while restoring the academic emphasis valued by the college.

- The high school senior may be fortunate enough to consider Barat College—one of the institutions involved in the Better Information for Student Choice projects. If attempts to obtain similar information about other colleges fail, the student may choose Barat.

- The university provost could talk with other administrators, faculty members, and students and then consult a psychology faculty member to develop a simple questionnaire that asks for student and faculty ratings of the college's facilities and programs. Using the results of this survey, he might design another form outlining various changes and courses of action. The results of these surveys could then be incorporated into plans for making changes on the campus.

- The dean of students could administer the University Residential Environment Scales to the experimental dormitories and the regular dormitories to learn whether the experimental ones had a greater sense of community and spirit.

- And the counselor working with potential dropouts could use the College Satisfaction Survey with them as well as with a sample of other students to assess the extent and sources of the former group's dissatisfaction. This assessment could lead to a major effort at remedying specific areas of dissatisfaction, curing more general causes of poor morale, and reducing attrition.

# 2

Alexander W. Astin

# Developing Information Systems About Student Activities and Opinions

—•❦•—

Scanning the literature on higher education administration might lead some readers to conclude that the educational environment, or climate of a college, has little to do with how the college is managed. Indeed, one is hard put to find any references to concepts such as learning, student development, and educational outcomes, let alone campus culture or environments. Instead, this

*Note:* The study that led to this chapter was supported by the Exxon Education Foundation.

literature—much of it written by either college administrators or scholars in the field of organization theory—focuses on issues of budgeting, planning, formal organization, leadership, decision making, and institutional politics. At the same time, the literature on college environments—most of it written by scholars in educational psychology or sociology—makes at best only token reference to the possible impact of administrative organization, management styles, and decision making on student development and outcomes.

The basic theme of this chapter is that the processes of environmental assessment and administrative decision making can and ought to be brought closer together. Its principal proposal is a mechanism for merging the two processes—a student-based management information system.

## A Student-Oriented Management Information System

Although most college catalogues claim student development to be a fundamental institutional purpose, the decision-making process in higher education—like the literature on institutional management—often ignores the implications for students of alternative courses of action. Even when administrators and faculty leaders have been offered extensive statistical data about the development of their students, they have had great difficulty in applying these data to policy decisions (Astin, 1976). And most decision makers lack such data. The computer-based management information systems (MIS) now used by many colleges and universities exemplify this fact: Except for simplistic information on enrollments, majors, and credits, these systems provide almost no information on students. Thus, administrators who rely on such systems are encouraged to view planning and decision making basically as a problem in resource manipulation. The "benefit" side of the decision equation reflecting the probable consequences for student development receives scant attention at best and in most cases is ignored altogether.

Seldom have those administrators who might be sympathetic to a more student-oriented MIS seriously attempted to develop one, because they believe such systems are simply unfeasible. A major assumption of this chapter is that such a system not only is feasible but also provides an opportunity to improve the quality of planning and decision making substantially, to use scarce educational resources much more effectively, and—in the long run—to improve the quality of the educational environment.

## Basic Plan for the System

Before focusing on the specifics of design and operation, it is useful to look at the premises upon which a student-oriented MIS would be based:

1. The principal function of planning and decision making in higher education is to enhance the environment for student development. While the other major functions—research and public service, for example—have considerable status in many institutions, no management system is doing its job if it ignores the implications of decisions for students.
2. The acquisition of resources—whether money, capital improvements, or additional staff—is regarded at best as an intermediate consequence of decisions; the ultimate consideration is how such resources can be utilized in the educational process to improve the students' environmental experience. In other words, the acquisition of resources is not an end in itself.
3. Student development is a multidimensional phenomenon involving cognitive skills, socialization, and career preparation. Developmental goals may be short-term (for example, learning calculus or child psychology) or long-term (for example, becoming a productive scientist or an effective parent). Although these different aspects of student development may be valued differently by students, parents, institutions, and the general public, the effectiveness of planning and decision making should be assessed in terms of the institution's contributions to these various goals.
4. The practice of administration is regarded as a kind of performing art. As with most performing arts, specifying the personal talents or behaviors required for effective performance is difficult. Most artists, however, recognize that the development of

performing skills depends heavily on a feedback system that provides some knowledge of results. Painters view the results of their brushstrokes, musicians listen to themselves sing or play, sculptors see and feel their products, dancers rely on feedback from their nerves and muscles to know the position of their bodies, poets and writers read their own works, and so forth. Some artists employ technical aids to enhance this sensory feedback (for example, dancers sometimes use mirrors and composers use pianos).

Practitioners in many fields outside the performing arts are similarly dependent on informational feedback. Physicians, for example, monitor the effects of their treatment programs through various physiological, chemical, and other measures of the patient's functioning. Even in business, executives and sales staff can assess the consequences of their policies and decisions through sales records and profit-and-loss statements. Educational administrators, on the other hand, ordinarily get very little feedback about the educational consequences of their policies and decisions. To be sure, they are inundated with information from a variety of sources, but this information is often unrelated to the educational functioning of the institution. Under these conditions, learning how to administer an educational institution is somewhat like learning how to paint blindfolded or how to play a musical instrument with one's ears plugged.

The student-oriented MIS would operate on a relatively simple feedback principle: Enrolled students would be monitored through an information system that regularly yields data on key aspects of any progress. Subsequent decisions about institutional policy and practice, including resource allocation decisions, would be designed to increase the correspondence between student development and stated developmental goals. The system itself would be continuously subject to change through one or more of the following mechanisms:

1. Redefinition of institutional objectives for students (addition of new objectives, reordering of priorities assigned to current objectives, sharpening definitions, and so on)

2. Modifications in the method of assessing particular developmental outcomes

3. Changes in the method of analysis or display of informational feedback.

Like any MIS, a student-oriented system would be designed primarily for use in planning and decision making. The need to make an educational decision implies two fundamental conditions: some desired outcomes, or ends, and two or more means to achieve those ends. The ends, of course, concern student development. Means might include manipulating certain aspects of the learning environment (for example, curricula and instructional methods), structuring the physical environment (for example, design and location of classrooms, buildings, and athletic fields), or establishing certain rules or regulations. Viewed in this way, *every administrative decision is predicated on the existence of a causal relationship between some educational outcome and a particular means selected to achieve that outcome.* In short, the administrator believes that, of all the means available, the one selected is most likely to produce the desired outcome. Thus, one purpose of the student-oriented MIS is to help administrators determine to what extent their decisions will lead to desired educational outcomes.

Traditionally, college faculty and administrators have been more means than ends oriented. The reward structure in higher education clearly reinforces this tendency, since administrators are rewarded not for improving the educational environment or for maximizing the development of the student but for acquiring a large share of higher education's limited resources: money, bright students, and highly trained and prestigious faculty. Also, the causal connections between means and ends are not well understood. Consequently, administrators must make decisions on the basis of a largely untested folklore about what does and what does not work. Thus, another function of the student-oriented system is educational: to help administrators develop a better understanding of how their actions are likely to affect students and to encourage administrators to think more in terms of ends than of means.

## Measuring Student Development

The success of any student-based MIS depends heavily on the relevance of the environmental and student outcome data to institutional objectives. While any given institution must develop its own specific measures, at least three outcomes are relevant to the educational objectives of most institutions. Measures of these "core" outcomes should be included in any student-based MIS:

1. *Successful completion of a program of study.* In its simplest form, this measure would involve a dichotomy: The student either completes a degree plan or drops out. A more sophisticated approach would be to determine if the students' undergraduate achievements are consistent with their original plans at entry. For example, if a student entered college to become a lawyer, simple completion of the undergraduate degree may not be sufficient, given the relatively stringent admissions requirements of law schools. Thus, admission to law school might be a more appropriate criterion of successful completion.

2. *Cognitive development.* Virtually all colleges and universities are concerned with students' cognitive development, but most institutions limit their assessment to the traditional grade point average. Since grades reflect only students' relative level of performance at a particular point in time, they may not accurately indicate what the student has learned. Thus, cognitive development probably should be measured repeatedly so that change can be assessed by comparing a student's performance level at different points in time. It is not feasible to obtain repeated direct measures of what students have learned; surrogate measures (for example, time spent studying and reports of knowledge acquired in various courses) can be utilized.

3. *Student satisfaction.* Since the undergraduate experience is often highly significant in individuals' lives, the students' perception of the value of that experience is one of the most important indications of program effectiveness. Overall satisfaction can be measured, but it would probably be more useful to obtain information on satisfaction with specific matters, such as with

teaching, curriculum, facilities, career preparation, extracurricular activities, and administrative services.

*Cognitive Growth.* Why institutions do not rely more on standardized tests to assess student progress in the cognitive area is somewhat of a puzzle. Many professors argue that the tests are inadequate: too superficial, incomplete in coverage, culturally biased, and so forth. However, professors' heavy reliance on these same tests to decide undergraduate admissions, advanced placement, and admission to graduate and professional schools belies these objections. Apparently, academics are willing to assess their students' performance but are reluctant to use these same measures to evaluate their own pedagogical efforts.

One difficulty in using standardized tests to monitor student development is scoring. Virtually every test maker today reports student performance only in normative terms: percentiles, standard scores, stanines, and so on. Such scores show how the individual performs in relation to others only. Although they are useful for selecting and screening (that is, identifying the "best" students), they are difficult to use for measuring change or growth. Without any absolute referent, it is difficult to know from successive administrations of such tests if or how much a person's performance level has improved. (The traditional letter-grade system used by most colleges suffers from the same limitation, particularly if students are graded on a curve.)

There is no good reason why such tests cannot be used to produce information on changes in a student's absolute level of performance: for example, in the number or percentage of items answered correctly. In addition, performance data on individual test items could yield important information concerning growth in specific areas of skill or knowledge. Psychometricians have discouraged testing companies from reporting results for individual test items on the grounds that such information is unreliable. However, individual-item data can be highly reliable if they are reported for groups of students.* If the colleges and universities that use stan-

---

*Data on individual-item performance of large groups have been used with considerable success in the *International Study of Achievement in Mathematics* (Husen, 1967).

dardized tests demand that results be reported in raw score form and that item data be included, the testing companies will probably oblige. Such demands could be made for most of the tests now in widespread use: the achievement and advanced placement tests of the College Entrance Examination Board (CEEB), the College Level Examination Program tests, the undergraduate program of the Graduate Record Examination, and the various devices used to select students for graduate and professional schools. The cost of providing this additional information would be trivial. Since so much care is devoted to writing and pretesting items—activities that account for much of the cost of standardized-test construction—the potential benefits from these efforts should not be lost in the construction of scales and the computation of percentiles and other normative measures.

Why do test makers persist in limiting their feedback to normative measures when such information is of limited value to students and institutions? There seem to be at least two explanations:

1. The psychometricians who control the technical aspects of the test industry have become mesmerized by the statistical properties of standard scores and by the elegance of the normal distribution, which underlies classical test theory. Thus, raw scores (such as number answered correctly or number answered correctly minus incorrect answers) are converted to normative scores, a procedure that eliminates the original units of measurement. Individual items, of course, have even worse statistical properties and must be lumped together in sufficient numbers to produce scales that form the appropriately shaped distribution with the proper degree of reliability.
2. The individually administered intelligence test, developed early in this century, served as a model for the group-administered tests used today. While the IQ score was not, strictly speaking, a normative measure, it prompted normative terms with a strong meritocratic connotation: *genius, average, dull normal, imbecile,* and so forth. The earliest large-scale applications of group testing were in the military, which, during the two world wars, was concerned with screening out illiterate and "mentally defective"

recruits and draftees and identifying superior candidates for
officer training. These applications were basically meritocratic:
finding the "best" and "worst" candidates. This view of group
tests continued after World War II, when the crush of applicants
forced many colleges to institute screening procedures that
could be applied on a large scale at relatively low cost. Normative scores provided a simple and seemingly fair means of identifying the best students. This meritocratic view of testing was
reinforced by the competitiveness of the colleges, in which the
"best" colleges are, of course, those with the highest-scoring
students.

This meritocratic orientation was reinforced by competitiveness at the international level in the 1950s and 1960s, when
many Americans interpreted the first Soviet Sputnik to mean that
many of the brightest U.S. students were not going to college. A
manifestation of this concern was the National Merit Scholarship
Corporation, which annually tested close to one million students
just to identify the 1,500 or so with the highest scores who could be
awarded scholarships to assure college attendance. Colleges, of
course, became highly competitive in their quest for Merit scholars,
and the number of scholars in the student body was widely regarded as a sign of academic quality. A similar competition developed among high schools.

Today, most faculty and administrators take the norm-
ative-meritocratic nature of testing for granted. Thus, concern with
student change, growth, or development is subordinate to ranking
students from best to worst. This interest has infected grading
practices, where instead of determining what students learn in a
course or in college, grades are assigned that compare students'
performances with each other. Employers and graduate schools
further reinforce these grading practices, since they conveniently
identify the best students.

There are no reasons why colleges should persist in these
practices other than habit and tradition. Using results from individual items and absolute or raw scores requires little additional

effort, regardless of whether the test is a national standardized test or an individual classroom examination.*

The importance of cognitive outcomes to both students and institutions suggests that any student-oriented MIS must include information on how and what students are learning. Since traditional college grades and the norm-based standardized tests are not suitable to this task, alternatives must be found.

*Affective Growth.* While student development in the academic or cognitive area can be monitored by modifying existing grading practices and standardized tests, measuring noncognitive or affective development may require developing new measures. Satisfaction with various institutional programs and services can be monitored with relatively simple student surveys, but measuring the development of traits such as social maturity, esthetic appreciation, tolerance, kindness, and citizenship may be a more complex task. Data concerning the affective side of the student's development presents certain interpretive problems: How can one evaluate an increase in, say, student dating? Is increased student participation in athletics a positive or a negative sign? Such interpretive problems should not, however, deter institutions from incorporating such data into their MIS. The mere availability of affective data may provide a basis for reformulating or at least sharpening institutional objectives.

A recent national study of student persistence (Astin, 1977) employed fifty different measures of development covering interests, personality, values, beliefs, and attitudes toward social issues. That such measures can be utilized productively in a student-based system is suggested by the fact that many of the measures were found to be sensitive to the effects of the college experience.

Student satisfaction is a useful category because it is relatively easy to assess and is widely applicable to the college experience. Students can evaluate not only their academic programs and instruction but also institutional services, such as orientation, reg-

---

*In this connection, Carver (1974) has suggested that traditional psychometric measures (which are sensitive primarily to individual differences) may not be as useful in assessing student progress as "educametric" measures (which are sensitive primarily to changes in students over time).

istration, financial aid, academic counseling, career counseling, personal counseling, health services, job placement, and campus housing. Even residential facilities can be rated on privacy, roommate assignment, quietness, food service, bathroom facilities, and programming (lectures and films). Students can evaluate extracurricular activities, opportunities for independent study, social life, work experience, contact with faculty members and peers, and so forth. While any institution must decide for itself which areas of satisfaction are most critical, student satisfaction is a rich source of outcome data for the MIS.

### Specifications for the System

A student-based management information system can take many forms. Suggestions provided here will cover only those features that are technically and politically feasible; almost any institution willing to invest modest resources can have such a system operational within a year or so.

The literature on MIS suggests at least six essential ingredients: data base, hardware, software, operating procedures, operating personnel, and users.

*Data Base.* There are three types of student data—entry, environment or process, and outcome. Entry data refer to characteristics of students at the time of enrollment, environment or process data to what happens to the students while enrolled, and outcome data to the students' degree of fulfilling desired educational or behavioral objectives.

Basically, entry data are of two types: background characteristics of students that are usually constant (sex, race, ethnicity, and socioeconomic background) and behavioral characteristics or orientations that can be influenced by the college environment (abilities, competencies, knowledge, social skills, beliefs, attitudes, values, career plans, and educational aspirations). The student data base should contain both types of entry information, since subsequent outcome variables can be affected by both. In addition, there may be some interest in tabulating process or outcome data separately for different types of students (for example, students of each sex). Whenever possible, entry information should also be collected earlier from potential students (that is, the entire applicant pool) to monitor characteristics of the pool over time and to study factors that influence students' acceptance of admission.*

Environmental or process information, which encompasses much of the data that can be collected on students, is primarily intended to reflect what is happening to students. The distinction between process and outcome information is often fuzzy. For example, the fact that a student switches majors can be treated as a change in process, since the student is now exposed to a different field of study, or as an outcome, since the student usually does the choosing. The distinction between process and outcome in this case is not a quality of the data; rather, it depends on how the data are used. Thus, if one is interested in the student's major field as an environmental variable (for example, how it affects an outcome such as the number of hours spent studying), the change in major can be regarded as a change in environment. If one is interested in how the student's choice of a major is affected by some other environmental variable, then the change is treated as an outcome variable.

Administrators who concentrate their efforts on acquiring resources often fail to recognize that their greatest potential resource may be student time. There is good reason to believe that educational environments are affected by how students spend their time (Astin, 1968a) and that the extent to which students achieve particular developmental outcomes is a direct function of the amount of time and effort that they devote to activities designed to produce these outcomes. For example, if an improved knowledge of history is regarded as an important outcome for history majors, maximizing the probability of this outcome is probably a direct function of the time that the students spend listening to professors talk about history, reading historical works, doing history homework, discussing history with other students, and so forth. Within certain broad limits, the more time spent in such activities,

*Institutions can obtain data on their applicant pools from the CEEB admissions testing program and the American College Testing program. Extensive entry data are available through participation in the Cooperative Institutional Research Program (CIRP) of University of California, Los Angeles, and the American Council on Education.

the greater the learning. The time spent attending formal lectures, taking notes, and otherwise attempting to comprehend the material constitutes a fraction of the *potential* time that might be devoted to activities that could contribute to historical knowledge and skills. Possible environmental interventions for controlling this time and effort would be to assign out-of-class work, to improve the quality or accessibility of library offerings in history, and to make lectures and other course materials available through audiotapes, videotapes, slides, and other media. However, it is important to distinguish between making such resources available and the student's effective use of them. An institution may have an excellent library and a wealth of media that students seldom use, or professors may assign homework that students fail to complete. In short, an effectively managed institution not only provides appropriate learning resources but also creates environmental conditions that encourage students to make effective use of those resources.

Most administrators do not recognize that virtually every institutional policy and practice has implications for the educational environment and for how students allocate their time and effort. So-called administrative matters that can affect students directly include class schedules, policies on class attendance, quality of faculty advising and counseling, regulations on academic probation and participation in honors courses, policies about office hours for faculty, and student organization procedures. Even nonacademic decisions can significantly affect how students spend their time in academic pursuits, such as decisions regarding the following: the location of new buildings, such as dormitories and student unions; rules governing residency; the design of recreational and living facilities; on-campus employment opportunities; the number and type of extracurricular activities and regulations governing participation; frequency, type, and cost of cultural events; roommate assignments; financial aid policies; relative attractiveness of eating facilities on and off campus; and parking regulations.

Some institutions may be reluctant to obtain time diaries from students because they assume the students' estimates will be crude and insensitive to differences among institutions and their policies. However, in a study of a national sample of 246 colleges made several years ago students were asked how many hours per week they averaged in various activities (Astin, 1968a). The variation among institutions was remarkable (Table 1). Regular monitoring of how students spend their time is another means to assess the consequences of administrative decisions. In short, the amount of time that students devote to pursuits directly related to desired developmental outcomes is an important informational component of the student-based MIS. In certain instances, such information can serve as a surrogate measure of student cognitive development.

In designing its data base, each institution should consider the entire range of potentially important student behavior. The study of 246 institutions identified more than 200 different aspects of student behavior. Even with regard to behavior relating to so-called academic matters, student bodies are capable of remarkable variation (Table 2). Nonacademic behaviors (dating, drinking, drug use, religious behavior, and participation in cultural events) show similar variations (Astin, 1968a). Which items will be judged relevant or potentially relevant to management will vary by institution.

The student data base must permit the user to follow trends or changes in environmental and outcome variables. To ensure this dynamic feature, the data must be organized either as a longitudinal file, with repeated measures on the same individuals, or as a set

**Table 1. Student Time Devoted to Various Activities by Freshmen**

| Activity | Lowest Institution | Median Institution | Highest Institution |
|---|---|---|---|
| | Mean Hours per Week | | |
| Studying | 16 | 28 | 39 |
| Attending class | 12 | 18 | 23 |
| Sleeping | 39 | 49 | 54 |
| Talking with other students | 7 | 13 | 17 |
| Reading for pleasure | 2 | 3 | 6 |
| Traveling to and from classes | 1 | 2 | 12 |
| | Percent Students Spending at Least 1 Hour Weekly | | |
| Working | 0% | 39% | 93% |
| Watching television | 3% | 47% | 96% |

*Note:* Data from a national sample of 246 institutions.
*Source:* Astin (1968a).

Table 2. Percentages of Freshmen Reporting Various Kinds
of Academic Behavior

| Behavior | Lowest Institution | Median Institution | Highest Institution |
|---|---|---|---|
| Dropping a course | 1 | 18 | 56 |
| Flunking a course | 2 | 19 | 57 |
| Changing majors | 4 | 26 | 43 |
| Changing career plans | 7 | 26 | 39 |
| Failing to take a desired course because of other requirements | 11 | 46 | 81 |
| Cheating on examinations | 0 | 11 | 38 |
| Checking out books from the library frequently | 15 | 56 | 89 |

Note: Data from a national sample of 246 institutions.
Source: Astin (1968a).

of successive cross-sectional files in which the same measures are taken on each successive cohort of students at certain developmental stages (for example, at the end of the freshman year). Longitudinal data files present certain difficulties in student anonymity, although techniques for virtually guaranteeing anonymity are available (Astin and Boruch, 1970). Successive cross-sectional surveys can be conducted with anonymous polling techniques. If the student enrollment is large enough and the desired breakdowns of data into student subgroups are not too fine, the institution can relieve the burden on any individual student by rotating the samples so that no single student is polled more than once or twice during the school year. This method, of course, requires some means of identifying which students have been polled.

A final consideration in designing the data base is comparative analysis with other institutions. If several institutions simultaneously collect comparable data, the potential value of the data in planning and decision making is greatly enhanced. Experience with more than 900 institutions over the past decade suggests that both faculty and administrators are likely to be more interested in student data if comparable data from other institutions are available. There are several mechanisms for generating comparative data on a multi-institutional basis: the Cooperative Institutional Research Program (CIRP); the Institutional Research Program in

Higher Education, conducted by the Educational Testing Service; and the Information Exchange Procedures project of the National Center for Higher Education Management Systems. State college and university systems and consortia of private colleges are other potential mechanisms for collecting multi-institutional data.

*Hardware.* Today practically any institution of modest size has the computer hardware to operate a relatively sophisticated student-based MIS. While one can talk about ideal hardware configurations and the relative advantages of tape drives and disk packs, such discussions tend to be meaningless outside of the context of the particular hardware configuration on the campus in question.

Nevertheless, there are two specific hardware questions to consider. The first is the method used to collect data and convert them to machine-readable form. If an institution conducts regular surveys of students or other members of the academic community, the typical procedure is either to keypunch the responses or to enter them directly into the computer through a terminal keyboard. An alternative technology is now feasible for institutions with even modest resources: the optical scanner or optical mark reader, which converts marks directly from a questionnaire or answer sheet onto magnetic tape or disk for subsequent analysis. This technique is extremely fast and, given adequate volume, much more cost-effective and accurate than keypunching.

The second hardware question is the use of remote terminals. Some advocates of greater MIS use conjure up a science fiction scenario in which each administrator has a terminal with typewriter, printer, or cathode-ray tube on his or her desk. As tempting as it might be to the technically inclined, this vision ignores the fact that most administrators perceive their work as dealing primarily with people rather than with machines. College administrators are not likely to use remote-access terminals but rather to train others to use them. To some extent, this response defeats the purpose of the terminal.

*Software.* A common error in designing management systems is to make the software too "passive." Designers, assuming that users know just what they want, design the software to accommodate highly sophisticated inquiries or requests. While responsiveness to user requests is certainly a useful characteristic of any MIS, equally important is that the system produce information that can guide or stimulate decision makers' thinking. If the system regularly produces reports on the achievement and behavior of students, decision makers will be hard put to ignore this information even if they do not initially request it. The software should be designed not only to anticipate what users are likely to ask for but also to regularly produce information that users are likely to need.

A simple example illustrates this distinction between active and passive systems: Take the seemingly trivial question of how much time students spend commuting from home to campus. If administrators were asked to list the eighteen most important items of information about their students, not 1 in 100 would list commuting time. However, this activity might become quite significant if a student-based MIS showed that commuting time increased greatly as a consequence of a major change in, say, parking regulations. The significance of this change would be even greater if it was accompanied by a decline in study time. Thus, the MIS should not be designed solely to answer specific questions anticipated beforehand but should be capable of *generating* questions that need solutions. As the data base and software are developed and as the system becomes more sophisticated and widely used, informational items seldom or never used can be dropped from the data base or eliminated from routine tabulations.

Determining the kinds of tabulations or reports to be routinely produced is critical to the design. Figure 1 shows a hypothetical example from one such report: data obtained from cross-sectional surveys of the last three freshman classes taken at the end of each academic quarter. Such data could be obtained on a rotated sampling basis so that no freshman participated in more than one survey.

These hypothetical data of how students spent their time are quite consistent with two major exceptions: The number of study hours has dropped off substantially during the past two quarters and the number of TV hours has increased slightly. The drop in study hours could be cause for concern, particularly if it is accompanied by a decline in the cognitive performance of freshmen. (Note the value of departmental examinations, standardized tests,

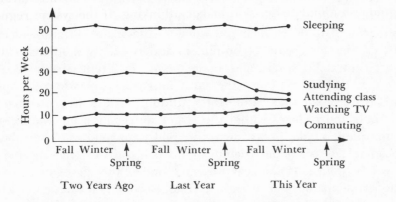

**Figure 1. Sample Output from a Student-Oriented Management
Information System: Quarterly Time Diary for Freshmen**

or other means of regularly assessing students' cognitive development.) Reporting this type of data routinely alerts administrators
and faculty to possible problems. If nothing else, such data stimulate further investigation into possible causes of the changes and
ideally suggest possible remedies. Even the limited data in Figure 1
suggest several explanations for the drop in study hours and rule
out other explanations. Clearly, the lost study hours are not being
spent sleeping or commuting. Also, data on hours spent attending
class do not support the hypothesis that students are studying less
because they are taking lighter class loads. However, the increase in
TV hours suggests that the current freshmen have a lower degree
of academic interest or motivation than previous freshmen.

The administrator who wants to determine if this hypothesis
is true can make use of the entry information in the data base. Do
the students have lower high school grades than students from
earlier years? Are their aptitude test scores lower? Do they aspire to
equally high degrees? Assuming that such entry data do not confirm these possibilities, other explanations could be considered
with the data. For example, are more of this year's freshmen enrolled in courses that require less work? This hypothesis could be
tested by tabulating the data separately for students in different
major fields or different schools or colleges within the university.

The software should be capable of tabulating student outcome data separately for a variety of subgroups that could be of
interest to administrators and faculty. Among the more relevant
subgroups would be men and women, students of different races
or ethnic backgrounds, commuters and residents, students with
different ability levels, and students with different curricular or
career interests. Perhaps the most important breakdown is administrative subunits within the institution. There are, of course,
schools and colleges within the larger universities, but the most
important single breakdown for policy purposes is probably
academic departments. Faculty members identify closely with their
own disciplines. If data are presented only in the aggregate across
departments, one can reject the results as irrelevant to one's own
department. The data in Figure 1 are not likely to pique the interests of most faculty members unless they are broken down by department. If the decline in study hours could be shown to occur in
certain departments but not in others, those departments would
probably be spurred to act or at least to investigate possible causes.

In the final analysis, of course, software must be designed to
reflect the specific needs and concerns of the institution—the
kinds of data being collected and the relevant user groups. Following are a few hypothetical examples to illustrate the wide variations
in data and user groups that are possible with a student-based
management information system.

Case 1. The administration of a liberal arts college begins to
collect and disseminate undergraduate ratings of instruction in
lower-division courses on a department-by-department basis. (This
example could apply as well to data on the quality of academic
advising, the availability of faculty to confer with students, and
other faculty activities.) Compared with other departments, the
quality of instruction in the history department is rated poorly. The
chairperson of the department calls a meeting of the faculty to
discuss the results and to obtain recommendations for action (if the
department fails to take such an initiative, the dean could formally
request that the department prepare a critical analysis of the survey
results with recommendations, if any, for action). The department
might take one of several courses of action. It could seek out more
detailed information about which courses, which instructors, and

which aspects of the instruction were producing the most dissatisfaction, or it could undertake a student-faculty review of the curriculum or even institute a program of in-service training for departmental staff. If the ratings remained poor over time, the administration might provide the department with data on the effectiveness of any efforts at remediation.

What if the history department chose to dismiss the rating data by arguing that students' negative reactions reflected the difficulty of the courses and that students were in fact learning a great deal in these courses? Such a situation illustrates the importance of having data on students' cognitive development, which would empirically test the history department's argument.

Case 2. The administration of a medium-sized state college that has been monitoring student persistence rates for several years notices a sharp increase in the number of nongraduating students who fail to return one fall. (Note that this example could apply to monitoring of many other student outcomes: satisfaction, hours spent studying, and so forth.) Given that its student data base has been well designed from the beginning, the institution could embark on a series of empirical investigations to diagnose the source of the increased dropout rate. Are the changes confined to just one class? Have the characteristics of more recent classes of new students changed? Are there fewer well-prepared students, more transfers, or more commuters? Is the increased dropout rate comparable across curricular subunits or do particular departments or schools account for most of the change? Do other student survey data (satisfaction with housing, instruction, and so on) show any corresponding changes that provide clues to the source of the problem?

Case 3. An institution has been operating a student-based system for several years and decides to make a major change in its program or structure (for example, changing to coeducation, expanding the facilities, adopting a new grading system, or establishing a new core curriculum). If the change was instituted for educational reasons, the data system would provide a means of determining if the change produced the desired results (changes in satisfaction, improvement in cognitive performance, increases in hours spent studying, and so on). If the change was motivated by economic concerns, the data system would help to determine possible side effects on the educational process.

*Operating Procedures and Personnel.* The most sophisticated student-based MIS is not likely to have an impact on decision making unless it is properly operated and interfaced with key administrators. The design and operation of the system should be a joint effort of key persons representing the major functions of the institution: budgeting and planning, academic affairs, and student affairs. It should *not*—as has been true of many earlier attempts to implement an MIS—be assigned to a single unit, such as the office of institutional research or student personnel. The operation, evaluation, and refinement of the system should be institutionalized, not simply assigned to an ad hoc group that disbands when the system is completed or the first report is published. Either the system should become a major part of the existing decision-making apparatus within the institution (for example, the academic policy committee or the budget committee) or a new administrative unit with real power should be created to design and operate it. While there are no simple formulas for forming such a group, a recent study of data use on nineteen college campuses suggests a number of guidelines (Astin, 1976):

1. The group controlling the system should be part of the top administration or at least have clear-cut administrative backing.
2. The chairperson should have recognized status within the institution, for example, the president or a top administrator.
3. The group should not be composed solely on political grounds, that is, chosen only because they represent special-interest groups. Members should be chosen for relevant skill or knowledge, concern for students, innovativeness, and willingness to consider new approaches to institutional governance.

Technical people who design the data base and associated software should either be members of the governing group or report directly to one or more members of that group. A common misconception about information systems is that decision makers do not have to understand how the system works but only how to use it. Users who lack understanding find it difficult to evaluate and control the system.

## Summary

This essay proposes to merge the tasks of institutional administration and environmental assessment by means of a student-based management information system (MIS). A student-oriented MIS not only is possible but also offers an opportunity to lead the administrative and decision-making processes of institutions in more productive directions. Decisions about resource allocation and other policy matters are difficult to evaluate in part because most institutions have no way to relate such decisions to student outcomes. An information system that routinely collects and displays such information is a means both to evaluate the impact of past decisions and to stimulate decision makers to consider the implications of future decisions for students.

C. Robert Pace

3

# Assessing
# Diversity Among
# Campus Groups

From the air the borough of Manhattan looks monolithic. On the ground one can find infinite diversity. But Manhattan's distinctive neighborhoods, whether Harlem, the Bowery, or Greenwich Village, are still clearly a part of New York City. Much of what gives New York its special character are its relatively permanent features—the tall buildings, the subways, the river, the city's history as a port of entry, and its commerce from pushcarts to Chase Manhattan. An element of permanence also accounts for the distinctiveness of other environments and institutions. One cannot describe Canterbury Cathedral without referring to its age, architecture, history, and tradition. The difference between Yale and the University of Minnesota is explainable in part by the land-grant college tradition of egalitarianism and public service that characterizes Minnesota.

In a chapter that considers subenvironments, and within a book that considers the practical uses of environmental measures, one needs to be reminded that subenvironments are parts of larger environments, that there are major differences among these larger institutional environments as well as differences within them, and that the valid reasons for measuring environments, large or small, are not necessarily pragmatic, managerial, or motivated by missionary impulses to reform.

Institutional differences, like individual differences, are interesting and important phenomena in their own right. The description and systematic measurement of institutional differences permit relationships to be explored, taxonomies and classifications to be developed, and the institutions to be better understood. The purpose of vocational interest measures is not to change students' interests but to identify systematically what they are and to compare them with other interests. So, too, the purpose of environmental measures has not been to change environments but to characterize them systematically and to compare different environments. This is not to say that measures of interest or environments are without practical utility or even that the test developers were not thinking of utilitarian potentials. Quite the contrary. The utility of vocational interest measures to vocational choice has been well documented. The best use of environmental measures to this time, however, has been as consciousness raising about the diversity of institutions and as contributing substantially to better research and better understanding of college impact on student development at national and interinstitutional levels.

Many useful generalizations have emerged from this research on college environments: (1) Students who come to college with highly unrealistic expectations about the environment are more likely to report difficulties in adapting to it and are more likely to withdraw than are students whose expectations are more realistic; (2) students' satisfaction with college is related to their perception of the environment as a friendly, congenial, and supportive community; (3) students' plans to attend graduate school

are related to the scholastic press of the environment; (4) when
students' personality characteristics are generally congruent with
environmental characteristics, they attain relevant objectives more
consistently than when these two types of characteristics are dissonant; and (5) certain environmental profiles or institutional types
are broadly related to students' self-reported sense of progress toward the objectives of liberal education, personal and social development, and vocational development.

The initial intent and the primary use of environmental
measures have been to describe and differentiate important
characteristics of the system of higher education. The object of
measurement has been the total institution—not student subcultures, the faculty, or the administration. The next application of
environmental measures, advocated in this book, is to describe and
differentiate subenvironments within an institution and to explore
how they relate to one another and contribute to or detract from
the institution's effectiveness. Instead of measures for institutional
comparisons, one would have measures for institutional case study.

## Evidence for Subenvironments

If most environmental measures have been constructed to
identify differences among institutions rather than among subenvironments within institutions, then what is the evidence that such
subenvironments exist and that they are important? There is an
extensive research literature on student characteristics, student activities, and student peer groups; on the characteristics of administrators and administrative styles, administrative roles, and the attitudes and values of administrators; and on the characteristics of
faculty members, their attitudes and values, their teaching, and
their influence on students. We will not review this literature.
Rather, we will select a few examples that are most clearly related to
environmental measurement and to differentiating subenvironments within colleges and universities.

One obviously cannot describe the environment or atmosphere of Harvard without considering the characteristics of Harvard students. What is the environment of France without the
French? The student characteristic that has been measured most
extensively is scholastic aptitude. One of the major distinguishing

elements of colleges and universities is their selectivity. The mean college aptitude test scores of entering freshmen at the most selective institutions are four to five standard deviations higher than those at the least selective institutions. While this range of difference is fairly well known, what is less well known is that within most colleges and universities, the difference between the highest-scoring student and the lowest-scoring student is about equally large (Darley, 1962). (Obviously, this is not true for a small group of highly selective institutions—California Institute of Technology being the classic example.)

The relevance of this fact to the study of subcultures lies partly in how this fact is related to measures of students' vocational interests and how students with similar interests and aptitudes tend to be concentrated in the same academic programs within the institution. Neither college aptitude scores nor vocational interest scores are randomly distributed across students in such diverse fields as education, business, agriculture, the physical sciences, engineering, social sciences, or the humanities. To the extent that concentrations rather than random distributions exist, the likelihood of academic subcultures exists. These empirical relationships generated the idea for the development of the Environmental Assessment Technique (EAT) (Astin and Holland, 1961). The EAT assumes that a student's major field in college corresponds to the student's ultimate occupational field. Students tend to enter majors that are generally congruent with or supportive of their interests, and this fact can be used to identify academic subcultures. In fact, there is evidence that the interests of students who change their major field become more congruent with the interests of students already in that field (Kojaku, 1972). In short, people with similar interests tend to find one another and to major in fields that are supportive of those interests. In order to identify academic subcultures, one might administer Holland's Vocational Preference Inventory (Holland, 1973) to the student body and then sort the results by academic major.

Another line of inquiry for sorting potential student subenvironments is illustrated by tests that purportedly identify different orientations or values among students. The best-known such effort is the Clark-Trow typology of student orientations (Trow, 1962), which is part of the College Student Questionnaires published by the Educational Testing Service (Peterson, 1968). This device simply asks students to relate their own orientations to college to one of four paragraph descriptions, which are assumed to reflect a collegiate orientation, an academic orientation, a vocational orientation, and a nonconformist orientation. The proportion of students in a particular college who identify with each of these four orientations suggests the kind of student subcultures that exist at the institution.

A similar instrument is the Student Orientations Survey (Morstain, 1976). This questionnaire identifies students' orientations or value systems with one of two essentially opposite dimensions—a preparatory, pragmatic, instrumental dimension and an exploratory, expansive dimension. This test seems to measure differences in cognitive style: a preference for specific, well-structured, sequential activities or for less structured, more open-ended, more flexible activities. If one administered this instrument to the student body and then sorted out the scores by academic major, students with the more specific, definite, pragmatic orientation would tend to be in certain academic fields, perhaps the physical sciences and engineering, rather than the social sciences, humanities, and the arts. These results would suggest the existence of differentiated academic subcultures within the university.

The Omnibus Personality Inventory (OPI) (Heist and others, 1968) can be used in a similar manner. One of the most interesting aspects of the OPI is the identification of individuals who possess what the authors describe as an intellectual orientation. This is evidenced by high scores on the scales measuring theoretical orientation, thinking introversion, complexity, and autonomy. Students so characterized are found in large proportions in some institutions and probably in certain major fields more than in others.

Age-old observations quite accurately describe the results of current research on student peer groups: Birds of a feather flock together, and people are influenced by the company they keep. One example of the latter is a study in which students were assigned to different living quarters according to major field or intended vocation; thus, in certain dormitories science students predominated by a ratio of four to one over those majoring in the humanities or social sciences, while in other areas the ratio was reversed. At the end of the freshman year, proportionately more of the students in the minority groups had changed their majors in the direction of the majority group (Brown, 1968). Another example is the longitudinal study of attitude changes in students from different Harvard houses, which showed that attitudes changed in the direction of the prevailing norm and that the extent of peer involvement was linked to the extent of change (Vreeland and Bidwell, 1965).

The primary basis for Astin's nationwide study of college environments (Astin, 1968a) was an instrument called the Inventory of College Activities (ICA), which Astin developed. This instrument attempted to measure different aspects of the environment, specifically the peer environment, the classroom environment, and the administrative environment, plus two other elements, the physical environment and the college image. While the study and the development of the instrument were motivated by an interest in revealing the extensive national diversity of environments, the ICA could also be used to study subenvironments within a given institution. The instrument, however, has not been widely used, although it could be. One of the interesting and particularly relevant findings of Astin's study is that the peer environment, the classroom environment, and the administrative environment sometimes interact in supportive ways and sometimes not. An analysis of such interactions would be of value in revealing the dynamics of subenvironments within particular institutions.

All of these studies of student characteristics, student activities, and student peer groups indicate the following: (1) There is considerable diversity among students within almost every institution; (2) students with certain abilities and interests are concentrated in certain academic disciplines; (3) students whose interests are compatible with certain academic groupings tend to gravitate toward those groupings even if they initially choose another major field; (4) student living groups, fraternities, sororities, extracurricular groups, and so on, attract students selectively and exert an influence upon them in the general direction of the group norm; and (5) college environments can be divided into different components, such as the peer environment, the classroom environment,

and the administrative environment, which can interact in supportive or nonsupportive ways.

Students are influenced by their peer groups, and a given
institution has many different peer groups whether it is large or
small. Students are influenced by the programs they pursue, and
every institution has different academic programs and majors.
Students are also influenced by the general character of the larger
institutional environment.

## Major Groups Within the Environment

The people at colleges and universities fall into at least four
readily identifiable groups of people—students, faculty members,
administrators, and an assortment of bureaucrats, clerks, and service personnel. Just as there have been studies of student characteristics, so have there been studies of faculty characteristics and
administrator characteristics. The fourth group has not been extensively studied to the present writer's knowledge.

Unfortunately, the studies of faculty members and of administrators have not been made with the intention of relating the
characteristics of those groups to student development or to the
interaction of students, faculty, and administrators. We know a lot
about faculty characteristics from the classic study of Logan Wilson
(Wilson, 1942) and the sociological analysis of Parsons and Platt
(1973), which dealt mainly with faculty members in the arts and
sciences, and from two of the reports published by the Carnegie
Commission on Higher Education (Ladd and Lipset, 1975; Trow,
1975). We know a lot about administrators from the recent study
of college presidents (Cohen and March, 1974), analyses of organizational and administrative styles (Millett, 1968), various studies
of organizational functions (Perkins, 1974), a study of department chairpersons (Dressel and others, 1970), and the study of
the unique role of academic administrators and administration
(Corson, 1975).

While students, faculty, and administrators are easily distinguished from one another by their activities and their roles within
the institution and in that sense form identifiable subcultures,

they do not therefore disagree about educational values and in-stitutional goals. In fact, the evidence seems to indicate that the three groups largely agree.

Many years ago in the Syracuse University self-study (Pace, 1949), students and faculty rated the importance of eighteen state-ments about educational objectives. While the two groups differed about the degree of importance that they attached to certain objec-tives, especially those related to personal and social development, the relative agreement between the two groups was very high (a rank-order correlation of .74).

In the large-scale study of changes in university organization (Gross and Grambsch, 1974), comparisons were made between the importance attributed to various educational goals by faculty mem-bers, administrators, and various groups external to the univer-sities. The faculty members and administrators substantially agreed not only on their ratings of the importance of the various goals but also in their perception of the sources of power and influence operating upon and within the institutions. The degree of congru-ence between the faculty and administrator rankings was very high (rank-order coefficients over .90).

In the use of the Educational Testing Service's Institutional Goals Inventory (IGI) in California colleges and universities (Peter-son, 1973), the various goal statements were rated by faculty mem-bers, undergraduate students, graduate students, administrators, and other groups. The ratings given by faculty, undergraduates, and administrators within institutions both of goals as they were in fact emphasized ("is" ratings) and as the groups thought they should be emphasized ("should be" ratings) were remarkably simi-lar. Moreover, the direction of differences between the "is" ratings and the "should be" ratings were consistently in the same direction for faculty, undergraduates, and administrators. In other words, even though there were often large differences between the "is" and "should be" ratings, the direction of those differences was always consistent.

None of these studies of educational values and institutional goals were specifically intended for an analysis of the internal envi-ronments of particular colleges and universities, although, of course, the data could be used for this purpose. Moreover, the instruments developed for these surveys of values and goals have not been described by their authors as environmental measures.

The most widely used measure for characterizing college environments has been the College and University Environment Scales (CUES) (Pace, 1969). CUES characterizes the institutional environment as a whole by the collective perceptions or consensus of the students; it was not designed to measure or identify possible subcultures. Nevertheless, many of the hundreds of studies using CUES as a measuring instrument over the past ten years or so have administered the instrument to different groups of students within an institution to find out whether the perception of the environment differed among subgroups or subcultures. For example, some studies have compared the perceptions between dormitory residents and members of fraternities and sororities, between resident students and commuting students, between students in different academic fields within the same institution, between black students and nonblack students, between men and women, between varsity athletes and other men students, between returning and nonreturning students, and between students and faculty. Although most of these studies have concluded that different groups tend to perceive the environment in rather similar ways, some have produced the contrary conclusion; thus, even an instrument not intended to reveal subcultures can nevertheless reveal them or at least suggest their existence. Another and perhaps more general indication of the existence of different perceptions within institutions is the fact that there is a substantial relationship (correlation of .45) between the number of items on which there is high consensus among students and the size of the institution—the smaller the institution, the greater the number of such items.

The validity of responses to the items in CUES rests on two assumptions: that the overall environment is comprehensible within the students' experience and that the students have been in the environment long enough to sense its dominant features and style. These assumptions are well supported in the liberal arts colleges, most of which are small and residential and have relatively few transfer or part-time students. Generally, they have been and continue to be comprehensible total environments. Interestingly, CUES has been used by at least three-fourths of all the liberal arts colleges in the country but by perhaps no more than a third or a fourth of larger institutions, where the assumptions underlying the validity of CUES responses are supported least. Most often, CUES has been used to determine whether differences in perception exist among various groups of students or units within the environment of the institution as a whole.

## Diagnostic Instrument Designed
## to Identify Subgroups

The rationale behind the construction of environment measures, particularly the College Characteristics Index (CCI) (Pace and Stern, 1958a), was the psychological theory that a reasonable matching of student and environmental characteristics would be predictive of better student performance and satisfaction. Thus, such a matching would be useful in the admissions process. However, the CCI, CUES, and similar instruments have not typically been used in this way. Their main use has been for institutional self-study and evaluation; for such a use, particularly in large institutions, a more diagnostic approach to measurement is clearly needed.

An early effort to provide a more diagnostic instrument was the construction of the College Characteristics Analysis (CCA), which was used in a study of nine colleges and universities specifically designed to measure and assess the influence of academic and student subcultures within college and university environments (Pace, 1964).

When the CCI was constructed, no systematic guidelines existed for selecting item content. Subsequent efforts to classify the item content of the CCI indicated that approximately half of all the items were related to students' interests, activities, and extracurricular programs, whereas only about a fourth dealt with such aspects of the environment as the faculty, the curriculum, and instruction, and only about a fourth dealt with administrative rules and procedures, facilities, and other special features.

The first order of business in constructing the CCA was to develop a blueprint for item content so that each aspect of the environment to be measured would be systematically represented.

There were 180 items in the CCA. The first set of 60 items referred to the college as a whole, covering such aspects as general rules and regulations, policies, procedures, and facilities. The second set of 60 items referred to academic aspects of the environment—characteristics of faculty members, courses, teaching, and so forth. In responding to this set of items, the student was first asked to identify his or her major academic field and then to answer the items with respect to that major field rather than with respect to the college or university as a whole. The third set of items referred to student aspects of the environment—student characteristics, extracurricular programs, and activities. In answering these items the students were requested to respond with reference to the students that they knew best, identified with, and associated with most commonly and to the extracurricular and informal activities that they knew about because they or their friends were involved in them. In other words, each student's answer referred to his or her own set of student acquaintances and activities rather than to the student body in general.

The CCA was also organized to measure four different environmental emphases, these being dimensions that had emerged from factor analysis of the original CCI. These emphases, or dimensions, of environmental press were (1) intellectual, humanistic, and esthetic; (2) friendly and group welfare oriented; (3) scientific and independent; and (4) practical and status oriented. Each of these four environmental press dimensions was measured by a set of forty-five items, fifteen reflecting administrative sources of press, fifteen reflecting academic sources of press, and fifteen reflecting student sources of press. This structure, with illustrative items, is outlined in Table 1.

One interesting way in which the CCA was used was to examine the relative contribution made by administrative, academic, and student sources to the institution's score on a particular dimension. These internal differences in the sources of environmental press were most apparent when the consensus method of scoring was used. For example, in one institution six items had a consensus of two to one on the scientific, independent scale. Five of those items came from the academic sector of the environment, one from the administrative sector, and none from the student sector.

In that same institution, twenty-one items had a consensus of two to one on the practical, status-oriented scale. Ten of those items came from the student sector of the environment, seven from the administrative sector, and only four from the academic sector. These differences in the sources of environmental press were reported in detail for each of nine different institutions, ranging in size from Bennington to the University of Florida.

The diagnostic potential of the CCA has not been exploited in subsequent studies mainly because the instrument was never officially published and thus never made available to other investigators.

At about the same time that the second edition of CUES was under construction, a longer diagnostic version was developed, modeled after the CCA. This 300-item test was tried out in a few large universities. The differences among subgroups within the universities, although not as great as the differences among subgroups across universities, were nevertheless considerable. The differences within institutions were smallest, as one would expect, on those items referring to the administrative or overall characteristics of the institution. Differences among academic subgroups were greatest on those items dealing with the academic environment and were substantial, although they were somewhat smaller on items dealing with the student environment.

The diagnostic version of CUES was used in a study of peer groups at UCLA (Herrscher, 1967). Six specific peer groups were identified—a dormitory section, a sorority, a campus service group, a political activist group, a departmental honorary group, and an athletic team. In responding to the student section of the test, students were instructed to answer the items by referring to their particular peer groups. The test was also given to a randomly selected cross section of students. In all cases responses to the administrative items referred to the university as a whole and responses to the academic items referred to the department or division of the student's major; in all cases except for the specified peer groups, responses to the student items referred to the students and activities that "one knows best."

Regardless of how students were grouped, the scores on the administrative items should have been about the same because all

**Table 1. Illustrative CCA Items**

| Source of Emphasis | Direction of Scale Emphasis | | | |
|---|---|---|---|---|
| | Intellectual, Humanistic, Esthetic | Friendly, Group Welfare | Independent, Scientific | Practical, Status Oriented |
| **Administrative** | | | | |
| Rules and regulations | Students are allowed to help themselves to books in the library stacks. | The student government has a responsible role in regulating student behavior. | Students who do not make passing grades are quickly dropped from school. | Student organizations must get administrative approval to take a stand on controversial issues. |
| Facilities | There is a theater on or near the campus specializing in foreign films. | Dormitories are nicely arranged for small informal gatherings. | Laboratory facilities in the natural sciences are excellent. | Athletic facilities are modern and well equipped. |
| Overall features | The school has an excellent reputation for academic freedom. | The school helps everyone get acquainted. | Students here are encouraged to be independent and individualistic. | There is a lot of fanfare and pageantry in many of the college events. |
| **Academic** | | | | |
| Faculty | Many of the professors are actively engaged in writing. | Many faculty members are active in community work—churches, charities, schools, service clubs, etc. | Many of the professors are actively engaged in research. | Faculty members always wear coats and ties on the campus. |

| | | | |
|---|---|---|---|
| Curricula | There are good opportunities for students to study and criticize important works in art, music, and drama. | Many courses are designed to prepare students for well-informed citizenship. | Accelerated or honors programs are available for qualified students. | Many courses stress the concrete and tangible rather than the speculative or abstract. |
| Instruction | Class discussions are typically vigorous and intense. | Students who are having difficulty with a course are encouraged to talk with the professor about it. | Frequent tests are [not] given in most courses. | Students almost always wait to be called on before speaking in class. |
| Student Characteristics | Students set high standards of achievement for themselves. | Students have a lot of group spirit. | Many students are planning careers in science. | Students are more interested in specialization than in general liberal education. |
| Extracurricular programs | Many students belong to departmental clubs: for example, French Club, Philosophy Club, Math Club, and so on. | Many upperclassmen play an active role in helping new students adjust to campus life. | Receptions, teas, or formal dances are seldom attended. | Student elections generate a lot of intense campaigning and strong feeling. |
| Informal activities | Many students are attracted to concerts and art exhibits. | Students often have small parties to celebrate pleasant events. | Most students [do not] dress and act pretty much alike. | There is very little studying here over the weekends. |

responses referred to the university as a whole. The data confirmed this prediction. On the academic items, one would expect that the variation of scores by academic groups would have been greatest on the scales that were most relevant to the academic, intellectual aspects of the environment. At UCLA this was true for the Awareness scale but not for the Scholarship scale. At other institutions one might reasonably expect significant differences among academic subgroups on the Scholarship scale. On the student items in the Community scale, one would expect differences between the peer groups and other groups because only the peer groups responded to the items by referring to a specific and presumably close-knit set of students. This expectation was confirmed by the data: The scores of peer groups on the Community scale were more than twice as high as the scores of the campus cross section. In other words, peer group members describing their own group reported a much greater sense of community in the environment than did a cross section of students or students in various academic fields.

## Guidelines for Developing
## More Useful Diagnostic Instruments

The Educational Testing Service was invited to make the diagnostic version of CUES available to other institutions on an experimental basis but has not done so. An instrument diagnostic of important subcultures within colleges and universities still needs to be developed and made generally available, particularly for the purpose of institutional self-studies. The previous experiences with the CCA and the diagnostic version of CUES were steps in this direction.

In designing a more broadly useful instrument, one might begin by conceptualizing three levels of environments—the overall institutional environment, the environments of subcultures, and the environment of the individual. Whether the personal environment can be determined or even whether it needs to be for an institutional evaluation rather than an individual evaluation are moot questions. However, descriptions of both the general institutional environment and the environments of important institutional divisions seem essential. Second, some indication of the nature of students' contact with the environment is needed. Since not all students are involved in all parts of the environment, knowledge about the experience base for students' perceptions must be known in order to interpret the students' perceptions. This would be especially important with respect to such experience differences as on-campus residence and off-campus, full-time and part-time status, and so forth. Third, although students may agree that something is characteristic of the environment, they may differ in how much importance they attribute to the characteristic. For example, a community college transfer student entering the university at the junior year or a commuter student may attach relatively little importance to certain characteristics of the environment that a full-time residential student would regard as very important. Fourth, a reasonable number of environmental characteristics included in the total item content should be changeable so that the faculty and administration reviewing the test results can alter the character of the instrument if they so wish.

A revised or new instrument should also have a clear content structure around which items can be grouped and scored. This content structure, which might be similar to that of the CCA and the diagnostic version of CUES, is necessary to assure that the final instrument diagnoses different segments of the environment and to determine the extent to which the various segments reinforce or conflict with one another.

The other decision in designing a new instrument involves the major dimensions of press to be measured. From factor analysis studies and other analyses of existing instruments, certain common or similar dimensions have emerged. All research studies have identified a scholarship dimension—that is, a dimension measuring reflectiveness, intellectuality, understanding, and academic achievement—and a community dimension—the degree to which the environment is perceived as being friendly, cohesive, and supportive. Most of the research studies have also identified an awareness dimension—one that measures esthetic expression, individuality, openness to criticism, and sociopolitical sensitivity—and a dimension related to the nature of control, supervision, organization, and status. Finally, many studies have suggested a vocational, utilitarian emphasis.

Over the past several years, Rudolph Moos and his colleagues at the Stanford Social Ecology Laboratory have used the collective perception approach to study a variety of organizations, including the military, industries, hospitals, and college residence halls (Moos, 1974). In every environment, three types of dimensions were found: (1) personal development dimensions—that is, achievement is relevant to the purposes of the organization; (2) relationship dimensions—that is, people are involved in the environment and support and help one another; and (3) system maintenance and system change dimensions—that is, aspects of order, organization, clarity, innovation, and so forth are involved in the control of the institution. The Scholarship and Awareness scales of CUES would be personal development dimensions in Moos's terms, the Community scale would be a relationship dimension, and portions of the Practicality and Propriety scales would be system maintenance dimensions.

In summary, a revised measure of college environment would (1) characterize the environment along four or five major dimensions, (2) have an explicit content structure so that different segments of the environment or sources of press could be identified, (3) characterize the environment at two levels (that of the college as a whole and those of significant subenvironments), and (4) enable the perceptions to be interpreted in relation to the students' experience base and the importance or relevance attributed to the various characteristics. Such an instrument would be a significant improvement over current measures, have diagnostic properties that would make it more useful in institutional self-study and evaluation, and advance future research.

A recent study at UCLA has attempted to incorporate at least some of the foregoing suggestions. The UCLA project, one of a dozen or so funded by the Fund for the Improvement of Postsecondary Education under the general theme of "Better Information for Student Choice," involved two elements. First, from the annual surveys of UCLA's college freshmen, sponsored by the American Council on Education, answers to the question Who goes to UCLA? were analyzed with respect to the backgrounds, characteristics, aspirations, and values described by the respondents. The second part of the study was addressed to the question What's UCLA like? For this purpose, a new instrument for characterizing the environment was constructed, and the highlights of the results obtained from a cross section of some 400 UCLA upperclassmen were reported. Thus far the results simply appear in a pamphlet entitled *UCLA: Who Goes? What's It Like?* (Pace, 1976), which is intended for high school students, high school counselors, and parents as an aid in choosing colleges.

The research of Moos and his colleagues influenced the development of the structure of the environmental measure for the UCLA project. We started by arbitrarily deciding that at least four personal development dimensions should be measured, because to varying degrees they are the concerns of most colleges and universities. These dimensions were as follows: (1) an intellectual, scholarly, academic emphasis; (2) an esthetic, expressive, creative emphasis; (3) a critical, evaluative, societal concern and personal commitment emphasis; and (4) an emphasis on vocational and occupational competence. Second, the project staff decided that relationship dimensions should be measured by at least three scales: (1) peer-group relations, (2) relations between students and faculty, and (3) relations of students with administrators and administrative offices. A separate set of items to measure the system maintenance and system change dimension was not constructed, partly because aspects of this dimension were included in other scales.

In selecting items for the new instrument, called the College and University Environment and Experience, we drew upon several sources. First, we looked at all items that had been used in any previous edition of CUES or its variations, such as the CCA and the diagnostic version of CUES, eliminated those whose content was clearly obsolete, and attempted to classify as many of the remaining items as possible under the personal development dimensions and the relationship dimensions that we had set up. Additionally, we interviewed groups of students who were majoring in different academic fields, plus selected groups of students in a dormitory, a fraternity, a sorority, a group of leaders in student government, and a group of black students. From these interviews we generated several hundred ideas for items, put together two somewhat similar versions of an instrument, and tried them out on a fairly good cross section of about 200 upperclassmen. From an analysis of those results, we selected what seemed to be the best items for the final questionnaire.

The first part of the final questionnaire consists of thirty-six items related to the students' major field—nine each related to the four personal development dimensions previously noted. These items were to be answered with reference to the students' major field. The second part of the instrument consists of three sets of nine items, each measuring the relationship dimensions—one set pertaining to peer-group relationships, one set to student-faculty relationships, and one set to relationships between students and various administrative personnel or offices. The final section of the questionnaire consists of statements about overall impressions of the university as a whole. The structure of this instrument, with illustrative items, is outlined in Table 2.

Results from the use of this instrument were obtained from a random sample of 400 UCLA upperclassmen, all of whom had been at the university for at least two years and who had been in their major field for at least one year. The results confirm the importance of academic and other subcultures and the ability of the instrument to reveal them. For example, on the first set of thirty-six items, there were significant differences among major fields on twenty-four out of the thirty-six items. On the items related to student peer-group relationships, there were no significant differences associated with major field; on the items related to student-faculty relationships, there was only one item showing a significant difference by major field; and on the nine items concerned with relationships between students and various administrative personnel or offices, there were only two that showed significant differences by major field.

Significant differences on the items dealing with peer-group relationships were found between those who lived on campus and those who lived at home and between transfer students and non-transfer students.

Some indication of the student's base of experience and his or her particular reference for answering various items was also built into the test. For example, for the statements regarding peer-group relationships, students were asked to indicate which was the largest source of their student friendships and activities—students in their fraternity, sorority, or dormitory, students in their major field, students in various extracurricular activities or other programs, or some other base that they could indicate. They were

## Table 2. Structure and Sample Items of the College and University Environment and Experience

*Part I*

Personal Development Dimensions of the Environment

1. Academic, scholarly, intellectual emphasis:
   "The professors here expect you to think, not just to memorize answers."
2. Esthetic, expressive, creative aspects of the environment:
   "Some of the faculty offices are attractively decorated with paintings, fabrics, plants, and so on."
3. Evaluative and critical emphases, societal concerns, and personal commitment:
   "Students are expected to question traditional values and assumptions."
4. Occupational and vocational emphases in the environment:
   "Most students in this field are mainly interested in the vocational value of the subject matter."

*Part II*

Relationship Dimensions

1. Among students and in student activities (the underlying dimension is from friendly, congenial, and supportive to impersonal, distant, and apathetic):
   "Students often help each other study and review for tests."
2. Between students and faculty (the underlying dimension is from friendly, helpful, and accessible to remote, formal, and impersonal):
   "Faculty are usually very helpful if you go to see them."
3. Between students and administrative offices and personnel (the underlying dimension characterizes such contacts as flexible, adaptive, and helpful versus rigid, rule bound, and impersonally bureaucratic):
   "Most administrators are willing to interpret regulations in a way that is helpful to individual or unusual cases."

*Part III*

Overall Features and Impressions

- There is no single dimension underlying the items in this section. Most of the items are of two types—first, some general feature of

the campus, and second, some indication of student satisfaction with that feature. Major features include the library, public events, cultural events, student facilities and services, and so on:
   "A lot of distinguished public figures come to the campus for special events—lectures, forums, and so on."
   "Many students find this a stimulating part of their college experience."

---

asked what they mainly had in mind when they answered the statements on student-faculty relationships—whether instructors in their major field, all their instructors, or all their instructors plus what they had heard from other students. With respect to items on the relationships between students and various administrative personnel or offices, they were asked to indicate roughly on how much personal experience their answers were based, the options being "many contacts," "occasional contacts," or "general reputation but little direct experience."

   The instrument obviously differentiates among academic subcultures and produces results that vary with the nature of the student's contact with the institution (for example, a resident or a commuter, a transfer student or a nontransfer student, or a person whose contacts with administrative offices have been frequent or a person whose contacts have been rare). Although some of the item ideas for the instrument were generated from conversations with UCLA students, much if not all of the item content is applicable to other large comprehensive universities.

   After the questionnaire was used in the UCLA project, it was slightly revised after various psychometric analyses were made: One item was eliminated, and seven other items were replaced by better items. Each of the nine-item scales in Parts I and II are appropriately homogeneous (the items all correlate positively with one another), discriminating (all items correlate positively with the scale score), and reliable (alpha coefficients between .60 and .80).

## Influence of Environment on Students

   To conclude this chapter, some observations should be made about the meaning of environmental measures and how they may relate to other observations that are crucial to fully understanding student development and college influence.

The college environment may be conceived of as the events and experiences that occur at a college, which reflect the purposes of the institution and its functions. Most current environmental measures reveal these purposes and functions by the clarity and strength with which the institution's constituents perceive them as a result of their own experience. The college—its curriculum, faculty, facilities, resources, and policies—exists before the student arrives. The question is to learn how students use the environment, how the nature and quality of what they do influences their own development, and how the environment presents opportunities and rewards for student responses. Given that there are three basic types of dimensions that characterize and differentiate environments (personal development dimensions, relationship dimensions, and system maintenance and system change dimensions), the problem is to identify the strength of these dimensions in different parts of the environment. An adequate instrument for characterizing the environment of a college or university helps reveal these differences among major segments of the environment.

In addition, the degree to which environments influence student development may depend on certain qualities of and relationships among these various dimensions as well as on the strength of each dimension. These qualities and relationships probably involve at least three more concepts that must be measured—intensity, pervasiveness, and congruence. A particular environmental dimension may typically be intense or bland; it may be pervasive across time and place or be sporadic or localized; and the emphasis felt in one part of the environment may be congruent or dissonant with the emphasis in another part of the environment. Any model for studying college effects must therefore identify the contexts in which different college events and experiences occur.

All learning and development in college involve some effort by the student. How much one learns depends on how much effort is expended. Effort, whether great or little, also has a quality dimension. The quality of cognitive effort can range from low-level activities such as memorizing facts, principles, and terminology to high-level activities such as application, analysis, synthesis, and critical evaluation. The quality of affective effort can range from disinterest and indifference to interest, enjoyment, and satisfaction. The quality of energy or behavior can range from passive to active, from silent spectator to active participant and public advocate. The effort made to gain quality or intensity of experience can vary from high to low. But the effort made to extend the *range* of events and experiences to which one is exposed can also vary. So, any model for studying college effects must also identify the quality of effort invested by the student in the educational enterprise.*

The student is surely accountable for the quality of investment or effort that he or she makes in furthering his own learning and development. Surprisingly, this dimension has rarely been measured in studies of student development and college influence. The college, of course, is accountable for providing the events and the environmental context designed to stimulate student learning and development. In evaluating higher education, we should not only ask what does college do for the student but also what the student does with the opportunities presented by the college. If we ask both of these questions and relate the answers to each other, we will focus on the educative purposes of colleges and universities and possibly enrich our understanding of how the student and the environment interact to stimulate student growth and development. It is the internal pattern, as well as the quality, of these interactions that must be measured.

---

*I am currently developing and pretesting a set of scales for measuring quality of effort.

# 4

*Rodney T. Hartnett*

# Evaluating
# the Faculty's
# Sociopsychological
# Environments

————————⟨∞⟩————————

When people speak of the college environment, they almost always refer to the environment experienced by students. As emphasized repeatedly throughout this book, the student environment is extremely important and merits careful and continuous assessment. But it is not the only environment on a college campus that deserves attention. Although some aspects of the student environment overlap with features of the environment for the faculty, administration, and nonacademic employees, some other aspects of the student environment are not important to these other groups, and vice versa. In effect, the academic environment might be described not as a series of separate environments but as one global environment, which has some elements (for example, size and location of the school) that are important to all members of the academic community, some elements (for example, library holdings and faculty teaching loads) that are important to two or more groups but not all, and some elements (for example, housing regulations for freshmen) that are important to only one constituency.

This chapter discusses those features of institutional and/or departmental life that are important to the faculty; that is, those features that characterize the nature and quality of faculty life. Surprisingly, faculty environments in higher education have rarely been empirically analyzed. A large number of studies, of course, have dealt with the backgrounds, characteristics, and attitudes of individual faculty members, including their political beliefs and affiliations (Spaulding and Turner, 1968); tendencies toward local institutional politics versus external professional matters (Gouldner, 1957a, 1957b); views about a wide variety of social, political, and economic issues (Lipset and Ladd, 1970); and the origins and backgrounds of faculty members in specific types of colleges (Donovan, 1964). However, analyses of the environment itself are uncommon. Furthermore, those environmental studies that have been conducted were prompted by fairly narrow interests. One of the earliest attempts to analyze faculty environments, for example, was the work of Lazarsfeld and Thielens (1958). Their study concentrated on the effects of government concern for national security on academic freedom and on faculty apprehension in the years following World War II. Similarly, numerous inquiries have focused exclusively on faculty participation in academic governance (Dykes, 1968; McConnell and Mortimer, 1971). Much has been written about the environments of nonacademic institutions, some of which has a direct bearing on the study of faculty environments (for example, Katz and Kahn, 1978; Pelz and Andrews, 1976), but research on the faculty environment in colleges and universities has been much less frequent, although there have been several noteworthy and refreshing examples, such as Hagstrom's work (1965) on faculty conflicts in departments with diverse specialties and Blau's analysis (1973) of the influence of the administrative structure of colleges and universities on academic scholarship.

In considering faculty environments, we shall discuss four general questions: (1) Why is it important to learn about faculty environments? (2) What are some of the more important dimensions of faculty environments? (3) How can faculty environments be assessed and how do the different procedures compare and differ? And (4) what are some strategies for interpreting information about the faculty environment?

## Why Study Faculty Environments?

There are two important reasons for learning about faculty environments. The first is based on the logic of institutional self-study: Faculty environment information can reveal aspects of institutional life that need attention and improvement. This reason corresponds to one of the major reasons for studying the student environment. Maintaining quality throughout the institution requires regularly updated information about both faculty performance and faculty members' feelings about their work place. In order to remedy a problem, the problem must first be identified, and to do this requires feedback from the faculty. We shall address the questions of what kind of information should be collected in what ways later in this chapter.

A second important reason for learning more about faculty environments is that by doing so we increase our knowledge about academic life and the effects of academic organization on the performance and satisfaction of the faculty. This reason is more subtle than the first and has less direct bearing on the formulation of educational policies and practices at a specific institution. But by conducting inquiries into the faculty environment, we will inevitably understand more fully how environmental factors are related to scientific and scholarly productivity and teaching.

The first reason might be briefly stated as *improving practice* and the second as *improving understanding*. Expressed in this way, it should be clear that progress in achieving the second goal—that is, an improved understanding of the social psychology of academic institutions—should directly affect progress in achieving the first.

It is also important to note that the quality of the faculty environment affects the quality of the student environment in ways that are not yet fully clear. More specifically, there is some evidence (Wilson and others, 1975; Hartnett and Centra, 1977) that some aspects of the faculty environment have important consequences for the extent and nature of student development.

## Important Dimensions of Faculty Environments

To paraphrase Kluckhohn and Murray's analysis (1949) of individual human differences, an academic institution is in some respects like all other institutions, like some other institutions, and like no other institution. An infinite number of features or qualities can be identified to describe a college or university faculty environment. The list is reduced considerably, however, if it includes only the important dimensions; that is, those aspects that not only are important in their own right but also distinguish among colleges or among academic departments. Five general categories of dimensions meet these criteria, which are listed in Table 1.

The first category includes those aspects that are obviously important to all members of the academic community. Moreover, these features influence many of the descriptors that follow. For example, size has been found to be correlated with many of the social psychological dimensions, and level of degree offerings with research activity and scholarly productivity.

Note that the first four categories might be called public dimensions, since most of this information is either well-known or readily available. The fifth category, however, clearly concerns private matters; these characteristics are rarely known by people outside of the academic community, and information about such variables is seldom available. In addition, the public indicators often cannot be changed. An institution's administrators cannot (or, in some cases, should not) do much about faculty unhappiness with the college's geographic location, type of control, facilities, and so on. The private environment, however, though by no means easily modifiable, can generally be changed.

This discussion suggests that focusing on the private dimensions will be more fruitful than focusing on the public ones. This does not mean that the public indicators are less important; indeed, such characteristics as size and level of offerings indicate a great

## Table 1. Five Categories of Important Dimensions of the Faculty Environment

*I. Basic Descriptions*
   A. Size
   B. Location
   C. Type of control (public, church)
   D. Source and degree of financial support
   E. Level of offerings (B.A., Ph.D.)
   F. Single sex, coeducational
*II. Responsibilities and Rewards*
   A. Salary
   B. Fringe benefits
   C. Teaching loads
   D. Opportunities for promotions and tenure
*III. Nature and Quality of Faculty*
   A. Training (percentage with Ph.D., origin of Ph.D.)
   B. Scholarly productivity (publications, works of art)
   C. Research activity (journal editorships, national committees)
   D. Peer ratings of quality of faculty
   E. Interest in (and seriousness about) teaching
*IV. Quality of Work Conditions*
   A. Offices (size, privacy, comfort)
   B. Library (holdings, services)
   C. Other facilities (laboratories, computer, art studios)
   D. Staff support (secretarial, other clerical, student assistants)
   E. Adequacy of parking; other general facilities
*V. Social Psychological Dimensions*
   A. Relations with colleagues
   B. Relations with administration
   C. Relations with students
   D. Opportunities to participate in academic governance
   E. Degree of academic freedom
   F. Institutional tolerance for diverse behaviors and life-styles

deal about other institutional variables. However, as characteristics that are already apparent and reasonably well understood, they need less examination. Consequently, the various instruments and techniques developed to assess faculty environments have tended to focus more on the private aspects of campus life.

## Measuring Faculty Environments

There are essentially two ways of assessing the faculty environment. One is to use information that is normally available in institutional records, and the second is to obtain information directly from faculty. (A third method—observation—has shortcomings so pronounced that we will not consider it here.)

Choosing between these two approaches depends on which aspect of the institutional environment one is interested in and for what purpose. Of the elements listed in Table 1, some information is readily available in institutional records, whereas some information can be obtained only by asking members of the faculty. Furthermore, sometimes different sources and kinds of information about a single indicator are desired. For example, one may want to know about the adequacy of certain resources (the number of books in the library, for example), which could be determined from institutional records. But it may also be desirable to determine faculty satisfaction with the library, in which case one must obviously go directly to the faculty members.

Information collected from faculty members can vary, both with respect to the method of obtaining the data and the nature of the data. Some sort of paper-and-pencil method (for example, questionnaires, rating forms, or check lists) is the most common technique of collecting information from faculty members, but interviews are also used. Indeed, faculty members were interviewed in several of the well-known attempts to assess aspects of the faculty environment (Lazarsfeld and Thielens, 1958; Caplow and McGee, 1958). Properly conducted personal interviews often provide a richness of information and a depth of understanding that cannot be duplicated by paper-and-pencil techniques. Interpreting interview data, however, can be particularly troublesome. In addition, because interviews are always time-consuming, they are quite expensive. As a result, paper-and-pencil approaches dominate data-collection procedures in the social sciences generally and faculty environment assessment specifically.

The basic types of information collected concern self-reports (including information on accomplishments, activities, attitudes, and opinions), perceptions of the prevailing organizational climate (including information on policies, practices, and emphases), and personal styles (including information on beliefs and orientations) of the other individuals in their immediate environment.) For greater detail regarding the self-report versus perceptual approaches, see the discussion by Baird in Chapter One. Data from available records are preferable to data from faculty members, since the former can often be retrieved more quickly and conveniently. Questionnaires, rating forms, and interviews require the cooperation of many people, and faculty members are often reluctant respondents. Still, good information about the more private dimensions of the faculty environment must be collected from members of the faculty by means of inventories or questionnaires.

Numerous institutional self-studies have employed "home-grown" questionnaires to determine faculty members' perceptions of current institutional practices, opinions about the priority and desirability of certain institutional goals and policies, satisfaction with various aspects of the institution, and so on. One of the chief advantages of locally developed questionnaires is that the content can be tailored to the institution being studied. A significant disadvantage, however, is the difficulty in comparing the information with that of other institutions, which sometimes hinders data interpretation.

To resolve this shortcoming of locally developed faculty questionnaires, a team of researchers in the late 1960s developed the Institutional Functioning Inventory (IFI). Though portions of the IFI can be answered by students, administrators, and trustees, it was designed specifically to be administered to the faculty. Since the IFI is considered more fully elsewhere in this book (see Chapter Nine), it will not be described in detail here. Very briefly, it consists of 132 statements about the institution, which are grouped under eleven dimensions or scales that were judged to be important aspects of college functioning. In general, the IFI concerns the private aspects of the faculty environment, which come under the social psychological category in Table 1.

Two important aspects of the IFI deserve further mention here. First, how does an understanding of the faculty environment obtained from an assessment of faculty members' perceptions differ from an understanding obtained solely from information available to the public? Second, how do faculty descriptions of the environment differ from descriptions by students and administrators?

Table 2 provides data relevant to the first question. These data were collected as part of the validation process for the IFI (Peterson and others, 1970). In general, these data indicate that many of the faculty perceptions are similar to information that might be collected from available records, but perceptual data nevertheless contribute useful additional information. For example, the Advancing Knowledge scale, which is a measure of institutional emphasis on research and scholarship, is fairly highly correlated with selectivity, library holdings, enrollment, annual contract research dollars, and faculty compensation, as we would expect. Obviously, more research is done at the larger, prestigious universities than at the small, liberal arts colleges with modest financial support. At the same time, however, the magnitude of the relationships makes it clear that none of the institutional descriptors could be substituted for faculty perceptions of research emphasis. Some selective institutions obviously do not stress research; some do not have large library holdings or high average faculty salaries. Though each of these descriptors is correlated with faculty perceptions, the faculty perceptions provide some unique information.

Similar analyses can be made of the other IFI scales in Table 2. In fact, the correlations between the institutional descriptors and the other IFI scales are somewhat lower than those for the Advancing Knowledge scale. This is not surprising, since the other scales all come closer to the social psychological category of information described earlier. Institutional Esprit (faculty morale) is not highly correlated with any of the institutional descriptors, though morale tends to be slightly higher at institutions that are more selective, attract students from higher socioeconomic strata, have a more

**Table 2. Correlations Between Selected IFI Scales and Published Institutional Data**

| Institutional Data | Freedom | Human Diversity | Undergraduate Learning | Democratic Governance | Advancing Knowledge | Institutional Esprit |
|---|---|---|---|---|---|---|
| Selectivity A (N = 57) | .40 | .33 | .24 | .48 | .49 | .30 |
| Number of library books (N = 60) | .32 | .35 | -.20 | .29 | .77 | .18 |
| Income per student (N = 60) | .24 | .09 | .32 | .39 | .34 | .43 |
| Faculty-student ratio (N = 60) | .21 | -.02 | .41 | .18 | .00 | .28 |
| Proportion of faculty with doctorates (N = 60) | .35 | .41 | .20 | .45 | .38 | .23 |
| Enrollment (N = 60) | .12 | .44 | -.54 | .08 | .61 | .14 |
| Annual contract research dollars (N = 22) | .29 | .38 | -.53 | .19 | .72 | .15 |
| Average faculty compensation (N = 51) | .68 | .65 | -.15 | .40 | .77 | .19 |

*Sources:* Peterson and others (1970); Centra, Hartnett, and Peterson (1970).

favorable faculty-student ratio, and so on. In other words, information about an institution's public features (such as size and faculty salaries) tells us little about the important private aspects of the faculty community.

Evidence that faculty perceptual information provides valuable information about academic climates was offered by another, more recent Educational Testing Service study of twenty-five doctoral programs in chemistry, history, and psychology. Faculty members were asked to report, by means of a questionnaire, their satisfaction with their work environment (Clark, Hartnett, and Baird, 1976). The scale consisted of six items dealing with personal relations among faculty in the department, satisfaction with opportunities to influence departmental decisions, and so on. Like the morale scale on the IFI, scores were found to be correlated with certain traditional descriptors of doctoral departments, such as reputation with peers, faculty research productivity, and adequacy of physical and financial resources, but the correlations were rarely very high. Faculty members' perceptions were clearly providing information about the program that was not available from other indicators.

In the introduction to this chapter, we made the point that the academic environment, rather than being made up of a series of separate environments, is one global environment with specific elements, each of varying importance to different campus groups. Analysis of faculty, administrator, and student IFI data appears to confirm this description. In a study based on IFI data gathered from these three campus groups at thirteen institutions (Hartnett and Centra, 1974), the existence of one general environment was supported by the generally high correlations between the perceptions of faculty and administrators, faculty and students, and administrators and students. Yet in spite of this overall agreement, administrators' perceptions were consistently more favorable than those of the faculty and students; for every IFI scale, the administrators' mean perceptions were higher than those of either the faculty or students. In some cases, moreover, the differences were fairly substantial, the most noteworthy examples being perceptions of the extent of faculty involvement in institutional governance, the level of faculty morale, and the extent to which the institution attracted faculty members and students with diverse backgrounds and points of view.

Thus, these data support both points suggested earlier. The campus environment is accurately described as one global environment with different elements having different degrees of importance for different groups. For this reason, faculty members' perceptions of certain elements of the environment will differ substantially from those of other groups, a fact that emphasizes the importance of obtaining environmental perception information from the faculty.

### Interpreting Faculty Environment Information

Earlier in this chapter we gave two reasons for studying faculty environments—one was to improve our understanding of the many factors that affect faculty performance. To use the language of the IFI, this is an Advancing Knowledge reason—we should learn more about environments because such learning is good and important in its own right.

A second reason, however, is more applied in nature and is central to any discussion of the utility of faculty environments information. This is the argument that knowledge of faculty environments will help in identifying institutional problems and areas that need improvement. This section of the paper discusses two strategies for using faculty environment information for such problem identification. These two strategies are (1) using environmental information to compare one institution with others and (2) using environmental information to trace the climate of one institution over a period of time.

College environment information is commonly used to compare the profile of one institution or department with that of other institutions or departments. Data are often more understandable when they are compared with those from some other meaningful reference group. In fact, without adequate and relevant comparison data, it is often difficult to know just what the collected information means. However, only similar data can be compared, and such comparisons are only useful when the other institutions are relevant to the one in question—that is, they are colleges with which one has some reason for wanting to compare one's own institution.

Useful and relevant comparison information is sometimes included in the technical manuals or other research literature that is available from the publishers of the inventory in question. The IFI, for example, was based on information collected at several dozen colleges and universities, and the data from these institutions were used to offer IFI users comparison information to assist in the interpretation of their own data. Similar comparison data is often available for standard inventories, though the comparison information is from institutions that are seldom of equal interest to all users. Furthermore, such information is rarely updated with revised norms.

Rather than relying on available comparison information, institutions can take part in multi-institutional projects that collect identical information. In effect, such a step establishes one's own comparison group, and such projects often produce more meaningful self-studies and a clearer understanding of a single institution's status.

One example was the project carried out by the Council of Graduate Schools and the Educational Testing Service (Clark, Hartnett, and Baird, 1976). Twenty-five universities collected information from students and faculty members about a variety of program characteristics that were thought to be related to program quality. Each participating university was then provided with a summary of their own information as well as with comparison information from the other institutions.

Figure 1 presents one example of how such information can be used. Both of the two departments considered are of moderate size (with about fifty full-time equivalent doctoral candidates in each) and place considerable emphasis on preparing scholars and researchers. In this figure student and faculty ratings of a variety of program characteristics are plotted on a profile chart, which also gives the full range of ratings for each characteristic across the twenty-five programs. Each institution can easily compare its program ratings with those of the other institutions as a group and thus obtain more meaning from its data. For example, the mean

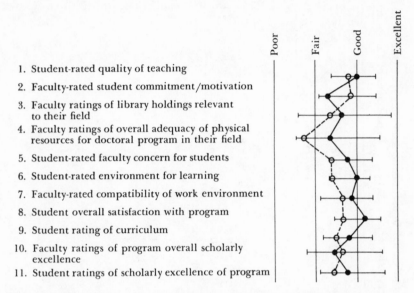

1. Student-rated quality of teaching

2. Faculty-rated student commitment/motivation

3. Faculty ratings of library holdings relevant to their field

4. Faculty ratings of overall adequacy of physical resources for doctoral program in their field

5. Student-rated faculty concern for students

6. Student-rated environment for learning

7. Faculty-rated compatibility of work environment

8. Student overall satisfaction with program

9. Student rating of curriculum

10. Faculty ratings of program overall scholarly excellence

11. Student ratings of scholarly excellence of program

*Note:* Horizontal lines with vertical "stoppers" represent the range of departmental mean scores on each variable. For example, the range of ratings was quite broad for indicators 3, 4, and 10. For details, see Clark and Hartnett (1977).

**Figure 1. Profile of Quality Ratings for Two History Departments**

rating (by students) of the faculty concern for students at the institution indicated by the broken line is about midway between "fair" and "good," a finding that might be judged positively by the institution's administrators and faculty members. However, the comparison data reveal that this rating is one of the lowest among the institutions participating in the project. Thus, the comparison data show faculty concern for students to be a departmental function that needs serious attention.

A somewhat different procedure for reporting the information gathered in this project is presented in Table 3. Here information about the faculty members' perceptions of the program academic environment and their involvement in professional activities are compared with the perceptions of faculty members at the other twenty-four programs, which are reported separately for

**Table 3. Example of Questionnaire Feedback Reports to Individual Departments: Assessment of Quality in Doctoral Education—Faculty Questionnaire Feedback, University of _____ Department of Chemistry**

| Faculty Perceptions of Doctoral Program Academic Environment | Your Dept. (N = 36 faculty) | | Larger Depts. (N =12 depts.) | Smaller Depts. (N = 12 depts.) |
| --- | --- | --- | --- | --- |
| | Freq. | Percent | Avg. Percent | Avg. Percent |
| 1-C. Different Personalities and Points of View Are Welcome | | | | |
| 1 Disagree strongly | 0 | 0.0 | 3.1 | 4.0 |
| 2 Disagree with reservations | 2 | 5.5 | 8.8 | 13.7 |
| 3 Agree with reservations | 15 | 41.6 | 39.5 | 40.4 |
| 4 Agree strongly | 18 | 50.0 | 46.7 | 40.1 |
| Other | 1 | 2.7 | | |
| 1-F. Common for Students to be Exploited | | | | |
| 1 Disagree strongly | 4 | 11.1 | 24.5 | 36.2 |
| 2 Disagree with reservations | 16 | 44.4 | 39.3 | 28.9 |
| 3 Agree with reservations | 10 | 27.7 | 23.2 | 19.0 |
| 4 Agree strongly | 5 | 13.8 | 11.6 | 14.8 |
| Other | 1 | 2.7 | | |
| 1-J. Faculty Feel Secure in Academic Freedom | | | | |
| 1 Disagree strongly | 1 | 2.7 | 3.3 | 3.2 |
| 2 Disagree with reservations | 0 | 0.0 | 7.3 | 5.5 |
| 3 Agree with reservations | 10 | 27.7 | 25.2 | 33.4 |
| 4 Agree strongly | 24 | 66.6 | 63.0 | 56.3 |
| Other | 1 | 2.7 | | |

Faculty Professional Involvement

| | | | | |
|---|---|---|---|---|
| 8-G. National Professional Association Office Holder | | | | |
| 1 Yes | 15 | 41.6 | 37.1 | 27.4 |
| 2 No | 20 | 55.5 | 62.2 | 72.3 |
| Other | 1 | 2.7 | | |
| 8-H. Regional Professional Association Office Holder | | | | |
| 1 Yes | 10 | 27.7 | 36.1 | 45.9 |
| 2 No | 25 | 69.4 | 63.4 | 53.8 |
| Other | 1 | 2.7 | | |
| 8-I. Journal Editor or Editorial Board Member | | | | |
| 1 Yes | 11 | 30.5 | 38.6 | 19.9 |
| 2 No | 24 | 66.6 | 61.0 | 79.8 |
| Other | 1 | 2.7 | | |
| 8-J. Article Referee in Last Two Years | | | | |
| 1 Yes | 32 | 88.8 | 92.8 | 89.5 |
| 2 No | 3 | 8.3 | 6.9 | 10.1 |
| Other | 1 | 2.7 | | |

large and small departments. As with Figure 1, the data for the institution in question take on added significance when compared with the data for the other institutions. For example, over 41 percent of the faculty members at the institution used in this example agree—either strongly or with reservations—that graduate students are commonly exploited at their institution. This may not have been cause for concern if it was not known that this figure was higher than the figure for either the larger or smaller departments participating in the project (35 percent and 34 percent, respectively).

Figure 1 and Table 3 are both examples of how comparison information can be used to learn more about an institution. Collecting information about the faculty environment and analyzing it in this way can be likened to a periodic physical examination. The purpose is to diagnose, by means of a reliable, systematic method, what the current health of the environment is. Such data can then be monitored over time to see what improvement or deterioration has occurred.

An example of examining environmental data over time to determine trends is presented in Table 4, where actual data pertaining to changes in the faculty morale at a small liberal arts college over a two-year period are presented. In this example, the improvement in faculty morale over the two-year period is striking. Between 1969 and 1971, the morale among members of the faculty improved dramatically. The percentage of faculty members agreeing with the statement "In general, faculty morale is high" rose from 40 percent in 1969 to 73 percent in 1971. The percentage agreeing with the statement "Generally, top-level administrators here provide effective educational leadership" rose from 60 percent to 85 percent. The figures for every one of the twelve statements evidence improved faculty morale.

The obvious question, of course, is Why? What happened at this college to improve faculty morale so tremendously in such a short period of time? In this case, the faculty members also reported, over the same two-year span, increased participation in institutional governance as well as an increase in the perceived level of academic freedom. That such changes are associated with improved faculty morale does not mean that they caused it, although

Table 4. Faculty Morale Change at a College: Percentage of Faculty
Agreeing with Various Statements at Two Different Times

| Statement | Percentage Who "Agree" or "Agree Strongly" | |
| | 1969 (N = 67) | 1971 (N = 71) |
| --- | --- | --- |
| Most faculty consider the senior administrators to be able and well-qualified. | 70 | 86 |
| Generally, top-level administrators here provide effective educational leadership. | 60 | 85 |
| Generally, communication between faculty and administration is poor. | 43 | 15 |
| Staff infighting, backbiting, and so on, seem to be more the rule than the exception. | 24 | 15 |
| The college is currently doing a successful job in achieving its various goals. | 62 | 82 |
| Close personal friendships between administrators and faculty members are common. | 43 | 75 |
| Compared with most other colleges, faculty turnover here appears somewhat high. | 79 | 47 |
| Although they may criticize some things, most faculty seem loyal to the college. | 61 | 75 |
| There is a strong sense of community here—a feeling of shared interests and purposes. | 28 | 55 |
| In general, faculty morale is high. | 40 | 73 |
| Faculty in general is strongly committed to acknowledged purposes of the college. | 61 | 79 |
| Most faculty would not defend the college against criticisms from outsiders. | 38 | 19 |

*Source:* Unpublished information assembled by the author from data in the files at the Educational Testing Service. The twelve items in the table constitute the Institutional Esprit scale of the IFI.

the hypothesis is strongly suggested. The point, however, is to illustrate the improved understanding and the curiosity that usually result from recurring assessments of the faculty environment. Periodic analysis produces more than just more facts—it also tends to improve understanding of the complex contributors to faculty environments and to heighten the need to learn more. In the long run, such inward-looking activities hold promise for improved educational practice.

## Concluding Comment

In this chapter we have introduced the notion of the faculty environment. We have indicated why it is important to assess the faculty environment and what some of the major elements of the faculty environment are, described several different methods for assessing the faculty environment, and discussed several analytic strategies for understanding faculty environment information.

Much of the chapter has focused on standard published measures suitable for use in assessing the private aspects of faculty environments. One of the major advantages of such instruments is that they often provide the user with useful comparison information. Nevertheless, locally developed environmental measures may sometimes be preferable, since they can be tailored to the special needs and characteristics of the institution.

In the last analysis, however, the potential benefits of assessing faculty environments and, more importantly, using such information when formulating institutional (or departmental) policy depend less on the specific nature of the measure employed than on carefully explicating the purposes to be achieved and meaningfully involving the faculty in the conduct of the inquiry. The latter point is particularly important. Those who have experience in various institutional self-study activities are familiar with the reluctance of faculty members to cooperate. As I have argued elsewhere (Hartnett, 1975), the involvement of faculty members in the planning and conduct of institutional self-studies is vitally important.

Finally, despite its advantages, a study of the faculty environment offers no panacea, suggests no easy solutions to institutional problems, and solves no complicated puzzles. However, when carried out with adequate planning, careful collection of relevant and useful information, and thoughtful interpretation and analyses, the final product is very likely to be extremely provocative and useful, improving understanding of the faculty environment and identifying aspects of the faculty environment that need attention and improvement. The final target, of course, is not just a more contented or satisfied faculty; it is a more effective and humane academic environment for all the institution's members, a place where student growth and development is most likely to occur.

5

*Norman P. Uhl*

# Collecting and Applying Social and Economic Information

⸺⸺⸺⸺⸺•·⟨∞⟩·•⸺⸺⸺⸺⸺

Long-range planning is the process by which an institution seeks to pursue its own destiny in accord with its own purpose. Informal and ad hoc academic planning was reasonably successful in the growth climate of the 1960s, but it has become less acceptable in the 1970s as the rate of growth and the flow of dollars into higher education have decreased. In today's environment, difficult choices must be made with regard to alternative uses of resources, and institutions that wish to win support must be able to demonstrate to their constituencies that they are managed in ways that achieve their goals with efficiency. Too often educators are unable to do so.

With numerous social programs vying for limited funds, members of Congress, legislators, alumni, and other sources of support need to understand the reasons for particular choices in budget requests. In order to communicate these choices, planning and decision-making techniques must be employed that these constituents understand. Programs and facilities must not be proposed as ends in themselves rather than as means to achieving educational and social purposes.

Using a formal model for long-range planning can be an important means by which an institution keeps academic purposes clearly in mind during decision making. In addition, use of a formal model can provide a way of communicating with laypersons and assure that important environmental information is employed in the decision-making process. As Alexander Astin noted in an earlier chapter, too often decisions are made without these data. One advantage of a formal long-range planning model is its early communication of the type of data needed for decision making.

Several models have been proposed that are claimed to improve an institution's long-range planning, such as the Phelps-Stokes' long-range planning model (Parekh, 1975), NACUBO's *A College Planning Cycle* (National Association of College and University Business Officers, 1975), NCHEMS's costing and data management system (National Center for Higher Education Management Systems, 1975), and ETS's HELIX (Educational Testing Service, 1975). Also, the Society for College and University Planning conducts an annual institute for college administrators at which several planning models are discussed. While the use of one of these planning models can eliminate the need for an institution to develop its own, an institution will most likely have to adapt the model it chooses to its own needs and resources.

In general, a long-range planning model has several stages:

1. *Mission:* What is the mission of the institution?
2. *Assumptions:* What assumptions about the internal and external environment will affect the mission and goals of the institution?
3. *Goals:* During the planning period, what should be emphasized in order to achieve the institution's mission more efficiently?

4. *Activities:* What activities can be undertaken to achieve these goals?
5. *Responsibilities:* What do the activities mean in terms of organizational responsibility? For what activities is each administrative office, school, or department responsible?
6. *Resources:* What resources do the activities require? Are the budget and resources directly linked to the programs?
7. *Evaluation:* Are the activities achieving their intended goals?

Regardless of the specific model used, a key step in improving communication with state legislatures, Congress, alumni, and other laypersons is to develop assumptions on the basis of external as well as internal environmental data. While environmental information has implications for each of the above stages, it is especially important in the development of assumptions and in assessing how well goals are attained.

To illustrate the use of external and internal environmental data in developing goals, examine the following goal and the assumptions upon which it was based. Notice how data were used from both the internal and external environments in developing the assumptions.

*Goal: To obtain accreditation for the school of business within the next five years.*

Assumptions leading to the formulation of this goal are as follows:

1. Enrollment will start to decline around 1980. This assumption is based on an assessment of the external environment, including national, regional, state, and local enrollment trends; changing attitudes regarding the value of a college education; and the job demand for college graduates.
2. In contrast to the school of education and the college of arts and sciences, the business school has great potential for increasing enrollment. This assumption is based partly on external data indicating that jobs will be available for business majors, especially in accounting, and that the local community has expressed interest in business courses at the master's level. It is also based on internal data resulting from an evaluation of present offer-

ings; an examination of faculty characteristics, including its strengths and weaknesses, tenure, and other policies; and the observation that the business major is becoming more popular with present students.

3. The major deterrent to attracting a large number of students to the business school is its lack of accreditation. This assumption is based on an assessment of employers and potential employers (external data).

4. It is feasible for the business school to obtain accreditation within five years. This assumption is based on examining the strengths and weaknesses of the present school (internal data) and comparing them with the accreditation criteria (external data).

5. With accreditation, the business school will help prevent an enrollment decline at this institution. This assumption is based on internal and external data already mentioned.

The above example illustrates the use of both internal and external environmental data in developing goals. The following section will discuss each of the seven stages, but emphasizing those two stages—mission and goals—in which environmental data are crucial. Since a major problem of many institutions is getting the environmental information into the planning system, a second section will describe one procedure for overcoming this difficulty.

### Importance of Environmental Information in Long-Range Planning

Each stage of the planning process will be discussed below in terms of its use of environmental data.

*Institutional Mission.* The mission statement, which refers to the general purpose of the institution, is usually decreed by the state legislature or by the board of trustees. It often describes who the institution is to serve, what the major emphases are (whether in liberal arts, research, awarding associate degrees, graduate work, professional training, or technical training), what programs leading to specific degrees will be offered, and other general purposes.

It is important to check periodically whether this mission

statement is consistent with the environment. For example, the mission of some institutions has been to serve a specific ethnic group or sex. However, due to certain events in the external environment, such as a decrease in the number of applicants or court decisions, it may be desirable to include other ethnic groups or to become coeducational. Such a decision may also require data on the internal (campus) environment, such as the effect of such a change on the morale and the intellectual climate of the campus as well as such obvious data as campus housing figures.

Information regarding the internal and external environments would also be important in determining whether to develop a program leading to a master's degree in a specific area. Formal assumptions about the internal and external environment should be made and then reviewed each year to ascertain whether changes are needed. After the annual review, the implications of the assumptions for the statement of mission should be examined.

*Assumptions.* The purpose of this stage is to identify those assumptions about the internal and external environments that have implications for an institution's mission and goals and that are likely to affect the institution's activities. Assumptions regarding the external environment will largely be determined by the primary region or constituency to be served; therefore, the assumptions for an international university would be quite different from those for a local community college. For example, a university with campuses in several countries would likely have assumptions concerning worldwide economic trends, while a community college probably would not.

Some external factors about which assumptions might be made and their possible implications for decision making are listed below. These implications affect not only an institution's mission and goals but also its programs.

1. Relevant international situations: Probability of war has implications for enrollment; improved worldwide transportation has implications for the curriculum (for example, it should develop a responsible citizen).
2. National attitudes toward higher education: The development

of a more negative attitude toward the value of a college education could lower the percentage of high school graduates applying for admission.

3. State aid to private higher education: This obviously can influence an institution's activities.
4. Price of goods and services: Energy price increases affect the resources needed for building operation and building construction.
5. National faculty salary trends: A buyer's market for faculty has implications for decreases in faculty salaries.
6. Competition from other higher education institutions: Greater competition for students has implications for market research, program development, admissions policies, continuing education, and so on.
7. Local and regional educational demands: These demands have implications for program development within an institution. For example, increased interest in new areas, such as ecology, might increase the number of courses offered in these areas; other demands might have implications for the continuing education program.
8. Federal programs: Different areas such as undergraduate and graduate education, student aid, funds for developing institutions, and funds for research have implications for programs, enrollment, and the types of students served.
9. Tuition: State policies and the rate of inflation can affect tuition rates, which in turn affect the implications for the socioeconomic levels of the students served.
10. Private support of colleges: Just as many private institutions are receiving more federal and state money, many public institutions are receiving more private money. This has implications for fund-raising plans.
11. Construction price index: As this index increases, less can be built for a given amount of money. This has implications for building plans priced several years ago.
12. Economic environment: Items such as the rate of inflation have implications for salary increases, tuition, and so on.
13. Technological advances: Certain technological advances such

as computer terminals, hand calculators, and new techniques in the design of buildings have implications for the instructional program.

14. Alternative education patterns: The use of alternative methods to classroom instruction (such as cooperative education and educational TV) has implications for designing the instructional program.

15. State aid to private higher education: An increase in this resource increases available income.

16. National and regional enrollment trends: These trends should be considered when projecting an institution's enrollment.

17. Local labor market: The availability of local help has implications for salaries and hiring practices.

The importance of developing assumptions about the external environment may be obvious, but in too many cases they are either developed informally or not at all. These assumptions should be reviewed and updated annually. Recording the data and sources used in making an assumption makes it relatively easy to check whether conditions have changed or whether additional facts should be considered at the time of the annual review.

Two examples of developing assumptions about the external environment follow. More examples showing the relationship between assumptions and goals are given in the section on goals.

*National and regional attitudes toward higher education.*

*Assumption 1:*   College-age youth increasingly desire alternative arrangements for obtaining a college education due to the increasing diversity of their values, attitudes, and learning needs (Yankelovich, 1974).

*Assumption 2:*   The planning and decision-making processes at both the institutional and state levels must be improved. State legislators are increasingly viewing higher education as merely one among a growing number of important social institutions, an attitude that makes it necessary to provide more detailed information in order to obtain favorable decisions. (For example, the North Carolina state legislature requested detailed financial data before it made a decision regarding allocation of funds to higher education.)

*Price of goods and services.*

*Assumption:* Nonenergy prices will rise at a rate of 10 percent annually for the next five years. Energy prices will increase more sharply, with electricity increasing as much as 13 percent per year, natural gas 18 percent, and oil 15 percent. These increases have implications for planning and designing buildings as well as for the operational budget. (These figures are taken from various government projections.)

Many aspects of the internal (campus) environment also have very important implications for planning and decision making. However, the parties gathering data for making these types of assumptions are different from those gathering data for making assumptions about the external environment. In most instances the relevant data for external assumptions are reported by outside agencies. For example, publications are available that show population shifts, birth rates, and number and percentage of students going on to college by age, sex, race, geographic area, and so on. In contrast, although several external agencies request some internal data, the institution itself must collect the data for internal assumptions. Examples of some areas for which assumptions need to be developed and data collected are given below. Every institution is probably collecting some of these data already, if for no other reason than to answer the requests of the Department of Health, Education, and Welfare.

1. Student interest in academic programs: Shifts in the popularity of certain academic programs have implications for future enrollment in specific majors.
2. Student attrition: Whether student attrition will increase, stabilize, or decrease has implications for many factors, including methods of instruction, financial resources available, number of faculty, and space.

3. Faculty and staff salaries and fringe benefits: This has implications for the ability of the institution to attract and hold high-caliber people.
4. Student aid: This has implications for the heterogeneity of the socioeconomic levels of the student body. If students from a low socioeconomic level are desired, appropriate student aid is necessary.
5. Campus morale: The morale of faculty, staff, students, and administrators can affect the learning environment of the campus.
6. Overall campus environment: Does the campus environment provide a positive force for achieving the goals of the institution? In what ways can it be improved? The campus environment should support the academic program and has implications for physical facilities, interpersonal relationships, degree and type of faculty-student-administrator interaction, the types of activities made available to students, and so on. The atmosphere of a particular campus results from such things as the nature of its students and faculty; the variety and emphasis of its academic programs; its various pressures, expectations, customs, procedures, and policies; and its relationship to political and cultural events in the larger society. One instrument that has often been used to measure the campus environment are the College and University Environmental Scales (CUES) (Pace, 1969).
7. Subenvironments: Just as the overall campus environment has many implications for planning and decision making, so do subenvironments, such as schools, departments, or support offices. A poor environment in a central office such as the registrar or admissions or in the English department can create problems throughout the institution if it is not identified and corrected immediately.
8. Learning environment: This is certainly a part of the campus environment, but it is separate because of its importance. Assumptions regarding conditions that stimulate learning certainly have implications for planning and decision making.
9. Characteristics of the general student body: Numerous student characteristics should influence planning and decision making. For example, the academic preparation of entering students

has implications for the academic program. Other factors such as family income, age, prior experience, and attitudes should also be considered in planning.

10. Characteristics of significant student subgroups: Sometimes in studying the general student body, the characteristics of important subgroups, such as racial minority groups, are masked because of their small numbers. If expanded minority group enrollment is desired, the characteristics of these subgroups should be examined to see how they resemble and differ from the general student body.

11. Student, instructor, and administrator expectations: Wide disparity between the expectations of students, faculty, or administrators and the realities of the campus has implications for possible changes in the institution's programs or organization. Sometimes such a disparity may lead to a better-informed group or groups; at other times it may result in a decision to change a segment of the institution, such as providing more opportunities for independent study or greater participation in planning.

12. Admissions effectiveness: Whether the institution can enroll only the types of students for which its academic program was established has implications for academic programs. For example, to keep its enrollment constant, an institution may have to enroll some students who do not have a sufficiently strong academic background to complete the standard freshman courses satisfactorily. In this situation the institution may need to add some remedial courses to the academic program or develop a special program to assist these students, especially during the first year.

13. Student-faculty ratio: This may affect the instructional methods employed (for example, the number of independent study courses and seminars or the amount of computer-assisted instruction).

14. Tenured-nontenured faculty ratio: This has implications for many factors, such as the ability to offer tenured positions to nontenured faculty, the ability to develop a new emphasis in a department, the expansion of program offerings, and the ability to hire senior faculty.

15. Expenditures per student: This is one measure of the effi-

ciency of the institution and has implications for enrollment in certain areas. For example, an increase in the number of students in some majors might greatly decrease the cost per student.

16. Program quality and productivity: These have implications for many factors, including the need for additional faculty with specific backgrounds.

17. Physical plant: The adequacy of the physical plant to support not only present needs but also future needs must be considered.

18. Existing and desired goals: It is useful to identify goals that an institution's populace see as being given importance and those that they feel should be given importance. The Institutional Goals Inventory (IGI) provides such information in terms of outcome goals and process goals. The outcome goals refer to the substantive objectives of the institution, while the process goals refer to internal objectives that largely relate to the educational process and campus climate.

19. Quality of teaching and faculty-student relationships: Instruction is the most important function for many institutions. On a campus having good teaching and good faculty-student relationships, most students would agree with the following statements: "The professors are dedicated scholars and thorough teachers who set high standards of achievement." "In their courses they keep their material up-to-date, clearly explain the goals and purposes, and stimulate good discussion." "In their relations with students, they are helpful, friendly, and interested in the students as individuals." One scale that assesses these characteristics is presented in the Professors scale included in Pace's *Higher Education Measurement and Evaluation Kit* (Pace and others, 1975).

20. Student satisfaction with courses: Student responses to evaluation instruments that measure such factors as clarity and appropriateness of objectives, presentation of subject matter, communication and motivation, instructional materials, and evaluation techniques provide a good indication of the degree of course satisfaction. Numerous student ratings of instruction are available. A complete system of faculty evaluation that in-

cludes student ratings is described in "A Faculty Evaluation System" (Uhl, 1976).

21. Quality of learning: The quality of learning can be divided into three areas: degree and complexity of intellectual engagement (including such factors as memorization of facts and terms, synthesis of materials, and analysis of situations), amount of interest and attitudinal involvement (such as disinterest, enjoyment, or satisfaction), and level of activity (whether passive or active). The Higher Education Measurement and Evaluation Kit (Pace and others, 1975) has a scale to measure these attributes.

22. Style of learning: The way students learn can differ from campus to campus, among students on a specific campus, and from course to course. Pace's kit (Pace and others, 1975) has two scales to measure this variable.

23. Student satisfaction with college as a whole: This would measure general student attitudes toward the institution and its educational program.

24. Notable student experiences: This would indicate what students feel are some of their most enriching and rewarding experiences at their institution.

25. Intellectual disposition of students: Pace and others (1975) use three disposition scales to measure intellectual disposition, regarding intellectual orientation, critical thinking, and scientific orientation. Intellectual orientation refers to the tendency to create, deal with, develop, and apply ideas. Critical thinking involves analyzing propositions and problems for their validity, viability, and resolution. Scientific orientation refers to the disposition toward scientific endeavors and analytical, scientific thinking.

The aspects of campus environment just listed are important to consider when developing assumptions for improving an institution. While some of these aspects (such as student attrition, faculty salary trends, and expenditures per student) are easily quantifiable, others are not. However, such instruments as the CUES, the IGI, the Institutional Functioning Inventory (IFI), the Student Reactions to College, and the Measurement and Evaluation Kit have been developed to assist institutions in analyzing unquantifiable aspects. These and other instruments are described in Chapter Nine.

Assumptions based on environmental data assist in developing specific goals for the institution. Examples of goal statements based upon these assumptions are presented in the next section. However, these assumptions can also be used to develop alternative strategies. For example, if an assessment of the environment leads to the assumption that current practices will result in an enrollment decline in three years, which could hurt the institution financially, the institution should start considering plans that would be likely to counter the predicted trend. Obviously, the assumptions about the internal and external environments would play an important role in developing these alternative plans.

*Goals.* The goals of an institution differ from its mission statement by being more specific, but they should support and not conflict with the mission statement. In many, but not all, instances, the goals will develop from assumptions that are supported by data on the external and internal environments. Below are two examples of goals, their associated assumptions, and supporting environmental data.

*Goal 1: To increase the enrollment by 2 percent a year for the next five years.*

This goal could lead to many quite different activities, depending on the assessment of the present environment. For example, if it was assumed that applications would increase by 25 percent next year, the action taken would be quite different than if a 25 percent decrease was assumed. Therefore, some assumption about the environment must be made in order to determine the best methods of achieving the goal. In this instance, the following assumption might be made: Unless special efforts are made to enroll students outside the 18-to-24 age group, and/or to make the curriculum more appealing, and/or to increase the effort in admissions, stable enrollment can be expected until about 1980, when enrollment will start to decline. This assumption is based upon the following data, which pertain primarily to the external environment.

1. The projected number of people in the normal college-age population (18–24 years) is expected to increase in North Carolina by about 4 percent between 1975 and 1980. From 1980 to 1985, it is predicted to decrease at about a 5 percent rate, and from 1985 to 1990 at about 7 percent. These are less than the declines for the nation as a whole (Southern Regional Education Board, 1975, 1976).

2. While private colleges accounted for only 15 percent of the enrollment in 1975 in the South, a figure most likely to continue declining, the community colleges are growing very rapidly (33 percent in full-time equivalent students from 1973 to 1975) (Southern Regional Education Board, 1975, 1976).

3. In contrast to the regional figures, in North Carolina the private sector accounts for slightly over 30 percent of the college enrollment. In addition, the private enrollment has not declined but has increased slightly (*Statistical Abstract of Higher Education in North Carolina,* 1900); in fact, in 1976–77 private college enrollment increased more (about 8 percent) than in any year in the past decade.

4. Beyond purely demographic data, the percentage of youth going to college within the traditional age group is decreasing, possibly because of a decrease in the value attached to a four-year degree or changes in life-styles. Fuller (1976, p. 67) reports that "between the fall of 1972 and fall, 1973 the proportion of 18- and 19-year-old women [as well as men] attending college dropped substantially." Thus, the end of the military draft would not explain this general enrollment decrease. Also, Fuller points out that the rising cost of attending college is probably not the only reason for this decrease, since the enrollment of students from upper-income families has also decreased.

5. The federal government continues to provide funds for those who cannot pay for their college education. About 85 percent of the present students receive financial aid. A reduction in the amount of financial aid for the institution would severely affect enrollment.

6. The number of non-college-age adults who are attending college is increasing, especially adults from ethnic minorities. (This

fact does not directly support the assumption but is listed because it has important implications for the enrollment goal.)

This assumption and the related environmental data, while not specifying the activities necessary to achieve the goal, do indicate the type of activities needed.

While the assumption for this goal was developed from external environment data, one of the assumptions for the following goal relates to the internal environment.

*Goal 2: To improve the intellectual climate of the campus.*

*Assumption 1:* A positive intellectual climate on campus is important for students to learn effectively and to develop interest in independent research.

*Assumption 2:* The intellectual climate on this campus is poor.

Assumption 2 is based on the following assessment of the internal environment:

1. Scores on the IFI were low, compared with the scores for other institutions, on the scales referring to the availability of activities, opportunities for intellectual and esthetic stimulation outside the classroom, and activities for advancing knowledge through research and scholarship.

2. Data collected from the IGI indicated that faculty, students, and administrators thought that the following areas should be given very high importance but were presently given only moderate importance: academic development (the acquisition of general and specialized knowledge, preparation of students for advanced scholarly study, and maintenance of high intellectual standards), intellectual orientation (a positive attitude about learning and intellectual work), advanced training (maintaining a strong graduate school, programs in the professions, and conducting advanced study in specialized problem areas), research (extending the frontiers of knowledge through scientific research), and intellectual/esthetic environment (a climate that facilitates involvement in intellectual and cultural activities).

3. Other data indicated a lack of faculty-student interaction out-

side the classroom, peer-group pressure to substitute social activities for intellectual activities, and a decrease in the use of the library facilities.

Again, these assumptions and the related environmental data help identify activities that may help achieve the goal of improving the intellectual climate of the campus.

Hopefully, these examples illustrate the importance of periodically assessing the internal and external environments for developing assumptions that can lead to important goals for the institution. However, identifying goals through assumptions about the internal and external environment is not the only process used to obtain an institution's goals. An institution cannot forget that its primary purpose is to educate students; therefore, the appropriate student outcome goals must be identified. The IGI is an instrument that not only assesses a part of the internal environment but also measures the importance attached to different student outcome goals by different constituent groups. The IGI consists of a series of ninety statements on possible institutional goals. Respondents indicate their views of these goals on a five-point scale ranging from "of no importance" to "of extremely high importance" both as the goals exist on campus and as the respondents would like them to be.

If it is desired to reconcile differences among constituent groups about the relative importance of these student outcome goals (or any other part of the IGI), the Delphi technique may be employed. This technique was successfully used for this purpose in five higher education institutions with quite diverse characteristics (Uhl, 1971, 1972). The objective of the Delphi technique, which was originally developed by the Rand Corporation, is to obtain a consensus of opinion without bringing individuals together in a meeting. The individuals complete a series of questionnaires that are interspersed with controlled opinion feedback. This mode of controlled interaction not only saves time and money but also permits the participants to think independently and helps them to gradually form a considered opinion. Also, it has the added advantage of keeping the individuals anonymous. In contrast is direct confrontation, as in a faculty meeting, which often results in the heated exchange, a reiteration of preconceived notions, an inclination to close one's mind to novel ideas, and tendencies to defend a previously taken stand and to be influenced by persuasively stated opinions.

The general procedure for employing the Delphi technique with the IGI is as follows: (1) The participants complete the IGI; (2) each participant is given the most common response to each goal statement and is asked to complete the IGI again and also to give one or more reasons if his or her opinion on a statement does not agree with the majority response; (3) each participant is again given the most common response among the group to each goal statement as well as the reasons why some participants did not agree with the majority and is again asked to complete the IGI. Although this procedure need not be limited to three steps, most Delphi studies have found that additional rounds did not result in greater consensus.

Once a decision is made about the goals that are most important, it is then necessary to determine how well they are pursued. While the IGI provides different groups' perceptions of the importance given to these goals, it is not intended to measure how well they are pursued. Other procedures, such as those developed by Pace and others (1975), Micek, Service, and Lee (1975), and Astin (1977), are more appropriate. These procedures are described in the review of available instruments in Chapter Nine of this book.

*Activities, Responsibilities, and Resources.* After the goals of an institution are determined, appropriate activities to achieve them must be identified and responsibilities for carrying out these activities must be assigned to different groups. Appropriate resources must be made available, if they are not already so, for implementing these activities. One of several procedures for relating activities to goals and assigning responsibilities and resources will be discussed later in this chapter.

*Evaluation.* While environmental data are extremely important in developing assumptions, they are essential to evaluation. Appropriate data are determined by the goals of the institution. In the examples previously discussed, the goals were to increase the enrollment by 2 percent a year for the next five years and to improve the intellectual climate of the campus. Obviously, to evaluate how well the activities are achieving these goals, each year student enrollment must be measured and the intellectual climate of the campus must be assessed. To be properly evaluated, goals must be explicitly communicated to the individual or group responsible for evaluation and sufficient time for collecting the data must be provided. The importance of communication and sufficient time cannot be overemphasized. A major reason why environmental data are not used more in decision making is because they are not available when the decision has to be made. In most instances this is not because the variables cannot be measured but because the evaluator was not given enough time. If assumptions based on environmental data are used to develop goals, and if all goals are formally communicated, the relevant information should be far more available. Of course, the decision maker must still make the decisions.

## Procedures for Collecting and
## Utilizing Environmental Information

The previous section discussed the importance of environmental information in the several stages of long-range planning. While many campuses realize this importance, very few have established a formal procedure to insure that this information is available when a decision must be made. Different procedures of varying complexity have been established to solve this problem. One example is presented in this section. While each institution must develop a procedure appropriate to its own organizational structure and mode of operation, the ideas and steps presented in this section should be helpful.

Success of this process depends on both administrative and faculty support. Faculty support can usually be obtained if they are given an important role in the process and are informed that the information will be used to determine the activities and budgets for each department. The process itself is involved, since it requires campus-wide participation. However, once the master plan is developed, the yearly updating process is relatively easy. The following steps are described for accomplishing the difficult tasks of collecting data and integrating them into the institution's planning system.

1. If no appropriate decision-making body already exists, a Planning and Budgeting Council should be created to develop the assumptions, mission statements, and goals as well as the master plan and budget. The majority of this council should be composed of senior administrators, with the remaining seats filled by faculty and student representatives. The chairperson should be the president or the chief academic officer, and the individual responsible for planning within the institution should serve as secretary. The director of institutional research should also be a member of this council.

2. This council could well establish three committees with university-wide representation of faculty members and some student representation: One should develop assumptions about the external environment that are relevant to the operation of the institution; a second should develop similar assumptions about the internal environment; and a third should revise or develop mission statements and goal statements for the institution. This third committee should consider mandates from the state legislature, the state governing board, and the board of trustees as well as catalogue statements and other pertinent documents and data in light of the assumptions developed by the other two committees. The chairpersons of these other two committees might serve as members of this committee to provide continuity.

3. As well as serving on the Planning and Budgeting Council, the director of institutional research should help all three committees to gather environmental data. The importance of these environmental data cannot be overemphasized; it would be very dangerous for an institution to base its goals on assumptions developed without supporting data. Usually the Office of Institutional Research is responsible for providing these data (which might regard enrollment, instructional programs, faculty, media, space, admissions, student attrition, student aid, campus climate, strengths and weaknesses of the institution,

and perceptions and value judgments regarding goals), as well as external data such as national and state enrollment trends and job market surveys.

4. The two committees for developing assumptions should submit their reports to the Planning and Budgeting Council. After receiving the comments of the council, the planning officer should synthesize these assumptions into one paper, incorporating any other data relevant to goals. This paper should then be reviewed by the Planning and Budgeting Council and sent to the Committee on Mission and Goal Statements.

5. The Committee on Mission and Goal Statements should develop the mission and goals for the institution as a whole and send these statements and related assumptions to the Planning and Budgeting Council.

6. The Planning and Budgeting Council should then review this document and send it to the faculty senate for review.

7. After receiving the faculty senate's review, the Planning and Budgeting Council should make any modifications that it feels are necessary. It should then send the document to all the departments with detailed instructions to examine and identify those goals that the departments feel they can support anytime during the next five years with specific activities. They should also identify other goals not listed that are important or that may become important to themselves over the next five years. For these latter goal statements, the departments should indicate their assumptions and supporting data. Then, for all goals, the departments should indicate the specific activities needed to achieve each goal for each quarter and their estimated cost. Students should be involved in this process, and each department should approve the final report as a whole.

8. These departmental reports should be sent to the appropriate deans, who should review all reports submitted and add recommendations. The reports and deans' recommendations should then be sent to the Planning and Budgeting Council.

9. The Planning and Budgeting Council should review, modify, and synthesize all the material. The resulting document should include the mission, goal statements, and related assumptions of the institution as a whole as well as the related assumptions

and goal statements for each department. In addition, the activities and estimated costs associated with both university and departmental goals should be included. This document should be consistent with revenue estimates. If certain activities cannot be supported by the estimated budget, tentative sources for the additional funds should be specified.

10. This document should then be sent to each support office (that is, admissions, registrar, counseling center, and development) with specific instructions to use the document when developing their goals and activities and estimating their costs.

11. The statements of goals and activities with their associated costs for each support office should be reviewed by the administrator to which it reports. After approval, the administrators should send the statements to the Planning and Budgeting Council.

12. The Planning and Budgeting Council should receive from the Financial Affairs Office revenue estimates with supporting data for the coming year as well as the coming year's enrollment projections.

13. The Planning and Budgeting Council should synthesize into one document the mission statement, goals, and activities with associated costs for each department and support office. Using the enrollment projections and the projected income figures, the council should attach priorities to these goals and associated activities and identify the office(s) or department(s) responsible for each activity as well as the estimated costs per department and office. This document should be sent to the president and board of trustees for approval.

14. After the plan is approved by the president and board of trustees, a copy should be sent to all offices and departments for their information and planning.

15. When the actual income becomes known, the Planning and Budgeting Council should review the plan to determine whether the activities scheduled for the coming year can be supported. Any changes should receive the approval of the president.

16. After the plan is approved, the Planning and Budgeting Coun-

cil should send it to the appropriate administrators, who should send out each department's and office's activities lists and budgets.

17. Each department and office should provide quarterly progress reports to the planning officer, who should compare each department's planned with actual activities and the associated costs with the estimated costs.

18. The planning office should synthesize this information into a quarterly progress report for the Planning and Budgeting Council, which should make any necessary adjustments in budget, personnel resources, and activity time estimates to best achieve the previously agreed-upon goals.

19. The director of institutional research should report to the planning officer how successfully each goal is being met so that this assessment can be included in the planning officer's quarterly report to the Planning and Budgeting Council.

20. At the end of the academic year, the Planning and Budgeting Council should assess the degree to which the activities were performed and the associated goals achieved, providing appropriate feedback to the departments and offices as well as to the faculty senate.

21. To update the plan for the following year, the Planning and Budgeting Council should review the assumptions and the mission and goal statements for the institution as a whole in light of updated internal and external data provided by the director of institutional research. These mission and goal statements and assumptions should be sent to the academic departments with directions to update their environmental assumptions and goal statements as well as their activities and associated estimated costs. These should be submitted through the appropriate deans to the Planning and Budgeting Council for synthesis and, after obtaining similar information from support offices, the council should set priorities for specific goals and activities. These should be approved by the president and board of trustees. This update procedure should be repeated each year so that the goals and activities are derived from up-to-date internal and external environmental data.

The above steps describe a procedure by which the input of environmental variables into the planning and decision-making process of the institution is continuous. Also, the described procedure formally involves a large number of people in the planning process. In addition to those members of the university-wide committees, each department, school, and support office develops its own plans. This greatly decreases the resistance to change, insures attention to important goals, and increases the ease with which the plans are implemented.

## Summary

In today's highly organized society, planning for the future is crucial for growth and survival. Planning is becoming a condition for staying in the race, for keeping up with people's expectations. The importance of the availability of environmental data for viable planning is illustrated and a formal procedure for collecting and utilizing environmental information in planning and decision making is described.

# 6

*Richard E. Anderson*

# Utilizing Interinstitutional Data to Evaluate Educational Policy

━━━━━━━━━━━━━━━━━━━━⌘━━━━━━━━━━━━━━━━━━━━

In response to decreasing enrollments, administrators at many colleges are broadening the mission of their institutions to expand the pool of potential applicants. Thus, liberal arts colleges are developing business and other vocational programs, religious colleges are becoming more secular, and single-sex colleges are becoming coeducational.

But does an expanded mission increase enrollments? If so, under what circumstances? What are the educational implications as well as the long-range competitive implications in terms of attracting more students and support? And how does such a change affect the educational environment of the institution as perceived by students?

The study reported in this chapter illustrates the use of environmental measures to answer these questions by comparing men's colleges and women's colleges with other single-sex colleges that have become coeducational and by comparing religious colleges with other religious colleges that have changed to a secular orientation. The chapter seeks to demonstrate the usefulness of environmental studies first by reviewing the differences among these groups of institutions and how they have changed over a decade as disclosed by the College and University Environment Scales (CUES), and second by offering a case study of how one of the colleges has used CUES in its strategic planning in order to become more competitive.

## The Decline of Pluralism

Pluralism has been a fundamental feature of American culture since colonial times, perhaps nowhere more than in the educational system. Differences in region, religion, ethnicity, sex, and race have all been important in shaping the diverse development of educational institutions, as has been the coexistence of public education and various forms of private education since the early nineteenth century.

However, pluralism in American education has recently begun to erode: The base of public education has expanded considerably while that of private education has diminished appreciably. Between 1949 and 1972, the proportion of private colleges and universities declined from 66 percent to 56 percent of all institutions of higher education; just between 1969 and 1972 enrollments in private institutions decreased from 33 percent to 23 percent of the total enrollment in higher education (West and Andersen, 1970; National Center for Education Statistics, 1974). Moreover, during the early 1970s, 138 private institutions closed, merged, or became publicly supported (Anderson, 1975). Public colleges, by virtue of their public support, tend to serve "mainstream" needs in higher education: They are virtually all coeducational (the only exceptions being in the Southeast), typically modest in academic standards, multipurpose in mission, moderate to large in size, and secular in orientation. Students whose educational interests are outside the mainstream might prefer a special-purpose college (such as a single-sex institution or a religious institution, but they will not attend such a college if they perceive that the "marginal utility" of attending it is less than its perceived "marginal cost" of high tuition. In 1970, the marginal cost of attending a private four-year college vis-à-vis a public four-year college was approximately $1,100 (Froomkin, 1972).

Consequently, special-purpose colleges find themselves in a wrenching paradox. Because of this price discrepancy, to be successful they must certainly be distinctive, since they cannot market their product at a price higher than the competition unless the product is unique and serves a special need. The higher the marginal cost, the greater the distinctiveness (marginal utility) must be (Stigler, 1967; Dorfman, 1967). However, the more distinctive the college, the smaller its potential market and the more difficult it is to maintain a full enrollment.

The problem of such colleges is not hopeless, of course. Some women's colleges, such as Hood, are thriving apparently because they are women's colleges, not in spite of this fact. And Oral Roberts University has attained national prominence as an evangelical religious institution. But when one adds to the price differential the societal trends of secularization and sexual parity, the monumental policy problems faced by these special-purpose institutions are apparent.

Most college officials recognize the importance of institutional distinctiveness, but because this quality is very difficult to measure and evaluate, they generally focus their attention on more immediate and measurable concerns such as enrollment, the student-faculty ratio, the salary schedule, and the budget. Their preoccupation with these data can obscure a more fundamental problem: the competitive strength of their institution. For many colleges, distinctiveness and thereby competitive strength depend on the provision of a special educational environment. If these colleges are to remain robust, their administrators cannot afford to dismiss environmental issues as illusive variables that defy analysis. No particular environment will be valued equally by all students, yet a certain type of environment will be attractive to a significant number of prospective students.

The task for college administrators is to promote the specific assets and character of their institution to those college-bound students who are interested in these qualities. This process of "market segmentation" has been the backbone of commercial marketing strategies for many years. Market segmentation does not require that colleges change their mission frequently to chase short-run consumer demand. Institutional missions should reflect institutional values, and successful market segmentation firmly roots long-run marketing strategies in those institutional values that serve long-term social needs (Hugstad, 1975). Once market segmentation is achieved, the college environment must be monitored so that undesirable changes can be avoided and institutional strengths can be restored.

Determining the financial and environmental consequences of two major strategic policy changes—from single-sex to coeducational status, and from a religious to a more secular orientation—provides a clear example of the value of environmental measures.

## An Example of Comparative Environmental Studies

To evaluate the effects of strategic changes across a variety of institutions, forty colleges that had used CUES during the 1960s were selected for study. All had been either single-sex or religiously oriented in the middle 1960s, but approximately half of them had become coeducational or secular, respectively, by 1975. These latter schools formed the experimental group for the study, while those retaining their original orientation were used as a control group.

At both the changed- and the constant-mission institutions, a tripartite methodology was employed. First, CUES was re-administered at each college during 1975–76 to assess environmental change on each scale after ten years. Second, enrollments and finances for 1965–66 and 1975–76 were compared. And third, key officials on each campus—typically, the president, the chief academic officer, the chief financial officer, and a trustee—were interviewed.

In looking at the findings (reported in detail in Anderson, 1977) with regard to enrollment trends, the institutions that changed or broadened their mission tended to grow while the others did not. Specifically, men's colleges that admitted women increased their enrollment by 34 percent over the ten-year period, and women's colleges that admitted men grew by 91 percent. In contrast, enrollment at the single-sex colleges that remained single-sex declined slightly. Similarly, at the Catholic colleges that became more secular, enrollment increased by 42 percent, while at those that preserved most of their religious orientation, enrollment declined slightly. The only exception to this trend occurred at Protestant colleges, where those that secularized showed less growth over the decade than the others, but this exception may be due to the fact that these colleges secularized in the early 1960s and increased their enrollment considerably before 1965.

These enrollment trends suggest that at least at Catholic and single-sex colleges, a broader mission does increase institutional attractiveness. But if data on campus environments are also considered, the benefits of such changes in mission are far more problematic, as the CUES scores shown in Figures 1 through 7 reveal. (The profile format for these figures is adapted from Pace, 1969.) All of the median scores are scaled against the normative data from a national sample of institutions, given in the CUES technical manual.

Figure 1 shows that, as perceived by their students, the environments of women's colleges that remained single-sex were generally the same in the 1960s and in 1975–76, characterized by an extremely polite and decorous orientation, a close sense of community, and high morale. Although their median Scholarship score was modest in the 1960s, they evidenced good student-faculty rapport and an emphasis on teaching as indicated by their Quality of Teaching score. By 1975–76, their high Community and Propriety scores had fallen somewhat, but they had made gains in Scholarship and Quality of Teaching.

The 1960s profile for women's colleges that became coeducational (Figure 2) is quite similar to the 1960s profile for women's colleges in Figure 1; however, by 1975–76, when about 25 percent of the students at these colleges were men, their environment was markedly different. Median Community and Campus Morale scores each fell over 30 percentiles, and Propriety score declined 25 percentiles. In contrast to the gains at women's colleges that remained single-sex, the median Scholarship, Awareness, and Quality of Teaching scale scores all also dropped. Initially, it was

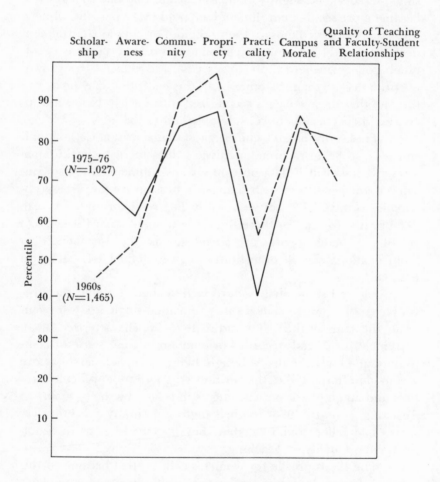

Figure 1. Median CUES Scores of Thirteen
Women's Colleges That Remained Single Sex

assumed that these changes might reflect the inclusion of men in the sample, in that men might not have changed the environment as such but simply responded in a systematically different manner than women to the items on CUES. However, when men's responses were omitted, the results were almost identical to those shown in Figure 2.

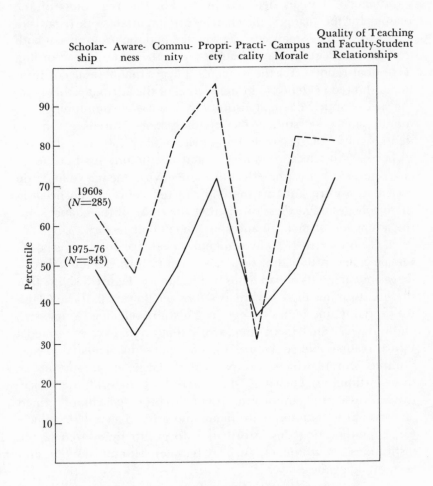

Figure 2.  Median CUES Scores of Five
Women's Colleges That Became Coeducational

These dramatic environmental changes measured by CUES cannot, of course, be attributed solely to a changed admissions policy. For example, the financial analyses showed that the colleges that had gone coeducational were in greater financial peril by 1975–76 than those that had remained single-sex: Among other problems, their institutional debt was twice as great. Possibly financial exigencies, rather than the admission of men, caused the environmental changes detected by CUES. But regardless of the reasons for the changes, the changes are important with regards to competition. The small size, the courses, and the programs of both groups of colleges remained attractive to their students according to student reports. Yet the women's colleges that became coeducational showed evidence of losing several of the attributes that form the special appeal of small institutions: a sense of community, high morale, and good student-faculty interaction. Moreover, the students at these colleges were almost twice as likely (30 percent versus 16 percent) to select social life as their institution's least attractive characteristic. Thus, the effect of these environmental changes on recruiting future students should be of real concern to officials at these colleges, regardless of whether the cause of the changes was the admission of men, finances, or some other factor.

Contrary to the environmental evidence for formerly all-female colleges, the admission of women to formerly all-male colleges appears to have had a positive influence. Figure 3 shows that these institutions increased their scores on almost all of the CUES scales. (Only one men's college in the study remained single-sex, and no special analysis was made for it that would have generated a figure comparable to Figure 1.) The gains on Scholarship and Campus Morale, which were particularly large, are important for these institutions. The CUES data not only agreed with the subjective impressions of administrators but also provided a more refined analysis of the campus environment and offered a credible vehicle for communicating this information to groups interested in the institutions' environment, such as trustees, alumni, donors, and accrediting agencies.

A pattern similar to that for women's colleges which had remained single-sex—modest alterations, both positive and negative—occurred at Catholic colleges that retained most of their

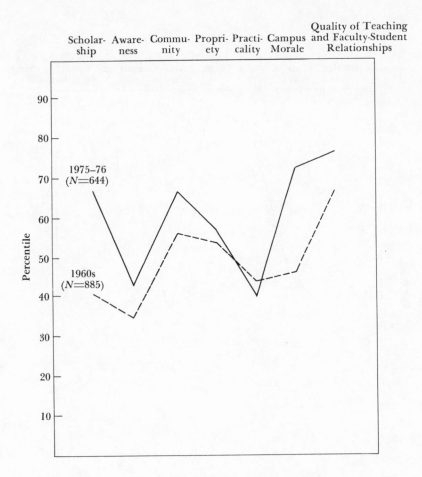

Figure 3. Median CUES Scores of Six
Men's Colleges That Became Coeducational

religious orientation (Figure 4). However, important and generally deleterious changes took place at Catholic colleges that became significantly more secular (Figure 5). Community and Campus Morale scale scores declined the most, 21 and 24 percentiles, respectively. The close resemblance of the 1975–76 profile to the national norm is cause for concern because it indicates a general decline in the distinctiveness of these secularized institutions.

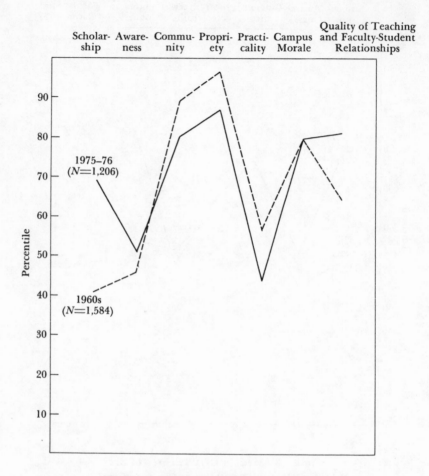

**Figure 4. Median CUES Scores of Twelve
Catholic Colleges That Retained Their Religious Orientation**

Figure 6 summarizes the CUES data for Protestant colleges that consistently pursued a religious mission. It indicates that these colleges changed very little in the ten-year period—a conclusion supported by the impressions of campus officials. The profiles of Protestant colleges that became more secular are presented in Figure 7. A comparison of the dotted profiles in Figures 6 and 7 clearly

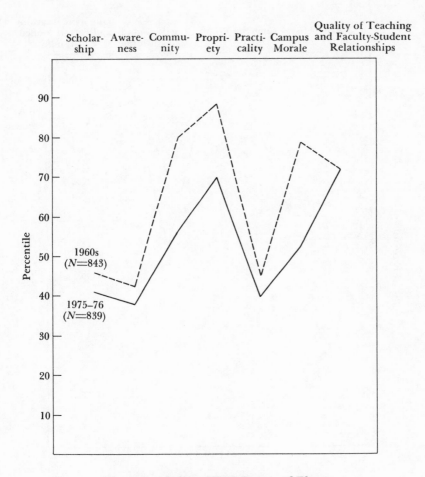

Figure 5.  Median CUES Scores of Eleven
Catholic Colleges That Secularized

shows that these two groups of colleges were quite different in the middle 1960s. Even then the secularized colleges had a profile that was only modestly different from a great number of colleges in the country, thus suggesting that these colleges were most likely in direct competition with other regional institutions. And, indeed, this was confirmed in conversations with campus officials.

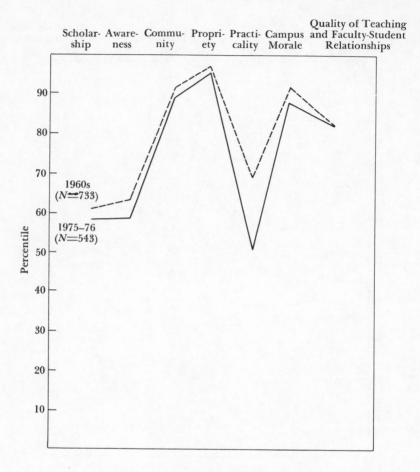

**Figure 6. Median CUES Scores of Seven
Protestant Colleges That Retained Their Religious Orientation**

As these figures undoubtedly illustrate, CUES was an invaluable tool for this comparative research project, enabling us to rely on more than just the impressions of campus officials. Although these impressions often agreed closely with the CUES data, they lacked reliability, particularly at those colleges evidencing environmental decay, where officials tended to equivocate. Under-

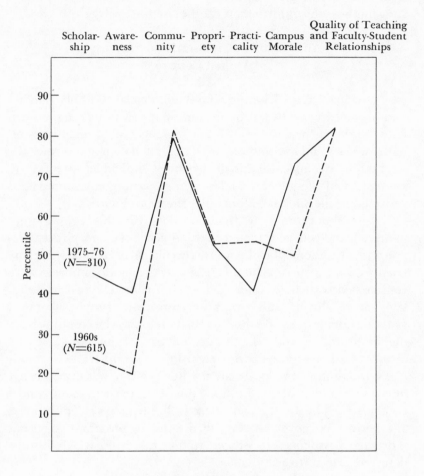

Figure 7.  Median CUES Scores of Six
Protestant Colleges That Secularized

standably, presidents of these colleges made more positive assessments than did deans, vice-presidents, and faculty. In addition, the
use of CUES provided finer gradations and distinctions for comparing elements of campus environments with national norms.

So far, the discussion of findings from this study has centered on changes in median scores, but naturally the changes at

individual colleges were often considerably more dramatic. The next section reviews the data from CUES for one particular college, showing how this information can be used by college officials.

## An Example of Institutional Studies: "Alpha" College

Alpha College has long served middle-class Catholic families and in the early 1960s was quite comfortable with its religious orientation. It was primarily staffed by members of a religious order, had low costs and low tuition, and had limited course offerings. Its strengths were an emphasis on teaching, individual attention to students, and the general quality of the learning environment, as reflected in the 1965 CUES profile, shown in Figure 8.

At about the time that the data for this profile were gathered, the college initiated both an academic and physical expansion. Additional faculty were recruited, particularly for the sciences, and a new science hall and two new dormitories were constructed with federal assistance. Unfortunately, several problems arose during this upgrading effort. Large numbers of Catholic families were becoming reluctant to pay the cost of private higher education, and a significant minority of the more able and affluent Catholic students were choosing to attend Ivy League colleges. In addition, the local state teacher's college was transformed into a comprehensive institution, thus offering the main constituency of Alpha College an attractively inexpensive educational alternative. Moreover, as a result of Alpha's physical expansion, mortgage payments necessitated tuition increases, which further deterred prospective students.

In response to these problems the college initiated a number of strategic changes: The admissions office, which once relied heavily upon referrals from counselors at parochial schools, was expanded and attempted to recruit students from the local public schools. To broaden the college's appeal, religious course requirements were eliminated and the student code was liberalized, although the college still maintained what officials considered to be "reasonable standards" of conduct. Recruitment literature was revised to describe the institution as a liberal arts college "with a

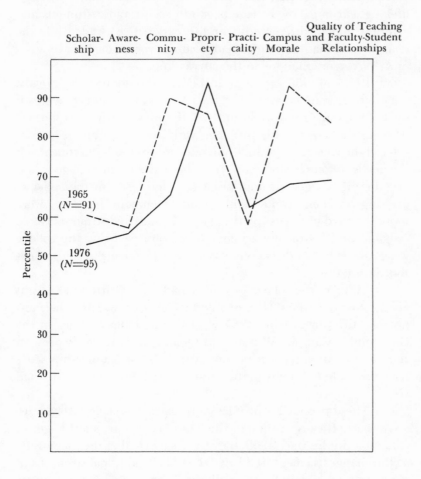

Figure 8.  CUES Scores of Alpha College

Catholic heritage," and administrators went out of their way to make their institution's academic freedom more publicly visible. For example, when students suggested a forum on abortion, the dean not only assisted in securing speakers representing both sides of the issue but also notified local media of the event. When the board of trustees was expanded so that the community could be better represented, a rabbi and a Protestant minister were included. Adopting the theme of "serving the community through lifelong learning," the college began to recruit older students and veterans and to offer credit for life experience. And, while the dean denied that the college had become "vocational," there was a new "career orientation" in the curriculum.

Between 1965 and 1976, enrollment did not increase greatly, although after an initial decline, the number of students rose steadily. During our campus visit in 1976, the president was expansive. Although acknowledging problems with student attitudes, he considered the college innovative and to be more closely "in touch with the needs of today's students." He projected that the college would become more vigorous and based this optimism on the college's growing academic reputation. Faculty members, however, were more reserved in discussing the changes. One cited strains between religious and lay faculty, while another observed that the college was growing in "six directions at once. . . . The name of the game is more students."

By 1976, the college obviously had a very different campus environment, as the CUES profile in Figure 8 reveals. The most notable differences from 1965 were considerable declines in the Community, Campus Morale, and Quality of Teaching scores. In spite of the attempted academic overhaul, the Scholarship score had also fallen. Interestingly, however, the Propriety score had risen.

These two CUES profiles were extraordinarily informative to Alpha's officials. Although they had been aware of changes in student attitudes since 1965, they were surprised at the magnitude of the changes as measured by CUES. The traditional strengths of the institution, except for its emphasis on propriety, were no longer perceived as distinctive by the students who were sampled in 1976. Instead, the college was rated modestly on most of the dimensions probed by CUES. The president was startled by these data, particularly by the decline on the Community scale. Seeking additional information, he and his staff reviewed the responses to individual items. They observed that the items most responsible for the decline dealt with student-faculty relationships rather than with relationships among students. Consequently, they wondered whether this fact was due to the increased number of lay faculty, declining morale among the religious faculty, or new types of students who were less receptive to the college's traditions. Although Alpha's score on Awareness had not changed, the item analysis showed that in 1976 queries about personal, poetic, and artistic concerns evoked more positive responses than in 1965, which were offset by more negative responses to items pertaining to political matters. Finally, the officials were puzzled by the increase in Alpha's Propriety score in spite of its liberalized student code. At least two explanations were possible: Perhaps as rules were discarded, the remaining regulations appeared anachronistic. Or vestiges of the college's past standards may have been especially onerous to new students.

The president and his staff did not accept the CUES data as conclusive evidence but as trouble signals, and they decided to collect more detailed information. Alpha's director of institutional research undertook a survey specifically tailored to the institution that focused on a number of the concerns raised by CUES. Its sample was large enough to make separate determinations about the perceptions of different student groups, such as part-time and full-time, traditional age and older, resident and nonresident, and Catholic and non-Catholic. The results of this study, combined with the CUES data, were the topics of a faculty forum. The strains caused by secularization were generally acknowledged, and the forum was expanded to include students and trustees. Students expressed a stronger sentiment for a Catholic education than was expected, and this and other important religion-related issues began to be resolved. The college instituted a number of short-run policies designed to improve the learning-living environment, and the faculty, recognizing Alpha's predicament, pledged their cooperation for further improvements. Whether this cooperation can be maintained is uncertain, but progress has been achieved. Moreover, Alpha's officials now plan to regularly and systematically gauge student perceptions so that they will not be surprised by "environmental drift" in 1985.

The changes measured by CUES are not always as dramatic as those that occurred at Alpha. However, its case should illustrate how CUES data can effectively inform and guide policy makers. The fact that Alpha's president sought to confirm and elucidate the signals given by the CUES profiles was important. He and his associates realized that seven scale scores cannot fully describe an organization as complex as a college. Aware of this limitation, they examined individual items and then undertook further studies to clarify particular interpretations. And they realized that they could effectively use environmental measures like CUES periodically to monitor the effects of policy decisions.

## Conclusions

Although administrators are usually aware of the problems facing their institutions, they often do not fully comprehend the magnitude of the environmental changes related to these problems. One reason is that they are preoccupied with data on deficits, debt payments, full-time equivalent enrollments, salary schedules, and contract negotiations. In solving these very real and complex problems, they can easily neglect the even more complex and seemingly amorphous problems about campus ambience. Moreover, while presidents may be sure that their college's student-faculty ratio is too low, they may not know whether campus morale is worse than it is at other institutions or than it was at their college five years ago.

Also, campus officials must recognize that enrollment decline and its financial consequences are not causes: They are symptoms. Students do not choose to attend an institution because its enrollment has risen or fallen; they choose on the basis of their perception of the educational experience that the school offers. In this regard, administrative attention to curriculum development and faculty development are important, but equally important—and perhaps more so for many institutions—is attention to environmental development. Formal environmental instruments can provide institutional leaders with valuable information about important issues that can be evaluated by administrators and faculty, the board of trustees, or the entire college.

Many of the problems facing the colleges studied in this research project are a direct result of the rapid expansion of higher education in the 1960s, the way in which American colleges and universities are financed, and general societal trends, which colleges cannot control. However, if college officials monitor environmental changes, they will be more able to maintain and build upon their institutional strengths and to stem undesirable trends. If these colleges can retain their unique vitality, they will continue to attract a special group of students and thus maintain their competitiveness.

7      *Francis J. Wuest*
*and Robert G. Jones*

# Anticipating Problems in Undertaking Campus Studies and Implementing Results

————————••⟨∞⟩••————————

This chapter discusses the lessons to be learned from a controversial series of studies about the educational and social environment of one university based on the use of the College Student Questionnaire (CSQ) and the College and University Environment Scales (CUES). The studies were conducted with authorization by the president. Groups of faculty, administrators, and students used the results to identify problems and to initiate actions for solving them, and some faculty saw the results as indicating central weaknesses in the educational life of the institution. However, five years after the completion of these studies, other faculty wished they had not been done, and administrators maintained that although the studies raised some serious educational questions, they failed to provide answers and could have damaged the institution's reputation.

The history of these environmental studies illustrates what this form of institutional research can and cannot do. It describes possible adverse reactions that should be anticipated when planning assessments of institutional life and offers some ideas about what to do and what to avoid when conducting assessments.

## The Institution

The university that undertook these studies is private, nondenominational, and highly regarded—particularly for its engineering and physical sciences programs. During the time of these studies, its three undergraduate colleges of engineering, business, and arts and sciences were all male, with a few women enrolled in graduate programs.

On the whole, the university's 3,200 undergraduate students were academically superior to the approximately 1,900 graduate students, with SAT scores for entering freshmen averaging 670 mathematical and 600 verbal. Its graduating seniors regularly receive scholarships and fellowships, including the most prestigious, for graduate study, and, at that time, 45 percent of them entered graduate school. The placement record of students who enter careers in business and engineering directly after graduation is outstanding. In a national survey of undergraduate colleges that have produced leaders of business and industry, the university ranks among the top twenty—outdistancing many other institutions that are larger, older, and more prestigious.

The 350 teaching faculty come, for the most part, from the best graduate schools. Their teaching, scholarship, and research are of good quality, and their overall publication record is average. Several instructors enjoy national and even international reputations, and many in engineering and business consult with major corporations and government agencies worldwide. As late as 1964, decisions affecting academic policy and the life of faculty and students were made by the board of trustees and administrators with, at best, only token consultation with the faculty. However, a new president that year, combined with changes in the governing board, greater assertiveness by an expanded and younger faculty regarding their role in governance, and demands by students for changes in social and academic regulations led to greater faculty and student participation in setting academic policy during the late 1960s.

Student social and cultural life has reflected the residence pattern of the university. At the time of the environmental studies, all freshmen were required to live on campus, were not permitted to have cars, and were housed in dormitories separated from those of the upperclassmen. Half of the upper classes lived in somewhat austere university residence halls that had identical, built-in furniture and rules against individual decor. These halls were organized into living sections, each of which was as selective as the fraternities and they lacked only the national affiliation and separate eating facilities of the Greek organizations. Most of the remaining upperclassmen lived in the large, luxurious houses of thirty national fraternities, while approximately 10 percent lived at home or in apartments off campus.

Student social life centered on parties in the fraternities or residence halls, several campus-wide events that included name-group concerts, and intramural and intercollegiate athletics. There were frequent incidents involving abuse of alcohol, property damage, and sexual escapades, but almost all were successfully treated as internal administrative problems requiring a minimum of publicity or police involvement. Relations with women were perhaps best reflected by the comment of the dean of student life, alluding to the profusion of *Playboy* foldouts taped to bedroom walls: "These guys wouldn't recognize a person as a woman unless she had a staple in her navel."

It would probably be fair to characterize the tone of the campus as primarily male, spartan, and competitive, emphasizing high academic achievement in quantitative terms. Until recently, admissions literature said, "The———University man works hard and he plays hard," and the head of the university's counseling center once described the institution as a "mental Marine Corps." Faculty members have tended to grade lower than those at colleges with similar admissions standards and reputations, and many academic departments have prided themselves on the rigor of their "killer courses," in which, for example, the class grade average up until the final examination was 40, with 70 considered passing.

Financially sound, with undergraduate tuition ranking among the very highest in the nation and with management consistently operating in the black, the university seems to have found a distinctive niche in the ecology of higher education somewhere between the highly specialized institute of technology on the one hand and the highly selective liberal arts college on the other.

## The Environmental Studies

The following information may help to explain at least some of the reactions to the studies of the university's social and learning environment, which were made during the late 1960s and early 1970s. Impetus for the studies can be traced to the arrival of the new president, which sparked a review of institutional regulations and procedures. This review followed three years of an interim administration and twelve years under a president who was extremely authoritarian. An ad hoc committee examined the effectiveness of faculty-administration communication in the formation of educational policy and decision making, and a committee on university organization rewrote faculty rules and regulations to assure broader faculty participation both in standing committees of the university and in departmental governance.

As a result of student government requests, the standing committee on student life (composed of elected faculty, appointed students, and ex officio administrators) considered updating social regulations, reforming the disciplinary code, and reducing perceived inequalities of treatment between residence hall and fraternity members. The dean of student life and two professors—one of them a social psychologist new to the university—proposed to the committee a $2,500 empirical study of the impact of the entire university's social environment on the student body to aid in the reforms. The president authorized the study, and the two professors and dean of student life became an ad hoc committee to conduct it.

*First Year.* In the first year of the study, both the CSQ and CUES were administered. During orientation week, before the start of their first semester at the university, a random sample of fifty freshmen in each of the three undergraduate colleges completed CSQ I, which ranked them on six scales—family status, family independence, peer independence, liberalism, social conscience, and cultural sophistication. At the start of the spring semester, random samples of second-semester sophomores and juniors representative of the residence halls and the fraternities received personal letters from the president asking them to complete CSQ II, which included six additional scales descriptive of upperclassmen: satisfaction with faculty, satisfaction with administration, satisfaction with other students, satisfaction with one's major, study habits, and extracurricular involvement. Initial response by the upperclassmen was small, but members of the Residence Hall Council and the Interfraternity Council helped boost the response rate by urging the students in the random sample to complete the questionnaire.

To the two study directors, the CSQ results were no surprise, reflecting the academically oriented, high-socioeconomic-status, and suburban and small-town background of the university's students. All student groups—freshmen and upperclassmen as well as engineering, business, and arts and sciences students—were above the national average in regard to family independence and peer independence. The engineering and business students were well below average in regard to liberalism, social conscience, and cultural sophistication, while the arts and sciences students scored above average in liberalism and cultural sophistication but average or slightly below on the social conscience scale. On satisfaction with the faculty, administration, other students, and their major, the engineering and arts and sciences upperclassmen clustered around the 50th percentile on all four scales, while business students ranked below average in their satisfaction with faculty, administration, and major and average in their satisfaction with students.

Upperclassmen in all three colleges scored below average in study habits and above average in extracurricular involvement.

That spring, CUES was also administered to a random sample of upperclassmen from each of the three colleges and from the residence halls and fraternities. Again the response rate was low. After working once again with the Residence Hall Council and the Interfraternity Council, the study directors completed the remainder of the sample by requesting volunteers from several large upper-division courses that drew students from many majors; a total of 275 respondents was ultimately obtained.

The version of CUES used in this first study translated the 150 true-false questions about the university into scores on five scales: Scholarship, Awareness, Community, Propriety, and Practicality. The differences among students from the three colleges and between residence hall and fraternity members on how they perceived the university environment along these five dimensions were negligible. Figure 1 shows the profile for all the students at the university across the five scales as well as the profiles for students at three other institutions—Swarthmore, Purdue, and the University of California, Los Angeles. As can be seen, the students perceived their university as markedly lower on the Scholarship and Awareness scales than did respondents at the other institutions. The university also ranked lower than the other three on Propriety and lower than Swarthmore and Purdue on Community.

The Committee on Educational Policy requested the CSQ data on freshmen for review in its study of the freshman year, including the impact of residence hall life on the freshmen. Some members of the committee viewed the results with alarm, interpreting them as low grades to the university on social conscience and cultural sophistication. But the findings from CUES were not circulated outside the Committee on Student Life, and the president authorized the continuation of the environmental studies into the next year without having seen the full results.

*Second Year.* At a student-faculty retreat just prior to the start of the academic year, one of a series sponsored each year by the dean of student life, the dean and the two study directors reported the results of both the CSQ and CUES surveys from the previous year. The campus leaders in attendance reacted calmly to the data,

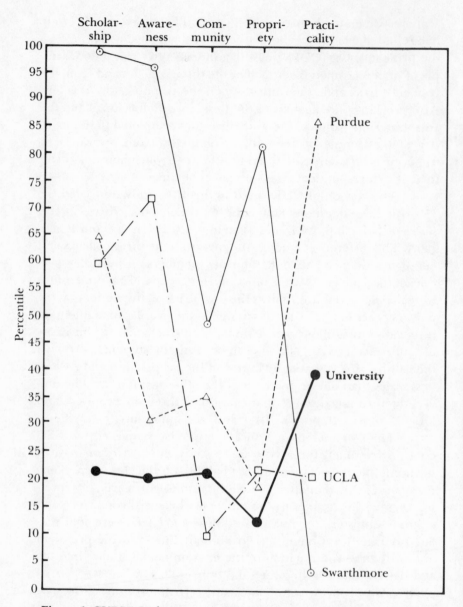

Figure 1. CUES I Scale Score Profile for Upperclassmen ($N = 275$) with Profiles of Three Other Institutions.

apparently seeing them as reflecting their own perceptions. But later in September, when the dean and the study directors briefed the president, the provost, and the vice-president for student affairs on these findings, both the president and vice-president seemed distressed by the students' perception of the university and puzzled by the mismatch between the students' perception and their own. The two study directors urged release of the data to stimulate discussion among faculty and students about the significance of the data for the university and about possible courses of action. However, the president, concerned that behavioral science data were too "soft" to serve as the basis for good decisions, responded that he was cool to the "indiscriminate divulging of results" without considering "whether such action would accelerate remedies to problems or conceivably make such remedies hard to find."

After consulting with his cabinet, the president recommended that the ad hoc committee conducting the studies be expanded to include the head of the counseling service, two faculty members with professional skills in statistics and educational measurement, and the new chairperson of the Committee on Student Life. At the president's request, these new members conducted an independent review of the instruments and procedures used in the previous year's studies as well as of the results. On the basis of this study, the full committee reported to the president in January that the results could be considered as a reasonable preliminary portrayal of life at the university and that they warranted further pursuit of the question "To what extent does the present image of the University reflect the image of the institution as desired by its constituency?" In a memo, the committee described possible lines of inquiry and urged continued self-evaluation as part of program development, but the president did not respond.

In February, student leaders from the student government and newspaper, who had heard some of the results of the studies from the student-faculty retreat and from other fragmentary reports, met with the president to learn how the results affected the ten-year plan that he was developing, which included new student housing and enrollment objectives. He indicated that he saw no connection between the environmental studies and long-range planning. When asked about the educational philosophy underlying the plan, he responded that the question of educational philosophy was a matter for the philosophers on the faculty.

As a result of the meeting, some of the student leaders wrote letters to the editor of the student newspaper analyzing the perceived ills of the university's academic programs and relating them to its social climate. They accused the administration of suppressing the results of the surveys, and the newspaper headlined one article on the studies "Environmental Plan Withheld." The editor interviewed the president about the surveys and quoted him as viewing them as "a very significant study with some startling results" and as noting that further study of the quality of university life was needed in order to know "how the non-academic part of the university experience can be more meaningful." The newspaper quoted the provost as saying, "the study is not yet complete. . . . We should resist drawing conclusions." The vice-president for student affairs was quoted as saying, "Although further investigation is justified, the study didn't tell me anything that worries me" and the findings were "not something to wring your hands about." But in an editorial, the student editor claimed that the study had uncovered "serious flaws" within the university that led him to state, "It is time for re-evaluation."

In an open letter to the president, the student leaders called for the results of the study to be released, for action to be taken in light of the results, and for the president to address the university community on these issues. The president agreed to the meeting, at which one of the study directors presented the results of CSQ and CUES, as shown in Figure 1. The president pledged to involve all campus constituencies in a continuing discussion about university plans and problems.

As a result of their analysis of the CUES data, the student leaders then asked the president to create a University Goals Committee "to examine possible ideal universities, compare the present university to these ideals, and find means to guide the university toward the ideal to which it aspires." They proposed that the committee consist of the president and two other administrators, three students, and three faculty members—including one of the two study directors.

The president accepted this proposal, and the committee was to begin work after the summer. During the summer, the two study directors, the dean of the college of arts and sciences, and another arts and sciences faculty member attended the annual Danforth Workshop on Liberal Arts, taking the tasks of interpreting the environmental data, planning further investigations, and selecting corrective actions if they were indicated.

*Third Year.* The fall semester was filled with activities generated by the students' demands of the previous spring: (1) The Danforth workshop team recommended that the university's self-study continue; (2) the dean of student life's student-faculty retreat was devoted to considering the university's goals; (3) the Educational Policy Committee renewed its study of the freshman year and recommended the creation of freshman seminars on interdisciplinary topics; (4) as a result of a weekend retreat discussing the issue of relevance in undergraduate education, which was led by the provost and attended by a group of faculty members, top administrators, students, and some members of the board of trustees, individualized majors were created and a procedure was established for adding temporary courses on topics of high, immediate relevance on short notice; and (5) the University Goals Committee established subcommittees to review the university's philosophy and goals, including one subcommittee on the "structure and scope of learning," which included the two study directors and which sponsored a second CUES study. At the start of the spring semester, the provost resigned and was replaced by a research chemist whom undergraduates perceived as hostile to their interests and to participatory governance.

The second CUES study, on real versus ideal university environments, was designed to determine three things: (1) how faculty members perceived the reality of the university, (2) how faculty members and students perceived an ideal university, and (3) whether the earlier CUES student data would be replicated with a different sample of students.

This study involved four different randomly selected groups: two groups of 63 faculty members each and two groups of 63 upperclass students each. All 252 participants were sent letters describing the study together with a copy of the CUES questionnaire instructions and an answer sheet. However, one faculty group and one student group were instructed to answer the CUES items from their own actual knowledge of the university (the "real" groups), while the other two groups (the "ideal" groups) were instructed as follows: "Assume that you are at the ideal university and are asked to be a reporter about it. You have lived in this environment, participated in its activities, seen its features, and sensed its attitudes. Answer each statement as to whether you expect it would be true or false about the ideal university."

The response rates were again lower than desired. Out of sixty-three members in each group, forty-one and forty-two faculty members and thirty-six and forty-two students responded in the ideal and real groups, respectively. The responses of the real group of students and the results of the first CUES study were almost identical, as a comparison of Figures 1 and 2 shows. As Figure 2 indicates, faculty responses regarding the university's real environment were comparable to student responses, although the faculty members ranked the university higher on the Scholarship and Propriety scales and lower on the Community scale than did the students. From these results, the study directors concluded that the small sample sizes did not seriously affect the reliability of the findings or introduce systematic biases in the data as a result of self-selection and nonresponses.

Next, the relationships between these perceptions of the real and the ideal university were studied. Figure 2 shows the profiles of the two ideal groups. Three relationships seemed particularly noteworthy: (1) The faculty and student respondents had almost identical conceptions of an ideal university. (2) The real university fulfilled the ideal regarding practicality for faculty and nearly did so for students, but it deviated sharply from the ideal on the four other scales for both faculty and students. And (3) the profiles of the ideal university were comparable to the real profile of Swarthmore, a highly selective liberal arts college (Figure 1).

By May, the University Goals Committee completed its work. In a thirty-six-page booklet for the board of trustees and the rest of the university community, it presented forty major recommendations, covering the entire scope of university life, which ranged from the broad and philosophical to the very specific. Over thirty

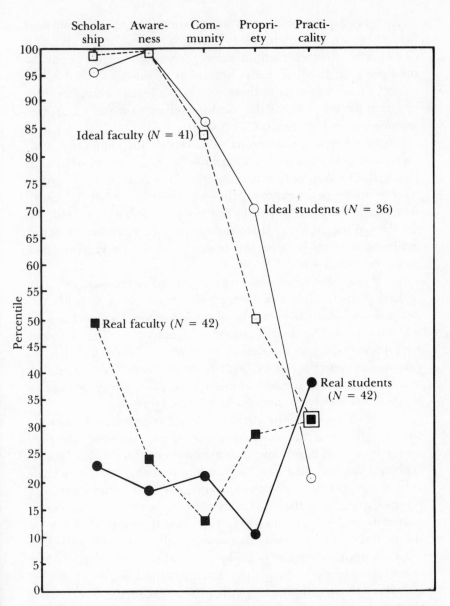

Figure 2. CUE I Scale Score Profiles for Upperclassmen and Faculty
under Two Conditions of Administration—real versus ideal.

people had participated in its deliberations, many of whom had helped launch or review the first environmental study and who came to the effort with attitudes and perceptions shaped in part by the results of that first study. A number of the issues they raised could be traced directly to those results, while the committee's description of "elements of the ideal university to which we aspire" stemmed from the second CUES study.

In a four-page appendix to its report, the committee summarized its real-ideal study and included a graph of the results as in Figure 2. The chairperson also described the study to the board of trustees in an oral report on the committee's recommendations. Afterwards, he was chastised by the new provost both for including the data in the report and for mentioning the study to the board orally, apparently because the provost felt the findings did not make the university look good.

Meanwhile, during the year the board of trustees had been making plans for a new residence hall complex to be built like the last one—without involving faculty or students in the planning, without considering the educational consequences of the plan, and without attending to the decline of student interest in living on campus. Despite protest by the University Goals Committee, the administration and trustees approved the plan, partly because so much effort had been invested in it by that time.

*Fourth Year.* The fourth year got off to an inauspicious start for the environmental study program. At the request of the provost, the dean of education, with assistance of some of his faculty, critiqued the real-ideal CUES study, and in their report they challenged the professional ethics and integrity of the study directors on the ground that they had chosen a poor instrument, misinterpreted it, used biased samples, and couched their interpretation of the results in biased, value-laden language. The study directors responded with a lengthy, point-by-point rebuttal and requested an open investigation of both the report and the critique. However, they received no response from the provost except that for the first time in nine years, one of them received no merit increase in salary.

A small experimental program of seminars for sixty freshmen was launched that year, the result of the earlier recommendation of the Educational Policy Committee. The freshman seminars were to have small enrollments and be led by senior faculty members with a commitment to teaching. Each seminar was to examine a broad topic that would provide students an opportunity to explore the impact of science and technology on society and the individual.

To explore the effects of the seminars on the students, the perception of the university by students enrolled in the seminars was compared with the perceptions of other students. An underlying hypothesis was that if freshmen had a personal, intense, stimulating learning experience in the seminars, their total experience of the university would be significantly and positively altered.

One of the study directors conducted this study, again using CUES (this director also led one of the seminars). In the study, the sixty students selected for the seminars were compared with two control groups of sixty other students each. The first group consisted of freshmen who had applied for the seminars but were not admitted because of enrollment limits, and the second of freshmen who had not applied at all. All three groups proportionately represented the entering freshmen in each of the three colleges (engineering, business, and arts and sciences).

The 180 students were asked to complete CUES in September when they first arrived on campus, again in mid-October, and again in mid-January after the seminars had ended. The first administration was assumed to determine the freshmen's expectations at the university; the second, an early assessment of the environment based on actual experience; and the third, a well-developed perception of the university. Presumably, if the seminars altered students' perception of the campus as measured by CUES, the alteration could be detected by the third administration.

In this study, a revised version of CUES—CUES II—was used, which consisted of 160 statements and included two additional scales, Campus Morale and Faculty-Student Relationships, or teaching quality. Ninety-four students, or 52 percent, responded to all three administrations of the instrument—thirty-three of whom participated in the seminars, thirty-one of whom had been denied entrance, and thirty of whom had not applied to the program. In order to provide comparable data, only the results for these ninety-four students were analyzed.

The data showed a dramatic shift from September to January. The September profile was comparable to those of the student and faculty perceptions of an ideal university illustrated in Figure 2, while the January profile resembled the profile for the real university obtained in the previous studies. Most of this shift had occurred at the mid-October testing.

On the two new scales, Campus Morale dropped from the 95th percentile in September to the 25th percentile in January, while Faculty-Student Relationships, or teaching quality, dropped from the 96th percentile to the 60th. Like the other studies, this survey demonstrated a marked difference between the perceived reality of the university and the ideal university, as well as producing a profile for the university quite different from those for other institutions. It also demonstrated, as had freshman socialization studies at other colleges, quite rapid formation of common perceptions of the environment.

The survey indicated that participation in the freshman seminars had no significant influence on these perceptions: The three freshmen groups showed a high degree of consensus in the September poll, greater variability by October, but again a high degree of consistency in January. Participants in the freshman seminars did adopt the same perceptions as the nonparticipants, if more slowly.

*Fifth Year.* The same professor administered CUES II for its final use in February by assigning each student in his introductory social psychology course the task of recruiting two respondents from the student's curriculum and residence area. Responses from ninety-four of the professor's students replicated the overall pattern seen in Figure 1, the real data of Figure 2, and the January results of the freshman socialization study. The only significant difference between these responses and those from the freshmen a year earlier was on the Campus Morale scale, on which these students scored near zero.

Later in the spring, the professor submitted to the president a report on the freshman seminars and suggested implications of all of the CUES studies for the future of the university. In June, he and the other study director left the university and took positions elsewhere.

*Summary.* Over a period of five academic years, 504 students and 42 faculty members at the university participated in six separate administrations of CUES to measure the university's environment. In addition, 36 students and 41 faculty completed CUES with instructions to indicate their conceptions of an ideal university.

These studies pointed up the qualities of CUES as well as of CSQ: Both were easy to administer—CUES in particular demanding little of the respondents—and both required relatively small samples to produce replicable results. Moreover, the five scales of CUES I and the seven of CUES II captured the flavor of the university according to student and faculty comments about the results. Both instruments came with excellent manuals, and comparative data from many kinds of institutions were readily available. In all respects, the instruments were of high quality. (The Institutional Functioning Inventory [IFI] and the Institutional Goals Inventory [IGI], which were not available when these studies began, provide a finer analysis along with many of the desirable features of CUES. For a real-ideal study today, the IGI could be used instead.)

In every administration over the five-year period, the instruments yielded similar results: The students ranked the university low on Community, Propriety, Awareness, and Scholarship according to norms based on the responses of a large national sample of students from a broad spectrum of institutions. The university's profile as perceived by faculty was approximately the same. These profiles were quite different from those of the ideal university as perceived by both groups. The ideal were more comparable to the real profiles of highly selective liberal arts colleges as perceived by students than to profiles of any other universities or colleges which could be located at that time.

These results, while not flattering, were not particularly explosive. However, they provoked intense reactions within the university community. Some members of the community raised common objections to the psychometric approach to environmental studies, such as "Perceptions can't be measured," "A few true-false items answered by a few students can't tell much about an entire institution," "That particular item doesn't have anything to do with scholarship," and the like.

In addition, some faculty and administrators claimed that

the two study directors and the sponsoring committees started with their own assumptions about what was wrong with the university and simply tried to confirm their assumptions through the studies. Others saw the directors as malcontents who wanted to stir up student and faculty unrest. Some considered them as dupes who were too open with student respondents, telling the students so much about the survey that the students could rig the results and present a false image of the institution. And others, particularly administrators, were concerned that the results would become known to parents, funding agencies, and neighboring institutions that competed for the university's students and reduce the school's funding and support. At the same time, some students and faculty sought to use the results for their own purposes, such as winning support for particular proposals, developing alliances, and even embarrassing the administration. As a consequence, the studies were only infrequently applied to program development and institutional policy making.

These difficulties need not have occurred. By evaluating the planning, implementation, interpretation, and use of the studies, we can develop tactics and strategies for applying their findings more constructively.

## Study Authorization and Conduct

At the university of this case study, the president approved and authorized the funds for each of the four research projects, and other administrators served as formal liaison on the projects, either directly participating in their planning and execution or simply receiving regular reports about them. Despite these formal connnections, a major flaw existed in the authorization and conduct of these studies: The president and his associates made no agreement with the study directors about purposes, interpretation, or dissemination of results before the studies were begun.

The study directors thought that they knew what needed to be done and why. They saw the environmental studies as part of a research project to assess the entire university climate and as a factor that would shape administrative decisions about new actions or further inquiry. But the president and his colleagues thought that the study of the nonacademic or extracurricular side of campus life was important as long as it did not interfere with more significant decisions involving educational policy, the building program, or the financial health of the university. Because they perceived the results from the first study to be negative, dissemination of results emerged as a sensitive issue. They worried about publicity, while student leaders charged that data were being suppressed. Inclusion of the second study results in the University Goals Committee report to the trustees angered the provost and led him to request the dean of education's critique of the study. The results of the final two studies were circulated only among administrators and members of the earlier study teams, and went, of course, into the rumor mill.

The study directors and others involved in planning the studies should have first worked out with the president and vice-president a clear understanding of the studies and their purpose in university planning. Also, the administration should have anticipated the likely outcomes of the studies and considered possible responses. Instead, everyone became locked into a relationship that exacerbated differences, and the studies kept going to no one's satisfaction. As a result, they were never used effectively to stimulate discussion and to guide decision making in promoting desirable institutional change.

Several recommendations can be made for administrators and those who direct environmental studies. The clearest message is to know what you are doing, why you are doing it, and for whom; establish clear understanding with everyone who is involved.

Also, administrators should have a definite purpose for studying their institution's environment, such as the purposes proposed by Leonard Baird in Chapter Eight. They should not expect an assessment of the environment to make decisions, plan actions, or solve an isolated problem. Such a study can help direct planning, decision making, and problem solving, and may suggest areas in which to conduct further analyses, but it cannot prescribe what to do.

Administrators should also understand how the instruments can help serve the functions just mentioned and anticipate the likely outcomes. If they lack expertise with the instruments, they should get advice from institutional research specialists or faculty members from the behavioral and social sciences.

For maximum benefit from a study, administrators should create a commission or committee made up of members from within the institution to plan and oversee the conduct and interpretation of the study. This committee will be particularly important if the motives of administrators or the study director are likely to be suspect or if the results of the study are likely to be distrusted. Its members should be chosen for the respect with which the campus community regards them, rather than for their special skills in research or measurement. If necessary, they can learn how to interpret the results of the study.

Most important, administrators should establish a clear agreement with those conducting the study about the purpose of the study, its design, and the interpretation and dissemination of its results.

Study directors should realize that to initiate a study without the endorsement of administrative leaders or a legitimate institutional body is risky. People whose lives are invested in an institution are often unenthusiastic about data collection or investigations that might embarrass them. Study directors should plan accordingly and anticipate likely reactions from all campus constituencies. If they seek institutional decisions or action regarding the results of the study, they will need support from the top. Without it, the most that they can expect are discussions of the results divorced from action. Thus, they should get an agreement in writing from the administration for what they plan to do and how they plan to distribute the results.

### Interpretation of Findings

At the university described in this chapter, agreement about the meaning of the results was difficult if not impossible to obtain because of the different intentions of the people involved in the study. The president, most administrators, and some faculty members sought interpretations that would dismiss or else disprove the CSQ and CUES results. They viewed "healthy criticism" as a good thing, but they read the CUES scores as low grades and attributable to bias or to agitation among hypercritical students. They questioned the quality of the instruments and the conditions of their use, even when their concerns were not supported by the follow-up analyses that they ordered.

At the same time, groups of students and faculty members used the data as a goad for reform, seeking to use the studies to mobilize support for their own purposes. They were aided in this goal by administrative actions that appeared to be suppressive but they created their own problems in interpreting the results. For example, because the profile obtained of the ideal university was similar to that of a highly select liberal arts college like Swarthmore, some students concluded that the university should become like Swarthmore without fully considering that such a change would be unrealistic and have profound consequences for the institution and its personnel. Others suggested solutions to problems related to surface indicators. For example, to improve the university's CUES score on Awareness, some advocated a major lecture series in which famous people would come to the campus, while others proposed hiring more faculty in the humanities and social sciences. To improve its score on Community, some people proposed meetings among students, faculty, and trustees.

The study directors failed to anticipate the emotions that the studies would release among these groups and the power of those emotions to shape different people's perceptions of the findings. As the professionals at the center of the activity, they offered their own interpretations as well as assistance to people who wanted to examine the data themselves. They made themselves available to administrators, but after their first data presentation, they were not summoned again. They worked with student leaders and faculty members on the several committees whose responsibilities involved institutional operations that were evaluated by the studies, but they erred in thinking that rationality alone would guide these groups in interpreting the data and overcome the administration's growing hostility.

Interpreting the results of any environmental study will always be difficult, especially to those inexperienced in survey and psychometric techniques. Thus, distinguishing between one's own experience of reality and the perception of that same reality by others as measured by a particular instrument will be a new and unfamiliar task to some. Those with no background in psychometrics may not know how a scale such as Scholarship is devised or what it means. And problems will arise in deciding how good or bad a given percentile score really is. Is anything below the 70th percentile bad? How poor is a score at the 20th percentile on Propriety?

Thus, our major recommendation regarding interpretation is to establish conditions that will encourage and support continuing dialogue about the results. For administrators, such dialogue is the key to a positive outcome from an assessment of the institutional environment. Hence, openly releasing the data is essential. Many people will know about the study directly or indirectly in any event, and secrecy may not only hinder full discussion of the results but also trigger strong, unwarranted negative reactions.

Administrators set the tone and establish norms for the community in interpreting the results and thus much is required of them: an effort to learn enough about the instrument to make an informed judgment about the meaningfulness of the data, a willingness to consider the interpretations of others, attention to the perceptions and motivation involved in opposing interpretations, and fairness in evaluating negative assessments in light of the institution's past achievements as well as failures. The commission can be particularly valuable to administrators at this point. Representing a broad range of opinions and trained to judge the results carefully, they can provide nonspecialist interpretations from several perspectives and emphasize that multiple interpretations are possible and that reasoned inquiry is encouraged. If the dialogues fail to reconcile major differences of interpretation, the commission might extend the inquiry so that additional information can be gathered to illuminate the differences.

For a study director, even more important than designing or conducting the study is assisting the campus community in interpreting the results. To do so, the study director must assume the related roles of teacher, guide, and critic. As a teacher, the director must explain technical details of inventory construction, reliability, validity, scale identification by factor analysis, norms, and the like, as well as provide comparative data from other institutions or the instrument's developer. As a guide, the director must demonstrate appropriate caution and set high standards in interpretation so as to avoid advancing a favored position or blocking those that seem less acceptable. As a critic, the study director may be the only person on campus capable of constructively criticizing some of the interpretations offered.

## Application of Findings

With no consensus about the purpose of the studies or the meaning of their results, little could be expected at the university described here about using the findings. Of those people who were inclined to act on the basis of the studies, some demanded a prescription of specific actions from the study directors, others condemned the instruments for not telling them what to do, and most became embroiled in a dispute resulting from conflicting interpretations. Meanwhile, those who had other plans proceeded without referring to the studies.

The administration and governing board of the university had their own plan for the future based on their assessment of the school's past achievements. Their priorities were: to design and build residence halls by primarily considering questions of cost rather than the quality of student life or the academic environment; to expand graduate programs that were already several times more expensive than undergraduate programs; and to increase faculty research through hiring highly visible, successful, and research-oriented faculty. The results of the environmental studies clearly did not mesh with these priorities.

In contrast, reformers among the faculty and student body sought to use the studies to rethink the philosophy and practices of the university and to explore and experiment with new possibilities for undergraduate education. They focused on residence hall patterns that enforced isolation, contrary to student expectations and desires; disparities between the decisions made by the administration and board and the reformers' concerns for learning and teaching; and a collegial ideal of institutional planning.

The study directors sought to use the studies to make program development responsive to student expectations about their university experience and faculty desires to improve their relationships with students.

The administration and board were able to maintain their priorities by selectively accommodating student and faculty interests—by absorbing and dismissing conflicting information, by rejecting purposes opposed to their own, and by adopting only those recommendations that were not at cross-purposes with their own priorities. Although some degree of tension and conflict can lead to creative problem solving, at this university the antagonists' values and goals were so dissimilar that the studies resulted in little action, discussion consisted of talk without communication, and personal relationships dissolved in suspicion, mistrust, and occasional recrimination.

If administrators hope to use environmental studies as a springboard to action, they must include the rest of the institutional community in the design and interpretation of the studies. With a willingness to explore the implications of the results, administrators can assume leadership in developing the plans. In those institutions where change is difficult, administrators will have to muster all of their diplomatic and political skills to make use of the results. However, administrators must alert faculty and other groups to the serious implications of the results for the future of the institution.

In contrast to this active leadership role, study directors should realize that they are not likely to be responsible for translating the results of the study into action. Indeed, they should be wary of taking responsibility for an action plan. Ideally, the dissemination and interpretation of findings will have brought other campus leaders to the fore. Study directors, perhaps more than anyone else, need to accept the fact that colleges are not changed easily or quickly. Along with other analyses, their environmental studies can provide an honest, objective look at their institution; but by themselves, the studies will rarely provide the impetus for major change. If the studies are successful, they will not be a unique episode in the history of the institution, as they were at this university. Instead, they will be used continuously in a constant process of self-study, in which study directors may be called on to design and conduct further analyses as part of action planning. Thus, study directors can profitably anticipate these future studies: What questions will need to be asked or are likely to be asked? And how can the answers best be found? Aiding such ongoing research—stimulating others to think about what is and what might be, promoting dialogue and debate based on study results about the meaning and possibilities of campus life, assisting others to take research-based action to make the possible actual—is essential for continual institutional improvement and can be the highest achievement of the environmental researcher.

# 8  *Leonard L. Baird*

# Using Campus
# Surveys for
# Improving Colleges

———————————•◦∞◦•———————————

This chapter demonstrates how to survey your college's environment in comprehensive detail. First, it describes some informal and nontechnical ways to better understand your college. Next it discusses some steps that can make your collection of systematic information more effective. These include defining your purpose, identifying variables that would affect your decisions, selecting instruments, planning actions, administering instruments, dealing with results, and implementing policy.

## Understanding How Your College Functions

Although the contributors to this volume have emphasized formal instrumentation for surveying colleges, decision makers can gain a better understanding of their college's functioning in other ways. Perhaps the most fundamental need is for decision makers, particularly administrators, to get out of their offices and find out what is happening on their campus and how people feel. It is easy to become engrossed in budget sheets, administrative memos, and legalistic arguments and to lose sight of the real needs, actions, and responses of the people in the college community. How can a decision maker avoid this trap? Some possibilities are outlined below. They are followed by a detailed discussion of information needed to make a specific decision.

*Informal Observations.* Go to the places where students and faculty congregate, such as the cafeteria, the faculty club, and the local hangouts. What are people talking about? What are they worried about? How are they reacting to current policies and practices? Sitting in on student and faculty meetings may also be helpful. What is going on there? What are the current concerns?

Also, experience aspects of student life. For instance, sit in on some large classes to see what the teaching is like, listen to the orientation lectures, and attend events that draw students to get an idea of what their out-of-class life is like.

Another clue to what is happening on campus lies in the *kinds* of groups that are forming or growing. Why do these groups exist? Do they represent a need for social activity, a desire for intellectual discourse, a concern for politics, or a reaction to institutional policies? What does their existence or success say about the college? Also, observe the use of campus facilities. Are students using the library? Do they check out books unrelated to class requirements? Do they stay in the library in the evening? What books are selling well in the student store? Is there a demand for art supplies? What kinds of lectures and concerts are being offered? Although informal observation of all these aspects provides only impressionistic data, it can lead to better ideas about what is going on at the college.

*Informal Conversations.* A more direct way to find out what is happening on campus is to talk with students and faculty. You might have lunch with small groups of students and faculty to talk about their concerns, needs, and enthusiasms. What do they do on campus? Where do they go and why? (For example, students may congregate at a nearby beer parlor because there is no place on campus where they feel as comfortable or welcome.) What do they think of current policies and practices? What misunderstandings about what is going on do they have and do you have? Particularly, are any policy decisions having unintended consequences?

Particularly with students, you might find out:

1. how and why they chose your institution,
2. if they had any difficulties adapting to the college in their first year,
3. what they feel they have learned,
4. how they think they have changed,
5. where they are living and how they like it,
6. what their interactions with professors have been like,
7. why they chose their major and how they like it,
8. whether they think there are significant subgroups on campus,
9. what kinds of political groups are active,
10. how they feel about current policies and administrative actions, and
11. how they would like the campus to change.

Talking with students in various classes may be helpful: The incoming freshman may have some erroneous ideas about the campus, the sophomore may be having difficulty coping with the demands of college life, and juniors and seniors may have particular perspectives about the preparation that they have received for work or further education.

Of faculty, you might ask:

1. why they happened to come to your campus, that is, what attracted them to your college,
2. what their interactions with students have been like,
3. their opinions about the degree of collegiality among professors
4. whether the campus is conducive to their research and scholarly activities,
5. what issues, if any, divide the faculty,
6. what issues, if any, separate the faculty from the administration, and
7. how they would like the campus to change.

Talking with professors who are new to the campus and those with many years of experience may be especially helpful. The first group is seeing the college with a fresh perspective and may question things that are taken for granted by others. The experienced group can provide long-term perspectives about the college, including how and why it has changed.

The questions suggested above are intended merely to start conversation. Obviously, they will elicit more specific comments about the college, which will probably lead you to ask other questions concerning the basis for the speaker's comments. After a number of such conversations, you should develop an appreciation of the general trends on your campus. (A comment is in order here for those who consider such conversations to be unnecessary or silly. It is very easy to assume that you know what people on your campus are thinking, but even well-informed people can be surprised by the direction, intensity, and diversity of opinion on their campuses. Sometimes they have also been surprised at the sophistication and quality of the comments and suggestions by students and faculty.)

As with informal observation, informal conversations provide chiefly impressionistic information. They are also an uncertain guide, since one or two articulate and persuasive people with strong, if atypical, views can easily sway your own opinions. However, informal conversations provide a useful way to gain some understanding of what people on your campus are thinking. These conversations can also serve as sounding boards for any proposed action and provide some indication of the success of enacted programs.

*Comparisons.* You can easily become accustomed to how things are done on your own campus. Familiar procedures seem to be the best and most reasonable. Possibly contentment with the status quo is warranted. However, comparisons of what is done on your own campus with what is done on other campuses can often be helpful. By visiting other schools you can gain new perspectives on your procedures and policies. When visiting a college similar to your own, you may concentrate on areas of greatest concern to you or on general similarities and differences in atmosphere. You might employ the informal observation practices suggested earlier and arrange to talk with some students and faculty. If you are considering a decision, policy, or action on your own campus, you might ask the following questions:

1. How similar is the procedure on this campus to the procedure we are considering for our own campus?
2. Are the general goals and specific objectives of this campus the same as or different from ours?
3. Are the participants similar? If not, how are they different?
4. How successful has the procedure been?
5. Does something in the general environment of this college account for the success or failure of the program?

The answers to these questions may help you make your own decisions.

*Documents.* Documents are often overlooked as sources of information about colleges. One of the most neglected is the report prepared for the last accreditation cycle. Prepared with great labor and at considerable expense, they are compilations of many data about the institution. If your college has prepared such a report in the last several years, you may find it very informative reading, giving you greater insight into your college. You may also discover statements that do not seem completely accurate or that do not tell the whole story.

Other document sources are the materials prepared for students, such as catalogues, disciplinary codes, and guides. Read these as would a student attempting to cope with life on your campus. What is the general impression of the college created by these documents—friendly, bureaucratic, rule bound, or concerned? What would it be like to be a freshman studying at your college for the first time?

Another stimulating document is the yearbook. What kinds of activities are emphasized? How important are extracurricular activities? Comparing yearbooks from several years can indicate whether fraternities and sororities are gaining or losing popularity and how student concerns have changed as reflected by the emergence and decline of various clubs and organizations.

The campus newspaper is another source of information. What activities are listed, what are the current issues on campus, and what needs do the ads reflect?

All of these documents, which should be easy to obtain, will provide you with a better picture of what your campus is like and how an existing or contemplated policy or action may affect the overall atmosphere. The materials chosen, their quality and accuracy, the skillfulness of your interpretation will determine how useful a review of documents will be. Although you may learn a great deal of information, it must be organized; however, it may not bear directly on the decisions or policies that you are considering. Of course, the documents will not provide comparative information on other institutions, but they are an excellent and informative place to start.

*Data on Hand.* Another sometimes neglected source of information is data in various reports. Some of the most informative reports are the profiles of freshman classes prepared by the College Board, the American College Testing (ACT) Program, and the American Council on Education and available at nominal costs. The College Board provides summaries of students' test scores, grades, high school subjects, ethnic groups, parental incomes, educational goals, special needs for assistance, intended fields of study, desires for advanced placement, high school and planned college extracurricular activities, and information about the high schools attended. The ACT Class Profile provides similar information but places greater emphasis on students' out-of-class accomplishments in such areas as writing, drama, and science; the reasons for the students' choice of colleges, and the students' vocational interests. The American Council on Education survey of college freshmen provides similar information but omits test scores and includes more information about students' occupational choices, life goals, and expectations about their college experience.

The individual college profiles can be compared with national normative data for all colleges or with data for colleges of certain types, such as two-year institutions. The College Board and ACT services also allow comparisons of students who applied and students who enrolled. All of this information can help you determine the kinds of students you are attracting and their goals, plans, and interests. Charting these profiles over several years can suggest how the ability, preparation, plans, and interests of the student body are changing.

Other factual information includes student attrition rates

and faculty turnover rates. Have these figures increased or decreased in recent years? Have the changes coincided with changes
in programs or policies? Has anyone talked with the people who
left to determine why they did so? Perhaps someone in the counseling office has talked with students who considered dropping out or
switching colleges.

A final source of data is the attendance figures for various
campus activities. Are sports activities well attended? Are classical
music concerts? Are art exhibits? What kinds of speakers have generated the most student interest?

All of this factual information must be interpreted with caution. For example, a decline in the test scores of incoming students
may represent a decline in the appeal of the college's programs to
bright students, or it may merely reflect a general national decline.
Similarly, a rise in the percentage of students choosing business and
health-related majors and a decline in the percentage choosing
traditional liberal arts majors may have nothing to do with the
quality of those programs but rather reflect the students' concern
for the job market. Perhaps most important, tying such factual data
directly to a decision is often difficult, and in other cases using
some data for judging a program or policy may be quite mislead-
ing. However, data, when used with caution, can provide valuable
and useful information about the nature of the student body and
the condition of the campus.

The sources of information discussed above are useful
mainly for making better-informed decisions. They enable the decision maker to improve his or her understanding of what is happening on campus and thereby (1) to understand the consequences
of current policies or programs, (2) to plan new actions more realistically, and (3) to anticipate the outcomes of future decisions more
accurately. The following sections outline some procedures that
can provide information that bears on decisions directly.

### Using Systematic Information

The information sources discussed so far are chiefly informal and unsystematic, lacking precision and detailed comparative
data. To evaluate an institution's environment and administrative

decisions thoroughly, the decision maker needs to have systematic information, which can be obtained either by using an available instrument, such as those described in Chapter Nine, or one's own. Of course, no instrument should be the sole source of information about the environment, but a well-chosen and well-designed instrument can provide comprehensive and systematic data.

Selecting and developing such an instrument are complex tasks depending on the nature of the college, the goals of the decision maker, and the politics of the situation. Although every situation is unique, the following sections will hopefully help colleges select or develop appropriate instruments.

*Identifying Your Purpose.* Although this advice seems self-evident, studies frequently neglect it. Institutional researchers often administer environmental instruments for no better reason than general curiosity—"How would our college look on these scales?" Occasionally a college can acquire useful information when this is the motive for a study, but a study will almost certainly be more useful if more specific purposes are developed. The following questions may help colleges clarify their purposes.

What Decision Do You Want to Make? This question is often difficult to answer because it requires careful thinking about the implications of the results of a study. Evaluating a program or policy is usually not very helpful unless one has determined what will be done if the evaluation is positive, negative, or neutral. Are you deciding whether to continue, discontinue, modify, restaff, or reorganize a program or policy? The more specifically you can describe the decisions you need to make and how environmental information would help you make the decisions, the better.

What Problem Do You Want to Solve? Sometimes identifying specific decisions that need to be made may be difficult; the issues of interest can be expressed only as general problems. For example, faculty morale may seem to be low, the turnover rate in the residence halls may be high, or enrollment may be dropping. Again, stating the problem in the clearest terms possible is helpful.

What Question Do You Want to Answer? Sometimes the purpose of a study is to gather information as a preliminary to later action. For example, information about what goals various groups feel the college should pursue in the future may help a college to formulate a five-year plan. Or you may simply want to know how students describe the academic rigor and friendliness of the college before you make any drastic changes. However, if at all possible, the use of the information should be clarified. At the very least, you should have a general idea about the needs that the information would fill. Would the value of the information obtained justify the expense? Would the information help in making later decisions? Which ones? How? These questions need to be addressed. At this point you may find it useful to invite and talk with researchers or administrators from colleges that have faced similar problems or conducted similar studies. Their experiences may help you clarify your own thinking and avoid many pitfalls. Appointing a small faculty-student group to plan the study may also be useful. Its ideas and effort may substantially improve the quality of the study.

*Identifying Relevant Variables.* After the decision, problem, or question is clarified, relevant variables may need to be identified. This step is critical to selecting instruments and planning the study. Identifying these variables may be made easier by considering the following questions.

What Results Do You Desire? For example, if your concern is the effectiveness of a new residence hall organization, what do you expect the new organization to accomplish? Do you expect better communications, higher morale, a greater sense of community, or stronger motivation for good grades? By listing the expected outcomes, you will also have a better idea of the specific purposes of your investigation and be better able to choose appropriate instruments.

What Are Your Assumptions About the Present Situation? This question is often one of the most useful, although it is often the most difficult to answer. If you are attempting to determine whether to change or maintain policies or programs, you must have certain assumptions about their nature and worth. How do you think they work? How do you think they affect students or faculty? Which features make them good or bad? By stating your assumptions explicitly, you will have a better idea about what you are looking for. For example, suppose you believe that the residence hall system should be improved and wish to try out some experimental arrangements. Exactly what is unsatisfactory about the present arrangements? Do you believe that there is too little group identity and cohesion? Do you think that there is little intellectual stimulation? It may be useful to list your assumptions about the present situation, then share the list with other people who will be involved in using the results of your investigation. Discussions with them can clarify the areas that need to be investigated.

Could the Decision Have Unintended or Unrecognized Consequences? New programs or policies may produce completely unexpected changes. For example, expanding the curriculum in some technical colleges to include more courses in the humanities and social sciences, intended to increase students' satisfaction with their education, has increased the rate of transfer to other colleges in some cases. Although most students *did* become more satisfied with the curriculum, some students became so interested in the new offerings that they decided to go to colleges where they could major in those fields. In short, all possible outcomes should be considered and eventually assessed by some measures; of course, the most important ones, positive as well as negative, should receive the highest priority in this assessment.

*Search for Pertinent Measures.* Once the important variables for a decision or investigation are identified, appropriate measures must be found. This step is more difficult than it might appear. Some suggestions follow.

Determining the Appropriateness of Existing Instruments. You should first examine existing instruments, which can be ordered from their distributors, to assess their appropriateness to your needs. Read the rationale given for the scales in the manuals—do not simply accept the scale names at face value. Look at the content and format of individual items in the scales that interest you most. Their applicability is a function of several considerations. First, does their content offer specific information that would help in making decisions concerning the areas in which the college is considering changes? How related are the questions asked in the instrument to the questions that the college wishes to answer? Are questions that would be important to the college left out? Might the items be subject to systematic bias at the college, either because of their wording or because of particular conditions at the college? Is there any evidence about the instrument's stability or the degree to which the instrument reflects change? Would the results be clear and interpretable? How representative of typical students or faculty are the groups that have completed the instrument before? How similar are they to the groups that would complete the instrument at the college? Has the use of the instrument led to changes in other colleges? Were there any problems in using the instrument? As you look at the instrument and its rationale, consider how it may stimulate new ways of thinking about your situation. You may decide to seek other information. At the same time, you should keep your need firmly in mind. Many people have been so impressed by the rationale of and rhetoric describing an instrument that they lose sight of their reasons for using the instrument in the first place. They have done studies of the rationale of the test rather than of their own problems.

Examining the Quality of the Instrument. Although the evaluation of an instrument for use in a college is similar to evaluations of instruments for use with individuals, there are significant differences. For example, the reliability of an instrument across colleges must be considered differently from reliability across individuals. The first represents the extent to which an instrument consistently distinguishes among *groups*, the latter among *individuals*. An instrument could be very reliable in one sense and unreliable in the other. For example, averaging the results of a test of student academic motivation might not reliably distinguish among Ivy League colleges but might distinguish among students *within* the colleges. Similarly, College and University Environment Scales (CUES) Propriety scores might reliably distinguish among Ivy League colleges but not among individual students. For most purposes, instruments should distinguish among colleges unless they are designed to distinguish among groups within colleges. However, reliability estimates across individuals can provide indirect evidence for the stability of the scales.

Similarly, the validity of most instruments should be based on their relationships to other information across institutions. Since the size and academic selectivity of institutions have pervasive effects on college climates, the relationship of these variables to the instrument should be described. In addition, other institutional characteristics should show plausible relationships to scores on the instrument. Similarly, if the instrument is designed for use within institutions, evidence should be available showing that it distinguishes among the groups that it was designed to assess.

The question of the accuracy with which the instrument describes a particular college is analogous to the validity of a psychological test for an individual. Whether a CUES profile accurately describes the climate of a particular college is similar to the question of whether the Strong Vocational Interest Blank accurately describes the interests of a particular individual. The only validity that can be presented as evidence is across colleges or individuals. The most important aspect of validity is the extent to which it provides accurate information for decision making and the evaluation of decisions. It seems reasonable to have more confidence in extremely high or low scores and in scores at small or single-purpose institutions, except for instruments specifically designed to assess subgroups within an institution.

Normative or comparative information should be based on a reasonable, ideally national, cross section of colleges. The most useful comparisons would, of course, be to institutions similar to your own. Also, the instrument should come with guides for interpreting the results that are clear and plausible.

Gaining Information About an Instrument's Previous Use. This step is often very productive, resulting in ideas for conducting your own inquiry and new ways of thinking about your own situation. The manual or interpretive guide is the first place to look for studies of situations like your own. However, many studies will have been conducted after the manual was published. Good places to look for descriptions of these various additional studies include Buros' *Personality Tests and Reviews,* the *Seventh Mental Measurements Yearbook* and the new *The Eighth Mental Measurements Yearbook.* The description of each instrument includes a comprehensive list of nearly all published articles and doctoral dissertations in which the instrument was used. A helpful feature is a page reference to *Dissertation Abstracts,* where you can read a summary of the study without ordering a copy of the dissertation. In addition, many of the articles cited are followed by a page reference to *Psychological Abstracts,* where you can read abstracts on articles that appeared in journals not available at your library.

Another useful source is the journal *College Student Personnel Abstracts,* which carefully monitors over a hundred journals and newsletters as well as papers presented at professional meetings and reports produced by various groups. Articles are grouped under headings such as "academic achievement" and "graduate students." You can look through the listings under the headings that are relevant to your situation during the most recent issues of this journal. You should also look at the listings under "college environment."

Another, more current source is the *Journal of College Student Personnel,* which probably publishes more articles on the college environment than any other journal. It also has an abstract section on student personnel and administrative issues. Finally, the Proceedings of the Association of Institutional Research often include reports of recent studies of campus climate and characteristics.

Look at these studies for information about the issues addressed, the hypotheses tested, the groups sampled, the conduct of the study, the analyses of the results, and the interpretation of the results. Such a review should help you clarify and focus on your own work. What were the central questions in these studies? Would one of the formulations of issues presented be better than the one you have in mind? Could you incorporate aspects of those formulations with yours? Which research design seemed best? Would it be applicable to your investigation? Do the articles reveal technical pitfalls to avoid? Do they employ a significantly different sample? Do some of the discussions include helpful ideas? By answering these questions you should be able to improve your own investigation.

Do No Existing Instruments Fit Your Needs? The content of assessment measures must be closely aligned with the purposes of administering the measures. For example, a measure of the overall campus climate would be less useful in assessing the effects of an innovative living arrangement than a specially constructed measure. In general, global measures will be less useful for specific, within-college decisions than specific measures. Often using a locally devised questionnaire that can focus on specific decisions is better than using a device developed for a national market that can address only general questions. Although you lose national comparative information, you increase the applicability of the results. Tailoring the question to the characteristics of the respondent also makes sense; for instance, the views of the faculty on tenure policies are more valuable than views of other constituents.

If you have a clear idea of what you want to find out, you can construct a questionnaire to obtain the information you need. For this purpose you do not need norms or scales. When the questions are well written, simple item information can be more useful even if scales can be developed. People on your campus, particularly in the institutional research office, the psychology department, or the sociology department, could probably help you to construct a good questionnaire. Several sources provide useful background information for developing and using questionnaires. Engelhart (1973) provides a helpful overview of the construction and use of questionnaires, discussing the problems of obtaining representative returns, writing questions, duplicating the questionnaire, writing cover letters, distributing the questionnaire, and tabulating the results. Two old sources that provide practical guidelines are Kornhauser (1951) and Nixon (1954). More technical guides include Bloom, Hastings, and Madaus (1971), Edwards (1954), Scott (1968), and Summers (1970).

Considering Other Purposes. Although you will most likely have a single reason for conducting your study, you should also explore other purposes that may be served. You should consult with staff in other parts of the college who might find the information to be gathered useful in their planning, evaluating, or projecting of changes. If several purposes can be met, the study will be much more cost-effective. To this end, you should carefully read the descriptions of the services provided by the instruments' publishers or scorers. Many provide analyses of the responses of subgroups and local option questions, both of which greatly increase the utility of the information gathered.

*Planning Actions Before Results Are Known.* Many people who have administered the instruments discussed in Chapter Nine found either that they could not link the results to the decisions that they had to make, that other people refused to accept the linkage, or that others did not agree on what to do with the linkage. Instead of employing a powerful tool for action, the user of the instrument may find that he or she has engaged in a useless academic exercise. The following are some suggestions for avoiding this outcome and making the most of the results.

After determining the decision you want to make or the question you want to answer, the variables you want to assess, and the instrument you plan to use, you must explicitly state your expectations and link your course of action to them. This involves setting up some decision rules that state the actions to be taken if any of the several possible results are obtained. In some cases this may be easy. For example, if an innovative program was compared with the traditional program and the scores on the instrument were not significantly different, then the cheaper program could be chosen. However, if the innovative program was not cheaper and entailed reassignment or disruption of staff, how much better than the traditional program must it score on the instrument to be justified? Although the process might be very difficult, it would be very helpful to get the proponents of both programs to agree on a score that would represent an improvement large enough to warrant adoption of the new program (or poor enough to warrant abandonment).

Obviously, many factors need to be considered to set these decision rules. For example, if the library closing hour is changed from 10 P.M. to 2 A.M., not only the users' satisfaction with the new hours but also their satisfaction with the services and facilities during the extended hours should be assessed, as well as their actual usage of the library at all times and their general attitude toward the library service. Other measures must also be considered, such as the costs of keeping the library open later, problems in finding staff willing to work the later hours, and any increase in book loss. In sum, although the instrument chosen should assess as many applicable attitudinal and behavioral aspects of a decision as possible, information on the financial, organizational, and other practical aspects of the decisions must also be considered. However, when other considerations can be kept fairly constant, it is very useful to produce decision rules for an investigation before it is carried out. That is, state the result that would support each particular option for action.

You must have clear understandings about the role that the

results will play in making a decision with the people who will make the decision and the people who will be affected by it. You should agree on the weight given to the results and the general course of action to be taken with each likely result. In this way, you can ensure that your study will be a factor in the decision making and avoid squabbling over the implications of the results.

You should also prepare for possible negative or even hostile reactions to the results. People can become very committed to either traditional methods or innovative programs and feel threatened when the results do not support their ideas. They may attack the validity of the instrument, the methods used, your impartiality and competence, or the logic of the conclusion.

*Administering the Instrument.* Helpful suggestions for distributing and collecting the instruments are given by Engelhart (1972) as well as by a number of writers on educational research and survey techniques. However, several points should be emphasized.

Because studies have shown that environment scores often differ among students, administrators, professors, and other campus groups, adequate sampling is important. If we wish to assess campus opinion and to understand the environment, we need to sample each important group carefully lest we remain ignorant of important differences and similarities of perceptions that could affect policy.

The views of the people most directly affected by a policy should be assessed. For example, if teaching innovations are being studied, professors as well as students should be consulted; when campus-wide changes are being evaluated, the perceptions of all the important groups should be taken into account. Furthermore, we will never understand how the general environment may be experienced differently by different groups without studying their responses. Some colleges may have not one but many environments, in which case each must be understood in order to understand the total environment.

The sample within the groups must also be representative and sufficiently large. Grande and Loveless (1969) found considerably different CUES results in several random and stratified samples. Their study warns us of the hazards of generalizing about the institutional climate from the views of small groups of students. The dangers may be particularly great if the scoring is based on the degree of consensus (Baird, 1973). In short, to assess the environment, care must be taken to sample appropriate persons and groups.

Sampling experts in the institutional research office or in the psychology, political science, or sociology departments could work out procedural details. Since the degree of accuracy of results increases until the sample size approaches 200, beyond which point it does not markedly increase, a good rule of thumb is to seek 200 respondents from each group to be sampled. The exception, as Peterson and Uhl suggest, may be the faculty; to avoid questions about the credibility of your results, sampling all faculty may be best if resources allow.

It is also important to elicit the cooperation of potential respondents so that your results will be representative. In addition to the usual cover letter (explaining the purpose and importance of the respondents' reply) and the usual follow-up notes, you can place reminder ads in the campus newspaper, try to get articles about the investigation in the newspaper, put signs on bulletin boards, and ask key people (such as residence hall supervisors or department heads) to remind students or faculty to return their surveys.

*Dealing with Results.* Once you have the results, you need to analyze them. Someone in the psychology or education department will probably be able to help you test for the statistical differences among groups at your institution or between your college's results and those of a normative or comparative group of colleges. Most manuals also offer suggestions for analysis. (The IGI manual has a practical discussion of these methods in Chap. 6.)

Once the statistical results are calculated, they must be summarized so that they can be understood and used by others. It should be fairly easy to make up a summary table that would show to what extent the results meet the decision rules. For example, in a study using CUES to determine the effects of an innovation, the results might look like those shown in Table 1.

In this case the main effects of the innovation appear to have been on the academic side of the college, as reflected on the

Table 1.  Ratings of Scores on CUES Scales After Implementation
of an Innovation

| | Decision Rule Level Reached | | |
| CUES Scale | Reject Innovation | Neither Accept nor Reject | Accept Innovation |
| --- | --- | --- | --- |
| Awareness | | | X |
| Scholarship | | | X |
| Community | | X | |
| Practicality[a] | | | |
| Propriety[a] | | | |
| Campus Morale | | X | |
| Quality of Teaching | | | X |

[a]No decision rule made.

Awareness, Scholarship, and Quality of Teaching scales. Although
the innovation did not produce the desired effects in the affective
area, as reflected in the Community and Campus Morale scores, it
also did not harm the affective area.

An important consideration concerning the instruments discussed in this book is the use of comparative information on other
groups of colleges. The normative data for different types of colleges offer another way to examine and assess one's own college.
Before investing a great deal of time and effort in using this comparative data, it is essential to know clearly why one wishes to make
such comparisons and with what type of college such comparisons
should be made. Moreover, in using comparative data, you must
realize that you are not comparing your own college with a particular college but with a *group* of colleges. Consequently, you also need
to know the size of the group.

Comparative information places the results for one's own
college in perspective. A high or low score on a particular scale may
seem less dramatic when compared with the data from other colleges; however, ordinary-looking results may appear quite significant in comparison. Differences of a few percentile points are
relatively meaningless unless they seem to form a pattern, which
can lead to insights about how your own college differs from
others. Comparative information also enables you to form an over-

all conception of how your college operates. A pattern of differences may make it apparent that your college is structured differently from most others; for example, it may be seen as more (or less) bureaucratic and authoritarian.

The most logical comparison group consists of colleges similar to your own. Similar colleges are likely to have similar problems, similar facilities, and similar ways of operating, and many colleges feel that they are in competition with other colleges of the same type. However, a comparison group made up of schools that are different from your own can also yield important information. For example, a Catholic or independent college located in an area containing mostly public colleges will find the results for public colleges relevant.

Preparing a Report. Communicating the results of the analysis can be extremely valuable to the college community; the importance of communicating cannot be emphasized enough. In many colleges the administration of the instrument involves many people. Furthermore, because the success of the administration naturally depends on the cooperation of the students, professors, and administrators who completed the instrument, these people deserve feedback about the results of their efforts. More important, if the results are to have any impact on the college, they must be understood by all the relevant groups.

The general report to the college should be kept simple and to the point. The overall picture must be presented as clearly as possible. The report might focus on general trends and include the details in an appendix, or it might be presented in several parts, each dealing with a single topic, such as teaching practices. Whatever its organization, it should present the information concisely and relate it to important and timely concerns of the college. Emphasis should be placed on the most important points and their implications for action. Several reports of about five pages each may be more effective than a single large report.

If an instrument is used at a college in order to gain information about particular issues, the report should focus on those issues. Furthermore, if people at the college would like to see a number of specific questions answered, the results provided by the instrument should be gathered in such a way as to suggest answers to those questions. Often a point-by-point listing of implications or suggestions is best.

Various techniques can be used to make the report more understandable. Comparisons and contrasts can be expressed in both words and graphs. Simple bar graphs are often useful, as are line graphs that show how two or three groups responded to related scales or questions.

It may be useful to change the focus or form of the report for different groups that have different interests, such as administrators, professors, and students. The tone and technical level should also be adjusted to each audience. Remember, however, that students, like everyone else, resent being talked down to and that most people, including freshmen, can understand a percentage.

The information that is most relevant to the purpose of your study should influence the nature of the tables and the comparisons that you report. Any important differences in the responses of different groups should be highlighted. Charts, figures, and diagrams usually present results more effectively than sheer numbers. Besides comparing different groups in the college, you may wish to compare your college's results with those of comparable colleges or with results from past administrations of the instrument at your college, or to compare the results for different divisions if yours is a complex institution. Some of the possible methods of presentation include the following (adapted from Peterson and Uhl, 1977):

1. Rank order of: (a) scale means from highest to lowest for different groups, (b) items from highest to lowest in terms of endorsement or means, (c) local option items, (d) means or items according to the magnitude of discrepancy between expectations and results or the difference between means for two groups
2. Profiles of scale means (possibly arrayed from highest to lowest)
3. Bar graphs and histograms depicting: (a) magnitude of scale means, (b) magnitude of the variation in responses (extent of consensus within groups as indicated by scale standard deviations)
4. Lists of: (a) items obtaining the highest or lowest endorsement or discrepancy value, (b) items grouped on some other concep-

tual or empirical basis (for example, whether they deal with the academic or the social environment or with the cognitive or affective sides of the college experience)

*Dissemination of Results.* Ultimately, the most important purpose of the instrument is to provide suggestions for decisions and action. The suggestions themselves, however, will not directly lead to better actions or decisions. The first critical task is to get the results to the people in the college. This section describes some ways to do this.

Written Reports. A good way to start getting the results out is to reproduce and distribute some brief reports on topics that are of interest to particular groups. The general report might also be made available to those who are interested. A series of articles might also be placed in the college newspaper or magazine. These methods, directed toward specific audiences, should be relatively impersonal.

Group Meetings. A more personal method is to make an informal oral presentation to small groups of faculty, students, parents, or others interested in the college.

Conferences. The results of the study and possible actions can be examined and discussed in conferences involving a large number of the college's constituents or representatives of college groups. Conferences can be organized in several ways. They may take place entirely within the college and involve only students, teachers, and administrators or certain other subgroups. They may also include the wider community of parents, board members or trustees, alumni, and other groups interested in the college. A conference must provide its attendees with plenty of time to assimilate and discuss the data. Discussions work best when the conference combines one or more general sessions with one or more small-group meetings.

The results can be discussed most effectively by organizing small groups to deal with particular topics rather than having everyone discuss all the results. It may also be useful to have one group consider the overall results and their implications for the school as a whole.

The composition of the discussion groups is particularly important. To be most effective, they should all include students.

Otherwise, there is a good chance that the groups will conclude that everything is all right as is. Students should be selected for their interest in a topic rather than for their achievement of honors or their membership in student government or other special group. The best discussion groups include a mix of different kinds of students.

The conduct of the discussion can make a great difference. The relevant data should be distributed to the group before the discussion so that each person will have a chance to understand them and think about them. It should be made clear that nothing students say will be held against them outside the discussions. Furthermore, students should be encouraged to talk, and professors and administrators encouraged to listen. Professors and administrators usually dominate conversations with students, and unless they are encouraged to listen to what students are saying, they may hear only themselves. This can be avoided by making a student the moderator. In any case, the moderator should not take part in the discussion but concentrate on encouraging participation and seeing that everyone has a chance to speak.

In these sessions the data should be regarded merely as stimuli for discussion; the talk is what is important. If a strong exchange on one subject begins, it should not be cut short so that other results can be discussed. If the results have been distributed beforehand, little discussion time need be devoted to detail. The main purpose should be to hear opinions about what the college is like, what needs to be changed, and how those changes might be carried out.

*Determining and Implementing Policy.* If the study has used the procedures listed above and has been tied into the decision-making process from the beginning, then the results should chiefly be viewed as supporting or eliminating various options. If, however, the results do not clearly support any option, other questions may need to be answered: Do the results provide clues for improving the policy or program in question? Do they show that the needs of particular groups are not being met? Do they suggest that a different scope of activity would be appropriate?

These and similar questions are also appropriate when the purpose of the investigation is to survey the success of existing programs or policies. For example: Do the results help identify problems of the faculty, the administrators, students in general, or particular groups of students (for example, commuters, working students, or minority students)? How do the results compare with information about the finances and personnel of the programs and policies? Do the results suggest that the college should expand, modify the form or function of a program, or create new policies or programs?

The contributors to this book have discussed many ways to use information from instruments to assess and improve the activities of colleges and to monitor the success of innovations. However, other writers have described the general principles of using information to shape institutions, some of which are quite relevant to the purposes of the colleges. The general roles of such information in planning are discussed in Kahn's book on the theory and practice of social planning (1969). Sarason (1971, 1972) has discussed some of the practical problems of implementing changes, particularly how the perspectives of various groups can hinder progress. Suchman (1967) has discussed the problems of administrative resistance and other barriers to systematic evaluation and the problems in using the findings. The readings in evaluation research, such as those edited by Caro (1977) and by Weiss (1972), provide many insights into the problems of using information and implementing change. These readings are particularly helpful since many describe programs in social action and in industry as well as in educational settings. The bibliographies on specific topics collected by Weiss and Caro provide more sources of useful information.

Caro's anthology is an extremely valuable source of information and ideas about evaluation, the evaluator, and the decision maker. Caro's introduction provides a succinct overview of the field of evaluation. Rodman and Kalodny describe the organizational strains on the researcher–decision maker relationship. House discusses the politics of evaluation in higher education. Weiss outlines many of the practical problems faced by evaluators. Deutcher writes on avoiding the goal trap in evaluation research, and Rossi warns of the "booby traps and pitfalls" in the evaluation of social action programs.

Also valuable is Rothman's book on the basis of ideas drawn from social science (1974). Although his book emphasizes programs for social change, Rothman discusses many useful points, including the variables that affect the performance of the practitioner, the organizational framework, the community and political setting of social change, and the problems of applying theory to practice.

### Conclusion: Using a Multidimensional Approach

Colleges are often concerned with general questions about their overall functions. Environmental measures can play a role in answering these questions. Evaluating college environments is not like evaluating the success of an experiment or a new product; it is evaluating an existing social and educational system "in situ" (Suchman, 1969). A college is a community of human beings with a history, mores, and long-standing human relationships. Therefore, the system model of evaluation advocated by Schulberg and Baker (1971) seems most appropriate. The system model evaluates "the degree to which an organization realizes its goals under a given set of conditions. . . . What counts is a balanced distribution of re-sources among all organizational objectives, not maximal satisfaction of any one goal" (Schulberg and Baker, 1971, p. 77). Important elements of the system model include (1) achievement of goals and subgoals, (2) effective coordination of organizational sub-units, (3) acquisition and maintenance of necessary resources, and (4) adaptation of the organization to the environment and to its own internal demands. (These internal demands include the pri-macy of the professor-student relationship, noted by Feldman and Newcomb, 1969, and Hartnett and Katz, 1977.) In my view, the systems model requires three types of information, each of which must be used carefully.

*Descriptive Information.* What is the college like? What is it doing? How does it compare with similar colleges? Although de-scriptive information seems easy to obtain, comparative informa-tion on even simple factual matters is often difficult to get, as Scriven (1969) has pointed out. For example, in a project to assess departmental quality at the graduate level (Clark, Hartnett, and Baird, 1976), we attempted to obtain a wide variety of information

but were able to use only a small portion of it. We found that
financial information was recorded and calculated in many different ways and was seldom summarized in a consistent manner. Student records were not updated or summarized. For example,
almost no department kept and summarized GRE scores of applicants and entrants over several years, and almost none could
give an accurate figure on student attrition. Virtually none knew
what their graduates of previous years were currently doing.

For a systems model to work effectively, methods for obtaining systematic information must be developed. In some cases, the
NCHEMS-MIS would be helpful. Most colleges are in a better position than specific graduate departments: They have figures on
attrition, average SAT scores, the number of professors, and so on.
In addition, certain environmental measures can provide baseline
data about student and faculty characteristics, attitudes, and
behaviors.

*Judgmental Information.* Is the college meeting its goals? What
are the effects of the college on the people involved? This is more
akin to the traditional goal attainment model of evaluation and
introduces familiar questions: Whose goals? What defines the goals
in the minds of different people? How does one define and
operationalize goals? How can the relative importance of goals be
determined? How can the economic, educational, and personal
costs of their attainment be assessed? Through a self-study, a college can consider these questions thoughtfully and eventually come
up with answers. Again, certain environmental measures can help a
college define its goals and assess the costs of attaining them.

*Analytical Information.* This type of information derives from
analyzing the above types of information in order to understand
the college. It would be used to answer questions such as the following: Why is the college performing as it is? What financial and legal
conditions affect the college? Does a particular college activity really produce the desired result? Does it produce any undesirable
results? To answer these questions, we must identify and measure
the independent variables (activities or college characteristics),
intervening variables (the causal process), and the dependent variables (the educational or scholarly effects). Once again, environmental information can provide data about all three areas or at

least some ideas that can help in interpreting the information. Ideally such information would be placed in an analytic model, such as path analysis, so that the direction and size of effects could be assessed. Obviously, such analyses would need to be based on research across a number of institutions. Although few colleges could conduct such research, most could capitalize on the general research that has been done on higher education, which would provide them with ideas that would help them to understand and improve their own situation.

### Recommendations

Using this information, you can implement the systems model and gain important insights into the operations of a college. By emphasizing the interrelationships among college characteristics, the systems model can produce a fairly accurate evaluation of the strong and weak points of an institution and suggest actions for improvement. The model needs to be applied in a way that is appropriate to the unique situation of each college, of course. Some methods for adapting the systems model to individual programs are discussed in several sources (for example, see references in Struening, 1975) and need not be repeated here.

Although the measures reviewed in this book do not assess all the information that would be needed for a systems model evaluation, they do identify a variety of indicators; the information they supply may be very useful.

### Summary

The development of measures that will aid decision making in any social institution involves technology, statistics, values, and judgment (Caro, 1971; Glass, 1971). The development is made even more complex if the approach used includes any interactions between persons and environment.

For example, a new program may appear to be successful because it attracts bright students and staff, because it gets more money than other programs, because its staff is extremely dedicated, because it is well organized, or because it emphasizes the particular outcomes used as criteria. The same considerations hold when we are comparing colleges. Thus, to understand the effects of a decision on a program, one would ideally have information about the antecedents, the processes, and the outcomes of the program (Bloom, Hastings, and Madaus, 1971). Likewise, to understand and thus to be able to change a college environment, one may need objective data from the input, process, and outcome areas. By choosing appropriate measures, one can assess all three. In some cases the same instruments can be used at different times for each purpose. Choosing the right instrument can be useful to decision makers who wish to make their decisions in a well-informed and sophisticated manner.

9

*Leonard L. Baird*

*and Rodney T. Hartnett*

# Directory of Leading Instruments for Assessing Campus Environments

————————•·◦⟨∞⟩◦·•————————

The following pages describe a variety of environmental measures. Each entry describes the content of the instrument, its reliability and validity, its availability, and, in some cases its development and strengths and weaknesses. Basic sources are listed for the reader who wants more information about the instrument, and some research studies are listed for the reader who wishes to see how the

225

instrument has been used. Finally, where available, other reviews are listed. The instruments are grouped by those that are currently available from a publisher, those that have been but are not now available from a publisher, and those that have chiefly been used in research studies.

### Currently Published Measures

*College and University Environment Scales (CUES),*
*Second Edition*

CUES is a perceptual measure, consisting of 160 items, that generates seven scores. Respondents indicate whether they believe each item is "generally true" or "generally false" of their college. The five basic 20-item scales, with sample items from each scale, are as follows:

- *Scholarship.* An environment characterized by intellectuality and scholastic discipline, intellectual achievement, and the pursuit of knowledge. Sample items: "Students set high standards of achievement for themselves"; "Most courses require intensive study and preparation out of class."
- *Awareness.* An environment that encourages concern about social and political problems, individuality and expressiveness through the arts, and tolerance of criticism. Sample items: "Students are actively concerned about national and international affairs"; "The school offers many opportunities for students to understand and criticize important works in art, music, and drama."
- *Community.* An environment that is friendly, cohesive, and group oriented. Sample items: "The school has a reputation for being friendly"; "The professors go out of their way to help you."
- *Propriety.* An environment that is mannerly, considerate, proper, and conventional. Sample items: "Students are conscientious about taking good care of school property"; "Students are expected to report any violation of rules and regulations."
- *Practicality.* An environment characterized by enterprise, organization, material benefits, social activities, vocational emphasis, and orderly supervision. Sample items: "Frequent tests are given

in most courses"; "There is a recognized group of student leaders on campus"; "It's important socially here to be in the right club or group."

Two new scales were added for the second edition:

• *Campus Morale.* The twenty-two items in this scale describe an environment characterized by acceptance of social norms, group cohesiveness, friendly assimilation of students into campus life, and a commitment to intellectual pursuits and freedom of expression. Intellectual goals are widely shared in an atmosphere of supportive and spirited personal relationships.
• *Quality of Teaching (Faculty-Student Relationships).* This eleven-item scale defines an atmosphere in which professors are perceived to be scholarly, to set high standards, and to be clear, adaptive, and flexible. At the same time, the teaching is infused with warmth, interest, and helpfulness toward students.

Some experimental items are included in CUES that may be incorporated in later versions. (Additional examples of CUES items are listed in Chapter One.)

Colleges may augment the CUES items with up to ten locally devised questions. The scoring service returns a sixteen-page printout and an abstract of each CUES item with the number and percentage of respondents replying in the scored direction. Similar reports for the locally devised questions are also available. Responses to four information questions, year of birth, sex, and educational status (student class year or faculty), and major field are also reported. Scores on the seven scales are reported for up to four mutually exclusive subgroups and the total group.

The instrument is untimed, but most students finish it in about thirty minutes, although a few may take as long as fifty. Scoring can be done locally, but most colleges employ the scoring service, which processes the questionnaires in approximately four weeks. Only group scores are provided, which are based on a consensus rationale. If two-thirds of the respondents believe a statement is true (or in the keyed direction), the statement is regarded as a clear indication of their view of the environment, and conversely. Scores for each scale are obtained by adding the number of items answered by 66 percent or more of the respondents in the scored direction, subtracting the number of items answered by 33 percent or fewer of the students in the scored direction, and adding 20 points to eliminate any negative scores. Thus, scores on the five basic twenty-item scales can range from 0 to 40, on the Campus Morale scale from 0 to 44, and on the Quality of Teaching scale from 0 to 22.

*Reliability*

Reliability across institutions, based on coefficient alpha, ranged from .89 to .94 for the five basic scales. Estimating reliability within an institution is much more complicated, depending on the size of the sample and the number of items that were close to being included in the scoring because they were endorsed by nearly 66 or slightly more than 33 percent. For example, a college could have a score of 5 on the Scholarship scale. However, perhaps five additional items were endorsed by between 60 and 65 percent of the sample. Upon readministration, all five additional items may be endorsed by over 66 percent, making the score 10 instead of 5. The manual reports a study of twenty-five institutions that administered CUES twice over one or two years or that surveyed different groups. It showed that 80 percent of the scores did not differ by more than 3 points and 60 percent did not differ by more than 2 points.

*Validity*

Validity information includes correlations of CUES scores with college size, average student aptitude, students' career and educational plans, Environmental Assessment Technique scores (see Chapter One), students' ratings of their political and religious preferences, students' activities, students' ratings of the quality of various aspects of their colleges, characteristics of students and faculty, and financial information. These correlations are generally quite plausibly consistent with the direction of the CUES scales; for example, small colleges have higher scores on the Community scale. It seems likely that CUES scores would be more accurate for small or single-purpose institutions. The CUES manual states that CUES was "not constructed primarily to serve [the] purpose [of] characterizing the environment of different parts of the institution." (Pace, 1969, developed a special version of CUES to measure subcultures in complex universities.) Still, research on CUES in complex institutions indicates consistent and plausible differences among groups.

*Norms*

Norms are based on a national reference group consisting of ten highly selective liberal arts colleges, ten highly selective public and private universities, twenty general liberal arts colleges, twenty public and private general universities, ten state colleges and universities, ten teacher's colleges, ten strongly denominational liberal arts colleges, and ten engineering and science colleges and universities. These colleges varied in geographic location, type of control, degree level offered, and enrollment so as to represent colleges across the country. (See Figure 1 in Chapter One.)

*Development*

The general approach and history of CUES is described in Chapter One. Between the publication of the first and second editions, Pace conducted studies of CUES results from different groups of reporters, the use of CUES in the admissions process, the assessment of community college environments, and the measurement of subcultures in complex universities. The last three studies resulted in adaptations of CUES for these special purposes. In addition, further psychometric work resulted in a reduction in the number of items from thirty in the first edition to twenty in the second, a revision of the scoring system from just those items on which 66 percent or more of the respondents agreed to the system described below, and the addition of two scales described above.

*Basic Source*

Pace, C. R. *College and University Environment Scales: Technical Manual.* (2nd ed.) Princeton, N.J.: Educational Testing Service, 1969.

*Research Studies*

Pace, C. R. *Education and Evangelism: A Profile of Protestant Colleges.* New York: McGraw-Hill, 1972.

In this book, prepared for the Carnegie Commission on Higher Education, Pace compares four types of colleges: thirty colleges such as Messiah, Eastern Mennonite, and Ursinus, which are affiliated with small evangelical and fundamentalist denomination; fifty colleges such as Shimer, Beloit, and Kalamazoo, which

are affiliated with major denominations that are not especially fundamentalist; forty universities; and forty liberal arts colleges. Both
of the denominational groups averaged below the other groups on
Scholarship and Awareness and considerably below the scores for
the group of liberal arts colleges. Both Protestant groups scored
considerably higher than the national median and about the same
as the liberal arts colleges on Community and Propriety. Finally, the
fundamentalist colleges were above the median on practicality, but
the mainline Protestant colleges were about average. However,
Pace emphasizes the fact that these colleges have a wide range of
scores on most of the scales. Examining the differences between
colleges that differed in the strength of their legal ties to their
denominations, Pace stated, "The more firmly and zealously a college is related to a church the more clearly it emerges as a distinctive college environment. And this distinctiveness is defined by
uniformly high scores on the characteristics labeled community,
propriety, and practicality" (p. 37).

Pace, C. R. *The Demise of Diversity?: A Comparative Profile of Eight
Types of Institutions.* New York: McGraw-Hill, 1974.

In this report for the Carnegie Commission, Pace compares
the eight types of colleges described above in the description of
norms. The basic data included questionnaire responses from
alumni of the class of 1950 in seventy-four institutions and from
upperclassmen in seventy-nine institutions. The questionnaires
asked about the alumni's activities, their knowledge and awareness
of trends in American society, their attitudes toward these trends,
their collegiate experiences, their sense of progress toward various
goals, and their descriptions of their environments on CUES dimensions. Pace found trends toward both greater and lesser diversity, but except for a trend toward less diversity on the dimension of
Propriety, there was no overall decline in the diversity of the college
environment. This study, concerned with the extent of pluralism in
American higher education, illustrates how environmental information can be used to address a question of national concern.

Chickering, A. W., McDowell, J., and Campagna, D. "Institutional
Differences and Student Development." *Journal of Educational
Psychology*, 1969, *60* (4), 315–326.

This article examines thirteen small, very diverse institutions. The authors found high correlations among the colleges' CUES scores and the average Omnibus Personality Inventory (OPI) scale scores of students. For example, scores on the OPI Impulsive-Innovative scale were highly negatively correlated with CUES Propriety scores. Similar results were found between CUES scores and the four typologies (vocational, academic, collegiate, and nonconformist) under which entering college students were classified. These results are taken as evidence of the self-selection of students who enter different types of colleges. The authors also concluded that during the college experience, students changed in their autonomy, impulse expression, estheticism, and practical orientation, irrespective of their mean score at entrance and irrespective of the characteristics of the college. However, the authors do report some impact of college on classification of students under the four typologies: Students in colleges scoring high on Practicality shifted out of the nonconformist orientation; all students in colleges scoring high on the Community or Scholarship scales generally shifted away from the vocational orientation, intellectual students shifted into academic or nonconformist orientations, and practical students shifted into vocational and collegiate orientations. Thus, there may be important interactions between students and college characteristics.

Feldman, K. A., and Newcomb, T. M. *The Impact of College on Students.* San Francisco: Jossey-Bass, 1969.

This book summarizes a great number of studies, many using CUES, which show that students have very idealistic views of the colleges they are about to enter. Almost all believe their college will be friendly, stimulating, and vigorous, irrespective of the descriptions by students who have been in the college for several years. This suggests that a general idealistic image of college is shared throughout the culture that is generally unrelated to the actual characteristics of colleges.

*Other References*

Buros, O. K. *Personality Tests and Reviews.* Highland Park, N.J.: Gryphon Press, 1970. Includes forty references to CUES.

Buros, O. K. *The Seventh Mental Measurements Yearbook.* Highland Park, N.J.: Gryphon Press, 1972. Includes ninety-nine references to CUES.

Buros, O. K. *The Eighth Mental Measurements Yearbook.* Highland Park, N.J.: Gryphon Press, 1978. Includes more references to CUES. These three references include doctoral dissertations as well as published literature. Additional references may be found in *College Student Personnel Abstracts,* especially in the sections on college environments. These abstracts include institutional reports as well as published articles.

*Availability*

Information about costs and services is available from Educational Testing Service, Princeton, N.J. 08541.

*Reviews*

There are reviews by Paul Dressel and James Mitchell in Buros's *Seventh Mental Measurement Yearbook* (1972). Dressel has also discussed CUES as well as other perceptual measures in his book *Handbook of Academic Evaluation* (1976).

## College Student Questionnaires (CSQ)

The CSQ consists of two questionnaires: Part I, covering students' backgrounds, attitudes, and plans, is designed to be used with entering students; Part II, which obtains information about students' educational and vocational plans, college activities, and attitudes toward their college, is designed to be used with students who have had one or more years of college. Each questionnaire consists of 200 multiple-choice questions, some of which are fairly complex. Part I can be scored for seven scales: Family Independence, Peer Independence, Liberalism, Social Conscience, Cultural Sophistication, Motivation for Grades, and Family Social Status. Part II can be scored for eleven scales: the first five described for Part I plus Satisfaction with Faculty, Satisfaction with Administration, Satisfaction with Major, Satisfaction with Students, Study Habits, and Extracurricular Involvement. Items use a variety of formats but most ask students to respond to a four-point choice.

*Reliability*

Reliability for the eleven scales of Part II ranges from .57 to .84, obviously not high enough to use the questionnaire with individuals but adequate for groups. Items that ask for factual information, which concern grades, major, religion, and so on, can be assumed to have reliabilities of .70 or higher (see Baird, 1976, for a summary of this research).

*Validity*

Validity information is of two types: correlations of individual items with scales, and group means. For example, the Liberalism scale correlated .32 with a preference for independent study, .37 with the Clark-Trow nonconformist type, and .44 with having no formal religion.

Mean scores on the Cultural Sophistication scale were highest among students majoring in the humanities and fine arts, followed by students in the social sciences, the natural sciences, education, engineering, and finally business.

The CSQ scales seem sensitive to changes among students, as evidenced by a large number of studies of various student groups over time. These studies compared students' CSQ scores before and after some college experience. CSQ scores have also been shown to differentiate among existing groups, such as fraternities, sororities, and residence halls.

*Norms*

Two types of normative information are presented. The first type, profiles of mean scale scores, is based on 700 students from sixteen institutions, who were selected from 6,680 students. The second type is comparative data, including response frequencies, scale means, and standard deviations for subgroups of colleges, such as Protestant colleges and universities (see Chapter One).

*Comment*

The scales that seem most useful are Satisfaction with Faculty, Satisfaction with Administration, Satisfaction with Major, and Satisfaction with Students. However, the variety of research studies suggests that the other scales are sensitive to changes in educational programs and structures. Thus, the CSQ can provide useful information. However, users should carefully examine the relevance of the CSQ scales to the problems that they are studying. Both CSQ booklets are lengthy, so users should determine whether the time required of students to complete the CSQ would be worthwhile.

One of the most common uses of the CSQ is for dividing students into subgroups on the basis of their responses to one item that asks them to choose one of four paragraphs that most closely corresponds to their views about education. These paragraphs were written to reflect the typologies developed by Clark and Trow: academic, nonconformist, collegiate, and vocational. The validity of this typology has been the subject of a great deal of research (for example, Terenzini and Pascarella, 1977). Whether choosing one of these paragraphs really means a student is a member of a subgroup in any sociological sense is unclear. However, investigators have found that answers to this item relate to a variety of other information about student behaviors and attitudes.

*Basic Source*

Peterson, R. E. *College Student Questionnaire: Technical Manual.* Princeton, N.J.: Educational Testing Service, 1968.

*Research Studies*

Hartnett, R. T., and Centra, J. A. "Attitudes and Secondary School Backgrounds of Catholics Entering College." *Sociology of Education,* 1969, *42,* 188–198.

Jones, J. D., and Finnell, W. S. J. "Relationships Between College Experiences and Attitudes of Students from Economically Deprived Backgrounds." *Journal of College Student Personnel,* 1978, *13,* 314–318.

Miller, L. D. "Distinctive Characteristics of Fraternity Members." *Journal of College Student Personnel,* 1973, *14,* 126–129.

Panackal, A. A., and Sockloff, A. L. "Factor Analyses of the College Student Questionnaires." *Measurement and Evaluation in Guidance,* 1975, *7,* 225–233.

Romine, B. H., David, J. A., and Gehman, W. S. "The Interaction of Learning, Personality Traits, Ability, and Environment: A Preliminary Study." *Educational and Psychological Measurement,* 1970, *30,* 337–347.

*Availability*

Information about costs and services is available from Educational Testing Service, Princeton, N.J. 08541.

*Reviews*

Reviews by Paul Dressel and Harrison Gough appear in O. K. Buros (Ed.), *The Seventh Mental Measurements Yearbook* (Highland Park, N.J.: Gryphon Press, 1972).

*College Student Satisfaction Questionnaire*

This is a ninety-two item questionnaire that yields scores on six scales, which vary in length from thirteen to seventeen items.

The items provide five possible responses ranging from "very dissatisfied" to "very satisfied." Scale scores are the sum of item responses. The six scales measure satisfaction with: (1) Policies and Procedures (for example, choice of classes), (2) Working Conditions (for example, comfort of residence), (3) Compensation (for example, amount of study required to attain good grades), (4) Quality of Education (for example, adequacy of teaching methods), (5) Social Life (for example, making friends), and (6) Recognition (for example, faculty acceptance of the student as worthwhile).

*Reliability*

The reliability of the scales (in a one-college sample) ranged from .85 to .92 with a median of .88.

*Validity*

Satisfaction scores have been found to be related to type of residence (for example, men in dormitories were less satisfied with social life than men in fraternities) and to year in college (for example, seniors were least satisfied with the quality of education).

In a second study, Betz and others (1971) subjected data from two groups of Iowa State students to factor analysis. They found good support for the Compensation, Social Life, and Working Conditons scales, fairly good support for the Recognition and Quality of Education scales, and inconsistent support for the Policies and Procedures scale.

In another study, Sturtz (1971) found that 110 adult women at Iowa State were more satisfied than 123 young women on the Quality of Education and Policies and Procedures scales and on an overall satisfaction score.

*Basic Source*

Betz, E. L., Klingensmith, J. E., and Menne, J. W. "The Measurement and Analysis of College Student Satisfaction." *Measurement and Evaluation in Guidance,* 1970, *3,* 110–118.

*Availability*

The College Student Satisfaction Questionnaire is available from Central Iowa Associates, Inc., 1408 Meadowlane Ave., Ames, Iowa 50010.

*Review*

A review by S. R. Strong appears in O. K. Buros (Ed.), *The Eighth Mental Measurements Yearbook* (Highland Park, N.J.: Gryphon Press, 1978).

*Institutional Functioning Inventory (IFI)*

The IFI is a 132-item instrument that consists of eleven scales with twelve items each. However, only the first 72 items are answered by students. Faculty, administrators, and other adults connected with the institution answer all the questions. The instrument's authors originally intended to assess "institutional vitality," while their current intent, as described in the manual, is to provide

> a means by which a college or university can describe itself in terms of a number of characteristics judged to be of importance in American higher education. The instrument assumes that different individuals and constituent groups will perceive the institution differently; the IFI thus affords the opportunity for study of sources of disparate beliefs about the work of the college. . . . In the most general sense, the purpose of the IFI is institutional self-study, carried out on behalf of institutional reform.

The eleven scales reflect this intent and are listed below, with sample items shown in parentheses.

- *Intellectual-Aesthetic Extracurriculum* (IAE) ("Students publish a literary magazine.")
- *Freedom* (F) ("Faculty members feel free to express radical political beliefs in their classrooms.")
- *Human Diversity* (HD) ("A wide variety of religious backgrounds and beliefs are expressed in the student body.")
- *Concern for the Improvement of Society* (IS) ("Most faculty on this campus tend to be reasonably satisfied with the status quo of American society." Scored direction is disagreement.)
- *Concern for Undergraduate Learning* (UL) ("Faculty promotion and tenure are based primarily on an estimate of teaching effectiveness.")
- *Democratic Governance* (DG) ("In general, decision making is decentralized whenever feasible or workable.")
- *Meeting Local Needs* (MLN) ("Courses are offered through which local area residents may be retrained or upgraded in their job skills.")

- *Self-Study and Planning* (SP) ("Laying plans for the future of the institution is a high priority activity for many senior administrators.")
- *Concern for Advancing Knowledge* (AK) ("There are a number of research professors on campus, i.e., faculty members whose appointments primarily entail research rather than teaching.")
- *Concern for Innovation* (CI) ("There is a general willingness here to experiment with innovations that have shown promise at other institutions.")
- *Intellectual Esprit* (IE) ("The faculty in general is strongly committed to the acknowledged purposes and ideals of the institution.")

There are two types of items: factual items, to which the respondent answers "yes," "no," or "don't know"; and opinion items, to which the respondent answers "strongly agree," "agree," "disagree," or "strongly disagree."

*Reliability*

Reliability, based on coefficient alpha, ranged from .86 to .96 with an average of .92. However, approximately 15 percent of the items correlated more highly with another scale than they did with the scale to which they belonged.

*Validity*

One important question about the validity of the scales is whether they are really necessary; that is, whether they provide enough distinct information to be considered separately. Fifteen (or 27 percent) of the fifty-five interscale correlations were .50 or higher. Furthermore, a factor analysis of the faculty means at the thirty-seven normative institutions suggested only four common factors, termed by the authors as Liberal (F, HD, IS, and CI), Community (SP, CI, IE, and DG), Intellectual (AK and IAE), and Ivory Tower (UL and MLN-reversed). However, the authors claim that the conceptual distinctions among the eleven scales and the preliminary nature of the instrument and its norms warrant the retention of the eleven distinct scales.

IFI scores were correlated with factual institutional data, CUES scores, and data from a study of student protests. Most of the correlations seem quite plausible: For example, library size and research funds are correlated with the Advancement of Knowledge scale; the CUES Practicality scale is negatively correlated ($-.54$)

and the Awareness scale positively correlated (.68) with Concern for Improvement of Society scale; and students' complaints about the absence of senior faculty and about the quality of teaching were negatively related to the Concern for Undergraduate Learning scale. Except for a few anomalies, the correlations generally support the validity of the scales. An analysis of a multigroup-multiscale matrix showed that faculty, administrators, and students generally described their campuses in the same ways, with the interesting exception that students did not agree with faculty or administrators about Democratic Governance.

*Norms*

Limited normative information is presented in the manual, which is based on the means of faculty scores at thirty-seven institutions. These institutions appear to reflect the diversity of American colleges in terms of geographic location, degrees offered, type of control, and selectivity, although they do not seem to be fully representative of all colleges.

*Comment*

As pointed out by Hartnett in Chapter Four, the faculty environment is partly subsumed by and partly independent of the total college environment. Analyzing the faculty environment in both respects is important. The IFI is the only environmental measure that is specifically designed to assess components of the environment that are important to faculty. Although some items now seem dated (one item refers to the Students for a Democratic Society, while another refers to Great Society programs), most items concern common academic situations that will remain part of academic life for many years. The institutional researcher who is concerned with the faculty environment might well consider using the IFI.

*Basic Source*

Peterson, R. E., and others. *Institutional Functioning Inventory: Preliminary Technical Manual.* Princeton, N.J.: Educational Testing Service, 1970.

*Availability*

Information about costs and services is available from Educational Testing Service, Princeton, N.J. 08541.

*Reviews*

Reviews by Paul Dressel and Clifford Lunneborg are included in O. K. Buros (Ed.), *The Seventh Mental Measurements Year-*

*book* (Highland Park, N.J.: Gryphon Press, 1972). Dressel has also reviewed the IFI in his book *Handbook of Academic Evaluation* (San Francisco: Jossey-Bass, 1976).

### Institutional Goals Inventory (IGI)

The IGI is a perceptual measure consisting of ninety statements of goals for a college. The respondent judges how important each goal is on the campus and how important it should be. Scores based on the "is" ratings and the "should be" ratings are provided for twenty goal areas (see Chapter One). The IGI requires about forty-five minutes to complete and must be scored by the publisher.

Colleges receive a printout showing the means and standard deviations for the "is" and "should be" ratings for the twenty goal areas for the total sample and for as many as five subgroups. The scores reported are simply the mean of the ratings given to four goal statements in each goal area. Colleges also receive a listing of the twenty goal areas ranked according to the discrepancy between the mean "is" and "should be" responses and listings of the "is" and "should be" results and their discrepancies for each of the ninety goal statements for the total group and for each subgroup. Colleges may obtain the same information for up to twenty locally devised goal statements. The results for seven background questions are also reported: role (faculty, student, and so on), field (for faculty) or major (for students), faculty rank, faculty teaching arrangement (full-time, part-time, and so on), age, student's class level, student's enrollment status (full-time day, part-time day, and so on).

*Reliability*

The manual reports reliabilities (coefficient alphas) for the twenty scales for both "is" and "should be" scores. Separate reliabilities are reported for faculty, administrators, community members, and college trustees. The median coefficient alphas ranged from .69 to .98 for the "is" scales, with the middle 50 percent of the scales falling between .83 and .90, and from .65 to .98 for the "should be" scales, with the middle 50 percent falling between .83 and .89.

*Validity*

The validity reported in the manual consists of correlations between faculty "is" responses and published institutional data, the significance of differences between the "is" and "should be" goals across the four types of institutions described in the norms section, and the correspondence between the highest and lowest scores of these groups to the predictions of nineteen specialists familiar with California institutions of higher education. In general, this information supports the validity of the scales, although the institutional data for six of the scales correlated so highly as to raise doubts about the amount of information provided by the scales. For example, Traditional Religiousness correlated .94 with whether the institution was sectarian, the Research Scale correlated .87 with the proportion of the faculty with doctorates, and the Advanced Training scale correlated .83 with the type of institution (counting a university as 3, a four-year college as 2, and a two-year college as 1). In addition, the manual reports a multigoal-multigroup matrix which suggests that the different groups attached similar meaning to the goal areas. Similar results are presented for factor analyses of the "is" and "should be" responses for each group, indicating that the groups saw the goals in basically the same dimensions. However, since the factor analyses generally resulted in the same five factors, a stronger rationale needs to be provided for retaining the twenty goal areas rather than scoring in five parts.

*Norms*

The comparative data currently available are based exclusively on California institutions. Percentile distributions for "is" and "should be" means for each goal area and discrepancy information, including percentile distributions, are provided for faculty, students, and administrators for four groups of institutions—eight campuses of the University of California, sixteen of the California state universities and colleges, sixty-six California community colleges, and nineteen California private four-year colleges. Norm information based on a nationally representative sample of institutions is reportedly in preparation.

*Development*

The IGI stems from the work of Gross and Grambsch (1968), two sociologists who analyzed the perceptions of institutional goals held by faculty and administrators at 68 Ph.D.-granting universities. Gross and Grambsch developed the basic "is" and "should be" format and used analytic techniques that were incorporated into the IGI. Other research on goals included Nash's

(1968) survey of academic deans throughout the country, the Danforth Foundation's (1969) survey of the goals of fourteen private liberal arts colleges, and Martin's (1969) study of changes in eight colleges and universities.

The Gross and Grambsch (1968, 1974) surveys of the goals of universities represent research that supports and illustrates the concepts behind the IGI. Faculty and administrators at the sixty-eight research universities that were surveyed in both studies described their university as emphasizing research and scholarly pursuits with students, with their own needs clearly given a lower priority. The second survey found a greater gap between the goals of the insiders—faculty and administrators—than did the first survey.

These research studies provided the background for the development of the IGI. Initially, a large number of goal areas were considered, and items were written to represent the areas. After review, the number of goal areas was reduced, and a trial instrument was developed. This instrument was tried out informally: areas lacking empirical or conceptual consistency were dropped; others that were concerns to the colleges were added.

*Comments*

Most organizational psychologists and managerial experts agree that one of the first steps in developing any rational plan for an organization is to determine its goals. In this respect, the IGI may serve a useful function. However, Lunneborg (1978), in his review of the IGI, suggests that colleges can no longer deal with such general goals. In his view, colleges now face decisions about specific allocations, such as spending money on the undergraduate social science program versus career counseling.

Although colleges do not have the luxury of exploring different goals that they had in earlier years, they still must examine these specific issues within the context of general goals. Even though obtaining consensus on any specific budget item may be difficult, it is possible to identify the general directions in which the college community would hope to move, and the IGI can help in this identification. Although disagreements among groups revealed by the IGI may not be easily resolved, decisions can be made more wisely if the extent of agreement and disagreement is known.

*Research Studies*

The "guide for using the IGI" (Peterson and Uhl, 1977) lists sixty studies that have used the IGI or a derivative. These studies, which chiefly report the goals of particular institutions as indicated by their institutional research offices or in doctoral dissertations, vary in sophistication and importance. However, a few multi-institutional studies illustrate the utility of the IGI. Peterson (1973) conducted a study of the goal ratings of all the major constituent groups associated with 116 colleges and universities in California. A report was then prepared for the California legislature, which was reviewing the California Master Plan. All constituencies in every type of institution supported the goals of Intellectual Orientation and Community; however, they perceived the existing situation as considerably below the ideal. The goals of Social Criticism/Activism, Social Egalitarianism, and Off-Campus Learning generally received low ratings. The constituencies of community colleges and private institutions had the highest levels of agreement about preferred institutional goals. Although the constituencies of the University of California campuses and the California state university and college campuses agreed about some goals, they differed on Vocational Preparation, Individual Personal Development, Innovation, and Freedom.

Peterson contended that such disparate views about basic goals must adversely affect the quality of work at an institution. In some instances, the off-campus public did not support the goals that they perceived their local campuses to be pursuing—a serious matter when the conflict concerns such goal areas as Freedom and Democratic Governance. Peterson recommended that colleges make an effort to help the public understand their goals and policies.

Bushnell (1973) adapted twenty-six items from the IGI to study the goal ratings of students, faculty, and presidents in a national sample of ninety-two community colleges. Although the groups agreed on most goals, presidents emphasized responding to community needs more than other groups, faculty emphasized students' personal development, and students emphasized easier admissions policies and more financial aid. There was greatest disagreement among faculty about applying quotas to the admittance of minority and low-income students. Bushnell concluded that community college presidents had greater concern for students than did university presidents.

*Availability*

Information about costs and services are available by writing the Institutional Research Program for Higher Education, Educational Testing Service, Princeton, N.J. 08541.

*Reviews*

Reviews by C. E. Lunneborg and M. Y. Quereshi appear in O. K. Buros (Ed.), *The Eighth Mental Measurements Yearbook* (Highland Park, N.J.: Gryphon Press, 1978).

*Student Orientations Survey (SOS), Form D*

The SOS is an inventory designed to assess students' attitudes toward various curricular and instructional possibilities. Students indicate the degree of their agreement with eighty items that provide four-point Likert responses. The SOS requires about thirty minutes, and scoring must be done by the publisher. Five of the ten scales (eight items each) assess a general preparatory orientation to college (that is, the extent to which students value college because it teaches useful knowledge, skills, and social roles). The other five scales assess an exploratory orientation to college (that is, the extent to which students value college for the opportunities it affords for exploring one's interests, ideas, and identity).

A scale in each group is concerned with students' attitudes toward (1) the purposes of higher education, (2) different modes of teaching and learning, (3) power and decision making in college, (4) peer relations, and (5) the role of the college in the community and society.

The preparatory scales are as follows:

- *Achievement* (Ach). Taps a practical, goal-oriented outlook that evaluates the college experience in terms of its future usefulness. (Sample item: "More college courses should be geared to the kind of job a student wants after college.")
- *Assignment Learning* (AL). Relates to a preference for structured teaching-learning arrangements with specific, clear-cut course

assignments. (Sample item: "An academic program is best organized into formal courses, with regular class assignments and examinations.")

- *Assessment* (As). Relates to student-faculty power relationships that emphasize formal evaluations by faculty of student work. (Sample item: "If there weren't any pressure on me to get good grades, I might slack off in my academic courses.")
- *Affiliation* (Affl). Deals with the importance of maintaining strong institutional loyalty and support (for example, belonging to organized extracurricular groups). (Sample item: "Active alumni generally render a great service to a college or university.")
- *Affirmation* (Affr). Assesses satisfaction with the status quo and the affirmation of the values of a peaceful and orderly society. (Sample item: "The society that tries to change too fast is headed for real trouble.")

The exploratory scales are as follows:

- *Inquiry* (Inq). Assesses the value students place on studying the relationships among various fields and the degree to which they endorse the view that learning is valuable for its own sake, irrespective of vocational concerns. (Sample item: "I like to study a given theory or new 'discovery' and consider what implications it may have for the future.")
- *Independent Study* (IS). Taps a preference for informal, less structured courses in which students set their own goals and standards and pursue their own interests with faculty supervision. (Sample item: "The teacher who wants students to do their best should allow them to pursue their own interests.")
- *Interaction* (Inter). Reflects a desire that faculty and students mutually plan courses, programs, and academic requirements. (Sample item: "Students should be involved with faculty in establishing degree and graduation requirements.")
- *Informal Association* (IA). Reflects a preference for informal relationships with peers and a dislike for formal, well-planned social events. (Sample item: "I would rather spend an evening with a friend or two than attend a planned social event.")

- *Involvement* (Inv). Assesses interest in social problems and political affairs and the desirability of students and faculty taking a stand on public issues. (Sample item: "College students should be meaningfully involved in correcting the injustices of our society.")

*Reliability*

In a sample of students in one institution, the coefficient alpha values reported in the manual ranged from .64 to .84. The median value was .77.

*Validity*

The evidence presented in the manual consists of correlations with other instruments and comparisons of students in different colleges and different curricula. Students who score high on the preparatory scales of the SOS tend to score low on Omnibus Personality Inventory (OPI) scales that measure intellectual disposition—(a preference for reflective thought and dealing with theoretical concerns, interest in art and espressive activities, and tolerance of ambiguity and uncertainty). In contrast, students who score high on the exploratory scales of the SOS tend to score high on the intellectual disposition complex. Students with high scores on the SOS preparatory scales tend to have low scores on OPI scales that measure openness and nonauthoritarianism. Students who score high on the exploratory scales of the SOS tend to have high scores on the same OPI scales.

Students who subscribe to the collegiate and vocational philosophies as described on the College Student Questionnaire tend to score high on the preparatory scales; those who subscribe to the nonconformist philosophy tend to score low. The pattern is roughly reversed for the exploratory scales.

Students in the humanities and social sciences tend to score low on the preparatory scales and high on the exploratory scales; male students in professional curricula tend to show the opposite pattern.

Subsequent studies have shown that students in traditional colleges who are dissatisfied tend to score low on the preparatory scales and high on the exploratory scales. Other studies have studied the relationships among SOS scores, SAT scores, and Rotter Internal-External Control scores (Pemberton, 1975), relationships among SOS scores and personality characteristics (Morstain, 1975), and discrepancies between faculty and student SOS scores and students' transferring out of the college (Stark, 1975). These studies provide mixed support for the SOS.

*Norms*

The only information available, based on 3,800 students in twelve colleges, is obviously preliminary; the author's attempt to subdivide the norms into four types of institutions is clearly premature.

*Comments*

At present, the SOS seems most useful for research purposes. Further work, especially in relating SOS scores to actual student behavior, may determine its ultimate utility.

*Availability*

The SOS is available from Barry R. Morstain, College of Urban Affairs and Public Policy, Rand Hall, University of Delaware, Newark, DE 19711.

*Reviews*

Reviews by A. B. Hood and C. R. Pace appear in O. K. Buros, *The Eighth Mental Measurements Yearbook* (Highland Park, N.J.: Gryphon Press, 1978).

*Student Reactions to College (SRC)*

Student Reactions to College (SRC) was developed to assess the opinions of community college students about different aspects of their college experience. Developed by Jonathan R. Warren and Pamela J. Roelfs at the Educational Testing Service, the primary intention of the original (1973) form of the SRC was to "help junior college administrators and faculty members learn what educational concerns junior college students had and how effectively they saw their needs being met" (Warren and Roelfs, 1972, p. 1). Five years after the original SRC was developed, a new version suitable for use in four-year institutions was produced. Both the two-year and four-year forms consist of 150 items (with slight wording differences) and report scores in nineteen areas:

- Quality of Instruction
- Form of Instruction
- Student-Centered Instruction
- Academic Performance
- Grading
- Studying
- Instructor Accessibility
- Involvement with Faculty
- Counseling and Advising
- Planning
- Programming
- Registration and Scheduling
- Rules and Regulations
- Administrative Procedures
- Campus Climate
- Organized Student Activities
- Help with Living Problems
- Financial and Related Problems
- Library and Bookstore

Space is also provided for up to twenty questions that can be written locally. Responses to these locally written questions are also tabulated and reported on the SRC summary data report along with the responses to the regular items.

*Reliability*

The reliability of the SRC was examined by comparing the responses of separate samples of students within the same institutions, which do appear to be consistent.

*Validity*

The validity of the SRC was examined by comparing the responses of students across different institutions. These responses differed considerably, suggesting that the SRC does distinguish among different student perceptions in different situations.

*Norms*

The fundamental information in the students' responses to the SRC items is the set of response distributions—that is, for each item, the percentage of students who gave each response. Responses are clustered into the nineteen groupings listed above, and the percentage distributions are provided. For the two-year institutions comparison data are based on the responses of approximately 15,000 students at forty-one colleges; for the four-year institutions,

2,500 students at six colleges.

*Availability*

The SRC is available from the Educational Testing Service, Princeton, N.J., which will also provide information about which institutions have used SRC, so that prospective users can contact those institutions to inquire about their results.

*Basic Sources*

Warren, J. R., and Roelfs, P. J. "Student Reactions to College: The Development of a Questionnaire Through Which Junior College Students Describe Their College Experiences." Research Project Report 72-23. Princeton, N.J.: Educational Testing Service, 1972.

*Students Reactions to College: Manual for Users.* Princeton, N.J.: Educational Testing Service, 1974.

*Students Reactions to College: Preliminary Comparative Data.* Princeton, N.J.: Educational Testing Service, 1978.

*Availability*

Information about costs and services is available from Educational Testing Service, Princeton, N.J. 08541.

*Reviews*

Reviews by Lawrence M. Aleamoni and Eric F. Gardner appear in O. K. Buros (Ed.), *The Eighth Mental Measurements Yearbook* (Highland Park, N.J.: Gryphon Press, 1978).

*University Residence Environment Scales (URES)*

The URES was designed to assess the environments of such college living groups as dormitories, fraternities, and sororities. The scales consist of nine to ten items each and measure ten dimensions. These scales and typical items are as follows:

- *Involvement* ("There is a feeling of unity and cohesion here.")
- *Emotional Support* ("People here are concerned with helping and supporting one another.")
- *Independence* ("People here pretty much act and think freely without too much regard for social opinion.")
- *Traditional Social Orientation* ("Dating is a recurring topic of conversation around here.")

- *Competition* ("Around here, discussions frequently turn into verbal duels.")
- *Academic Achievement* ("People here work hard to get top grades.")
- *Intellectuality* ("People around here talk a lot about political and social issues.")
- *Order and Organization* ("House activities are pretty carefully planned here.")
- *Student Influence* ("The students formulate almost all the rules here.")
- *Innovation* ("New approaches to things are often tried here.")

The initial items for these scales were developed by interviewing students and college housing personnel and by searching the literature. The resulting items were subjected to a variety of analytic and statistical techniques, including group differentiation, item subscale correlations, factor analysis, and analysis of the social desirability of the responses. Forms for assessing students' ideal residence group and expected residence group are also available.

*Reliability*

Statistics indicate adequate reliability for comparison of group means. Internal consistency estimates ranged from .77 to .88, and test-retest from .59 to .74. Some evidence is provided for the reliability within groups as well as among groups.

*Validity*

The validity of the URES is suggested by a series of studies. Some have correlated URES data about dormitories with other information about dormitories (Gerst and Sweetwood, 1973); others have used the URES to construct a typology of student living groups (Moos and others, 1975), related URES scores to the influence of living groups on students' vocational choices (Hearn and Moos, 1976), and studied the effects of "megadorms" (Wilcox and Holahan, 1976).

*Norms*

Normative data are based on URES scores for students in 168 living units at sixteen colleges.

*Comment*

Although other environmental measures have been adapted for analyzing small units, this instrument is the only one specifically designed for this purpose. However, the basic ideas behind the

scales in URES were derived from work on the environments of
psychiatric wards (Moos, 1974). Although the scales seem sensible,
they were developed to fit into a preconceived framework. Perhaps
other scales would have been developed if a different approach
had been used. However, research suggests that the URES scales
assess important aspects of the residence environment.

*Basic Sources*

The development of the URES is described in the following
   articles: Gerst, M. S., and Moos, R. H. "Social Ecology of University Student Residences." *Journal of Educational Psychology*, 1972,
   *63*, 513–525.

Moos, R. H., and others. "A Typology of University Student Living
   Groups." *Journal of Educational Psychology*, 1975, *67*, 359–367.

Smail, P. M., DeYong, A. J., and Moos, R. H. "The University
   Residence Environment Scale: A Method for Describing University Student Living Groups." *Journal of College Student Personnel*,
   1974, *15*, 357–365.

*Availability*

   The URES can be ordered from Consulting Psychologists
Press, 577 College Avenue, Palo Alto, Calif. 94306.

*Reviews*

   Reviews by Fred Borgen and James Mitchell, Jr., appear in
O. K. Buros (Ed.), *The Eighth Mental Measurements Yearbook* (Highland Park, N.J.: Gryphon Press, 1978).

### Previously Published Measures

*College Characteristics Index (CCI)*

   The CCI is an instrument consisting of 300 statements that
respondents identify as being typical or atypical of events in their
college setting. Originally developed by C. Robert Pace and the late
George Stern (Pace and Stern, 1958a), most of the subsequent developmental and research work was carried out by Stern and his
colleagues at Syracuse University; consequently, the instrument is
commonly associated with him.

   The CCI has its theoretical origins in the work of
psychologist Henry Murray, who postulated that personality is a
function of various personal needs and environmental pressures.

According to Murray, each personal need has a corresponding environmental pressure (or "press"). In the college setting, for example, a student need for achievement (as indicated, say, by a student's enjoyment in taking tests or entering contests) would have a corresponding press for achievement in the environment, as evidenced by tutorial and honors programs, advanced placement, extensive out-of-class preparation among students, and so on.

The 300-item CCI consisted of thirty 10-item scales but was generally scored and reported in terms of eleven factors. These factors were as follows:

- *Aspiration Level*—environmental press for intellectual and professional achievement
- *Intellectual Climate*—environment emphasizing scholarly activities in the humanities, arts, and social sciences
- *Student Dignity*—emphasis on student self-determination and personal responsibility
- *Academic Climate*—concern for academic excellence in traditional areas of humanities, social sciences, and natural sciences
- *Academic Achievement*—emphasis on high standards of achievement.
- *Self-Expression*—environment offering numerous opportunities for the development of leadership potential and self-assurance
- *Group Life*—environment offering numerous opportunities for group activities and reflecting a concern for the welfare of fellow students
- *Academic Organization*—press for purposeful and planned organization and structure
- *Social Form*—emphasis on social skills, social position, and role
- *Play-Work*—heavy student social life; many opportunities for parties, dancing, drinking, and informal dating
- *Vocational Climate*—emphasis on orderliness and conformity in student-faculty relationships and few opportunities for esthetic experiences

Developed on the basis of a personality theory that places approximately equal importance on individual needs and environmental pressures, the CCI was originally intended to be used in conjunction with a measure of individual student needs, the Activities Index (AI). The AI was developed under the assumption that an individual's needs may be inferred from either behavior or reported behavioral preferences. Since it was a measure of student needs rather than environments, we shall not describe the AI here, but the fact that the CCI and AI were intended to be used together should be kept in mind.

*Reliability*

Reliability for the thirty CCI scales varied considerably, averaging about .70—high enough to justify use of the CCI for comparing groups of students.

*Validity*

Stern, his colleagues, and numerous other users of the CCI have done extensive research on the validity of the CCI. One of the most complete sources of information is Stern's *People in Context* (1970). In general, some inferences made from CCI profiles are valid; others are not. For details, the reader is urged to consult some of the references listed below.

*Norms*

The norms for the CCI were based on a sample of approximately 2,000 students from thirty-two colleges and universities. Unfortunately, the sample is not based on institutions but on individuals (Layton, 1972). As a result, the CCI user is forced to compare an institutional mean with a score distribution based on individuals. Furthermore, the institutions included in the norm group are not representative of the national distribution of American colleges and universities. Large private institutions are omitted entirely, and large state universities are underrepresented (Skager, 1972).

*Basic Sources*

Stern, G. G. *Scoring Instructions and College Norms: Activities Index and College Characteristics Index.* New York: Syracuse University Psychological Research Center, 1963.

Stern, G. G. *People in Context.* New York: Wiley, 1970.

*Reviews*

Reviews by Wilbur L. Layton and Rodney Skager appear in O. K. Buros (Ed.), *The Seventh Mental Measurements Yearbook* (Highland Park, N.J.: Gryphon Press, 1972). (This volume also includes an extensive listing of references.)

*Other References*

McFee, A. "The Relation of Students' Needs to Their Perceptions of a College Environment." *Journal of Educational Psychology,* 1961, *52,* 25–29.

Pace, C. R., and Stern, G. G. "An Approach to the Measurement of Psychological Characteristics of College Environments." *Journal of Educational Psychology,* 1958, *49,* 269–277.

Saunders, D. R. "A Factor Analytic Study of the AI and the CCI." *Multivariate Behavioral Research,* 1969, *4,* 329–346.

Stern, G. G. "Environments for Learning." In R. N. Sanford (Ed.), *The American College: A Psychological and Social Interpretation of Higher Learning.* New York: Wiley, 1962.

Stern, G. G. "Student Ecology and the College Environment." *Journal of Medical Education,* 1965, *40,* 132–154.

Walsh, W. B. *Theories of Person-Environment Interaction: Implications for the College Student.* Iowa City, Iowa: American College Testing Program, 1973.

## Institutional Self-Study Service Survey (ISSS)

Unfortunately, this service is no longer available. Nevertheless, it deserves a description here because it was used by many colleges and universities during the early 1970s and because the questionnaire itself (but not the service) can still be obtained.

The ISSS was a product of the American College Testing Program, designed to provide colleges with student opinion regarding institutional policies, practices, faculty, service, and programs and to appraise student development. Data for the ISSS were gathered by means of a 247-item questionnaire that covered three basic areas:

- *Student Goals and Aspirations*—vocational choices, vocational role preferences, educational aspirations, importance of various college goals
- *Student Development*—intellectual pursuits outside of class, nonacademic achievements in college, student ratings of progress in achieving selected college goals
- *Student Collegiate Experience*—instructors, college services, selected policies, practices, and facilities

The ISSS was developed as a research service, not simply as a questionnaire. Users received a research report that included cross-tabulations of ACT scores and student responses to items in the three basic areas and correlations between academic performance during college and student responses.

When the ISSS was first published, normative data were available for 41 institutions.

*Basic Sources*

*The Institutional Self-Study Service Manual: Research and Planning.* Iowa City, Iowa: American College Testing Program, 1970.

*Manual for the ACT Institutional Self-Study Survey.* Iowa City, Iowa: American College Testing Program, 1969.

*Review*

A review by James V. Mitchell appears in O. K. Buros (Ed.), *The Seventh Mental Measurements Yearbook* (Highland Park, N.J.: Gryphon Press, 1972).

### Inventory of College Activities

The Inventory of College Activities (ICA) was developed by Alexander Astin to identify environmental stimuli that are observable by students and reportable by means of a questionnaire. According to Astin, the ICA was developed "as an objective means of describing and measuring some of the important differences among the environments of undergraduate institutions" (Astin, 1972a, p. 1). The word *objective* is crucial to understanding the logic of the ICA, which is based on a stimulus theory of the college environment that emphasizes observable behaviors or events that are "capable of changing the student's sensory input" (Astin, p. 1). The ICA, then, represents an environmental measure that differs significantly, both in content and theory, from perceptual measures, such as CUES or the IFI, or measures that focus exclusively on student characteristics.

The ICA contains 275 items representing environmental stimuli from four broad categories:

- *Peer Environment*—student competitiveness, dating behavior, leisure-time activities, use of automobiles

- *Classroom Environment*—extraversion of instructors, student familiarity with instructors, severity of grading, student participation in class discussions
- *Administrative Environment*—severity of policy against drinking, cheating, demonstrations against institutional policy
- *College Image*—school spirit, emphasis on athletics, flexibility of curriculum

*Reliability*

The reliability of the ICA was calculated by comparing the responses of two separate groups of students within each college (the same procedure employed by Warren in examining the reliability of the SRC). The reliability is definitely high enough to describe groups of students.

*Validity*

The validity of the ICA has been examined by means of two procedures: a factor analysis (which provides evidence for the construct validity of the ICA) and the relationship of ICA scores with scores for the same institutions on CUES and the Environmental Assessment Technique. For many of the ICA scales, these correlations offer convincing evidence of validity.

*Norms*

Comparison information for the ICA is available from over 34,000 students at 246 colleges and universities; however, these data were collected in 1962. Users of the ICA should collect more recent data to make more meaningful comparisons.

*Basic Sources*

Astin, A. W. *Manual for the Inventory of College Activities.* Washington, D.C.: American Council on Education, n.d. (Also available from National Computer Systems, Survey Research Services, Minneapolis, Minn.)

Astin, A. W. *The College Environment.* Washington, D.C.: American Council on Education, 1968.

*Research Study*

Clearly the single most important publication on research using the ICA is Astin's *The College Environment* (1968a). In many respects, this research testifies to the value and importance of a stimulus approach to the assessment of college environments—

more so than the ICA technical manual. Examining data from students who had completed their first year at over 200 institutions, Astin clearly demonstrated, in rich detail, the dramatic diversity among America's colleges and universities.

*Review*

A review by James V. Mitchell appears in O. K. Buros (Ed.), *The Seventh Mental Measurements Yearbook* (Highland Park, N.J.: Gryphon Press, 1972).

*Other References*

Astin, A. W. "Personal and Environmental Determinants of Student Activism." *Measurement and Evaluation in Guidance,* 1968, *1,* 149–162.

Tupes, E. C., and Madden, H. L. "Relationships Between College Characteristics and Later Performance of College Graduates." *Educational and Psychological Measurement,* 1970, *30* (2), 273–282.

## Measures Used in Research Studies

### Academic Alienation Scales

These scales are based on a political model of the academic system derived from such sociologists as Easton and Seeman. A basic assumption of the model is that "the more students' inputs to the system are restricted or discouraged, the more students would manifest feelings of academic alienation" (Long, 1977, p. 17). In this model, then, students' feelings of alienation are not due to their personal attributes but rather to features of the environment. Academic alienation is seen in terms of five components: (1) cynicism about academic goals and their implementation, (2) meaninglessness of the purposes and operation of the university, (3) powerlessness in influencing the governance of the university, (4) negative emotions toward university administrators, and (5) negative evaluations of university administrators. Long developed brief (three- to twelve-item) scales to assess each of these dimensions. Typical items corresponding to each of the dimensions above are: (1) "The educational goals at this university are irrelevant to the attainment of a good education by students"; (2) "Most of the rules at this university are relatively useless and to accomplish anything I often have to disregard them"; (3) "How much influence do you think [this university's] students have on the following groups and individuals in achieving their needs and demands?" (student rates the board of trustees, the university president, and administrators on a six-point scale); (4) "What is your feeling for [this university's] administrators? (student responds on a nine-point "feeling thermometer," ranging from 0° [very cold or unfavorable feeling] to 100° [very warm or favorable feeling]); and (5) "Assuming that this ladder represents university excellence and that rung nine represents a university with the most presidential excellence where do you think [this university's] president falls on the ladder?"

*Reliability*

Coefficient alpha values reported by Long (1977) ranged from .67 to .92.

*Validity*

Long (1977) reported that these scales were correlated with the following scales he developed to measure political climate: Authoritarian Governance, Student Desires for Student Independence, Student Desires for Participation in Governance, and Positive Feelings Toward Student Activism. Long (1976) found that the student scores on the academic alienation scales and their perceptions of the political climate distinguished among groups that had different degrees of attachment to their college. Students' scores were unrelated to their personal characteristics.

*Norms*

The only norms available are the mean scores reported by Long (1977) for students at Southern Illinois University.

*Comments*

These scales were designed to examine some research hypotheses. They may be of greatest interest to researchers concerned with similar hypotheses. However, some of the simple assessments of views of the president, administrators, or trustees may be helpful to administrators concerned with the views of students about the former groups' accessibility, responsiveness, and competence. Furthermore, colleges that believe in the importance of students feeling part of their university and its decisions may find these scales a good barometer of students' opinion.

*Adaptation of the Semantic Differential Technique*

The Semantic Differential Technique, developed by Osgood (Sinder and Osgood, 1969), presents a concept and asks respondents to rate on a scale the applicability of opposing adjectives. For example, for the concept "myself," three scales might range from "warm" to "cold," "bright" to "dull," and "strong" to "weak."

Besides the TAPE technique, reviewed below, there have been a variety of adaptations of the semantic differential technique, which have chiefly been used in research studies of specific topics. They are described here to alert the reader interested in similar questions to the devices used in other studies. Birnbaum (1972) asked students to rate four-year colleges and two-year colleges as well as an ideal college on a forty-item, seven-point semantic differential instrument. In this case, the instrument included such items as "There aren't many student activities" and "There are a lot of student activities"; "Most classes are large" and "Most classes are small"; and "There is a lot of competition for high grades" and "Students don't compete much for high grades." Birnbaum found that four-year colleges were rated more positively than two-year colleges and that the image of four-year colleges corresponded more to that of the ideal college than did the image of two-year colleges. Birnbaum factor analyzed the scale and found three factors: social activities, supportive interpersonal environment, and intellectual climate. This study illustrates that the semantic differential technique can be adapted for various uses. Appropriate polar adjectives can be chosen for most problems and concepts. Possible concepts include "the counseling center" and "the cafeteria."

Long (1976) provides another illustration. He asked students at Southern Illinois to rate the ideal university, Southern Illinois, and the university president on a twenty-five-item, seven-step semantic differential and related the semantic differential responses to students' political self-identifications. (Students chose one of seven terms, ranging from "reactionary" to "moderate" to "radical.") Using stepwise multiple-discriminant analysis, Long found that conservatives tended to prefer an ideal university that was less active, less liberal, and more structured than did liberal students. Conservatives also saw the university president more favorably and the university as more progressive and democratic than did liberals.

*Environmental Satisfaction Questionnaire (ESQ)*

The ESQ, which consists of two parts, is designed to be diagnostic: It helps to pinpoint problem areas and indicates treatment interventions. In Part One, students indicate whether any of eleven areas are problems for them by choosing one of five options, ranging from "strongly agree" to "strongly disagree," for each area. Examples are: "My major is preparing me for a job"; "My advisor has been helpful to me"; and "I personally feel valued as a person at [college name]." In Part Two, students describe the referents for each problem identified in Part One, how they are coping with those problems, and recommendations for easing the problems.

*Comment*

No reliability, validity, or normative information is provided for the ESQ, but such information may not be needed with an instrument of this sort, since it is more a technique for identifying local situations. It might be used in two stages. A fairly open-ended questionnaire might survey broad areas of student experience, and the replies could be used to identify specific problem areas to be investigated with a second questionnaire. As a problem-oriented technique to determine local concerns, the ESQ technique may be more useful than the standardized, sophisticated measures offered by various publishers.

*Basic Sources*

Corazzini, J. G., and Wilson, S. "Students, the Environment and Their Interaction: Assessing Student Needs and Planning for Change." *Journal of the National Association for Women Deans, Administrators, and Counselors,* 1977, *40,* 68–72.

Corazzini, J. G., Wilson, S., and Huebner, L. "The Environmental Satisfaction Questionnaire." *Journal of College Student Personnel,* 1977, *18,* 169–173.

*The Environmental Satisfaction Questionnaire.* Fort Collins, Colo.: Rocky Mountain Behavioral Sciences Institute, 1976.

*Inventory of College Characteristics*

Thistlethwaite (1959, 1960, 1963) revised the College Characteristics Index to reflect those items and variables that discriminated among colleges having different effects on students' motivation for advanced study. Eventually, as reported by Thistlethwaite and Wheeler (1966), the measures consisted of fourteen scales designed to assess the environmental presses experienced by freshmen and sophomores (lower class scales) and twenty scales designed to assess those experienced by juniors and seniors (upper class scales).

Each lower class scale was composed of ten true-false items, with five items keyed true and five items keyed false. Students were to respond in terms of all students and teachers. The scales consisted of nine scales assessing the faculty press for Affiliation, Directiveness, Enthusiasm, Achievement, Compliance, Supportiveness, Humanism, Independence, and Vocationalism and five scales assessing the student press for Competition, Estheticism, Reflectiveness, Social Conformity, and Intellectualism. Typical items were "The faculty usually demands strict compliance with all course requirements" and "The competition for high achievement is intense."

The twelve upper class scales were composed of eight items each and used five-point Likert ratings. Students were to respond in terms of the professors in their major field from whom they had taken most of their courses and fellow students with whom they had associated most frequently. Twelve scales assessed the faculty press for Positive Evaluations of Students' Ability, High Academic Standards, Independent Thinking, Enthusiasm for Intellectual Values, Advanced Training, Convergent Thinking, Adequacy as Positive Role Models, Excellence of Teaching, Availability to Students, Affiliation, Compliance, and Structuring of Major Field of Study; eight scales assessed the student press for Intellectualism, Unfavorable Self-Evaluations, Cohesiveness, Rebelliousness, Playfulness, Status, Opposition to Faculty Influence, and Openness to Experience. Typical items were "Their [faculty's] evaluations of my academic performance convinced me that I had a flair for course work in this area" and "They [students] occasionally plotted some sort of escapade or rebellion."

*Reliability*

The reliability of the lower class scales ranged from .59 to .85, with a median of .73. The reliability of the upper class scales ranged from .57 to .87, with a median of .74. Initial data were based on 2,919 students who had taken the National Merit examinations and entered one of the 140 most popular colleges. Subsequently, Thistlethwaite (1968, 1969) administered twenty-three of the scales to a panel of 1,178 students enrolled at 50 colleges.

*Validity*

Thistlethwaite showed that some of these scales were related to students' plans to obtain advanced degrees. For example, students tended to raise their aspirations when professors were enthusiastic, encouraging, and inspiring and to lower them when professors emphasized vocationalism and when their fellow students opposed the faculty's influence. Thistlethwaite (1969) also showed that students who entered different fields had changing patterns of experience as assessed by some of these scales. For example, entry into the physical sciences was accompanied by increases in faculty and student presses for science and advanced training. Entry into the humanities was accompanied by an increase in faculty press for humanities and student press for estheticism.

*Comment*

The National Merit Scholarship Program conducted the original research. The program was vitally concerned with the identification and encouragement of academically talented students. Consequently, the Merit researchers concentrated on the environmental characteristics of colleges that were associated with promoting student ambitions. That is, they tried to identify the college variables that encouraged very bright students to continue on to advanced studies. Although the Inventory of College Characteristics was developed for research purposes, it may have utility on certain campuses.

*Purdue University Environment Scales*

This is an adaptation of CUES used to study differences in the perceptions of student groups and student personnel workers. It consists of a ten-item Academic scale (similar to the CUES Scholarship scale), a ten-item Community scale, a ten-item Awareness scale, and an eleven-item Personnel Services scale. The first three were adapted from CUES items. The last scale consisted of such items as "Most student personnel workers (dean of men, dean of women, residence hall managers, and counselors, etc.) understand student concerns" and "Financial aid programs meet the needs of most students requiring assistance." Responses were on a five-point Likert scale (ranging from "strongly agree" to "strongly disagree").

*Reliability*

Test-retest reliability was estimated at .71.

*Validity*

To determine content validity, Purdue student personnel workers and professors of psychology and education reviewed the items. Noeth and Dye (1973) compared the perceptions of 299 student personnel workers with students in each class sorted by sex. The students and the personnel workers largely agreed about the academic environment, but personnel workers saw the sense of community and the degree of individual freedom for students to be higher. The largest differences were on the Personnel Services scale, on which personnel workers scored considerably higher. Noeth and Dye suggest that the individual item responses highlight areas where student personnel workers could improve the environment.

*Basic Source*

Noeth, R. J., and Dye, H. A. "Perceptions of a University Environment: Students and Student Personnel Workers." *Journal of College Student Personnel,* 1973, *14,* 527–531.

*Availability*

The Purdue University Environmental Scales are available from Richard Noeth, American College Testing Program, Box 168, Iowa City, Iowa 52240.

*Questionnaire on Student and
College Characteristics (QSCC)*

The QSCC was developed by Centra (1968) to describe the college environment accurately by including information on students' perceptions of their institutions, their behavior during college, and their personal backgrounds and characteristics. After an initial tryout in 8 colleges, Centra (1970) obtained data from students in 214 colleges, which were subjected to a variety of factor analyses. First, the seventy-seven items that asked for students' perceptions were analyzed separately. (These items asked students either to indicate whether statements were true or false or to rate their agreement with statements on a four-point scale.) A typical item was "Faculty members tend to be aloof and somewhat formal with students." The factors obtained were termed Restrictiveness, Faculty-Student Interaction, Activism, Nonacademic Emphasis, Curriculum Flexibility, Challenge (academic), Laboratory Facilities, and Cultural Facilities. From these analyses, factor scores based on two to nine items per factor were computed. The median coefficient alpha reliabilities of the scales was .86, and six of the eight scales had reliabilities of .84 or higher.

In a second analysis, the eight factor scores just described were included with thirty-four student self-report items about their behavior in college (for example, the extent of their involvement in intramural athletics or dramatic productions) plus objective information about the colleges (such as percentage of students in residence halls, books in the library per student, and student SAT scores). A factor analysis yielded six factors: athletic emphases versus cultural activities, size and cliquishness, academic elitism, activism and flexibility, student satisfaction with their college, and social life. A second, multimethod factor analysis yielded ten factors. The first four were similar to those obtained in the standard factor analysis, supporting the meaning and stability of those factors. The remaining six factors included regulation, fraternity and sorority emphasis, emphasis on science, and three other factors with unclear meanings.

The colleges that had participated in the administration of the QSCC had been encouraged to use the results in their self-descriptions for the "College Life" section of the College Board's *College Handbook.* Interestingly, 53 percent did not use the results at all, 9 percent used them for only one to three sentences, 13 percent used them for as much as a short paragraph, and only 25 percent used them extensively.

Centra (1970) provides the means and standard deviations for each of the seventy-seven perceptual items and lists the items that were used in the factor scores. However, there is no normative information on the factor scores. Besides the validity suggested by the factor analyses, the correlations between the perception factors and student self-report data and the published objective institutional data are reported.

The chief users of this instrument would likely be other researchers who would like to replicate or extend Centra's work.

*Transactional Analysis of Personality
and Environment (TAPE)*

The TAPE questionnaire is a semantic differential instrument. Students are asked to rate certain concepts (College, Self, Students, Faculty, Administration, and Ideal College) on 52 "scales." Each scale consists of eleven points between two polar adjectives, such as artistic-pragmatic and materialistic-idealistic, and the students indicate where they would rate the items for each concept on each scale. In this way, the students indicate their perceptions of their college. On the basis of a three-mode factor analysis, the fifty-two scales were reduced to thirteen factors. Although these factors would presumably be more stable than the scales, most analyses using TAPE have concentrated on the scales. In the middle of the questionnaire, the students also respond to sixteen questions about their satisfaction with their colleges' environment.

*Reliability*

In a small sample study reported by Pervin (1967b), test-retest means and means for two samples were all .95 or higher for the concepts of college, self, and students. However, when the reliability was based on individual subjects, the correlations were .59, .70, and .58 for these concepts.

*Validity*

The chief validity presented for TAPE lies in Pervin's investigation of person-environment congruency and satisfaction. Pervin (1967b) found that large discrepancies between Self and College were moderately related to dissatisfaction, especially nonacademic dissatisfaction. Similar results were obtained by Per-

vin and Rubin (1967). Pervin and Smith (1968) used a modified
TAPE with a sample of Princeton students who were members of
eating clubs. The College concept was changed to "My Eating
Club." Again, incongruency was related to dissatisfaction. Finally,
Pervin and Rubin (1967) found that discrepancies between Self
and College, Self and Students, and College and Ideal College were
related to the students' thoughts of dropping out of college for
nonacademic reasons.

*Norms*

None.

*Comments*

This technique can be adapted to a wide variety of research
uses. For example, instead of comparing College with Ideal College, one could compare "This Dormitory" with "Ideal Dormitory";
instead of studying discrepancies between Self and College, one
could study discrepancies between Self and "My Major Field."
However, the practical implications of such studies may be limited
by the general nature of the scales and the lack of normative information. Some of the semantic differential scales described elsewhere may be more useful.

*Basic Sources*

Pervin, L. A. "Satisfaction and Perceived Self-Environment Similarity: A Semantic Differential Study of Student-College Interaction." *Journal of Personality,* 1967, *35,* 623–634.

Pervin, L. A. "A Twenty-College Study of Student × College In-
teraction Using TAPE (Transactional Analysis of Personality and
Environment): Rationale, Reliability, and Validity." *Journal of
Educational Psychology,* 1967, *58,* 290–302.

Pervin, L. A. "The College as a Social System: Student Perception
of Students, Faculty, and Administration." *Journal of Educational
Research,* 1968, *61,* 281–284.

Pervin, L. A. "Performance and Satisfaction as a Function of
Individual-Environment Fit." *Psychological Bulletin,* 1968, *69,*
56–68.

Pervin, L. A., and Rubin, D. B. "Student Dissatisfaction with College and the College Dropout: A Transactional Approach."
*Journal of Social Psychology,* 1967, *72,* 285–295.

Pervin, L. A., and Smith, S. H. "Further Test of the Relationship Between Satisfaction and Perceived Self-Environment Similarity." *Perceptual and Motor Skills,* 1968, *26,* 835–838.

## University Climate Questionnaire

This research instrument was developed at the University of Maryland from essays written by black and white students. These essays were used to generate a pool of 294 items describing university life, from which 115 were chosen for the final form of the questionnaire. Students indicated the extent of their agreement with each item on a five-point scale. After the items were factor analyzed in separate black and white samples, six factors were identified in a sample of 138 black students and five factors in a sample of 730 white students.

The six black factors were titled Institutional Racism, Nonacademic Atmosphere (concerning the learning process), Social Isolation (difficulty in meeting and talking with people), Personal Racism (among individual students), Nonclassroom Related Activities, and Attempts at Communication (among students and between students and the administration). The five white factors were titled Impersonal Academic Atmosphere, Administrative Neglect, Social Interaction (atmosphere conducive to meeting and talking with other students), Racism, and Racial Separatism (lack of interaction).

The blacks scored substantially higher on the scales reflecting racism as well as on the Administrative Neglect and Impersonal Academic Atmosphere. Other differences were statistically significant but smaller.

*Reliability*

Internal consistency (KR-20) for the scales showed the median reliability to be between .65 and .70. Predictably, students of one group tended to have less reliable scores on the scales developed for the other group.

*Comment*

This research is important in showing that black and white students not only perceive the college environment differently but also perceive it along different dimensions. Each group finds certain aspects of the environment more salient than does the other group.

*Basic Source*

Pfeifer, C. M., and Schneider, B. "University Climate Perceptions by Black and White Students." *Journal of Applied Psychology,* 1974, *59,* 660–662.

*Availability*

Copies of the University Climate Questionnaire may be obtained from C. Michael Pfeifer, Jr., Westinghouse Behavioral Safety Center, Box 948, American City Building, Columbia, Md. 21044.

### Miscellaneous Measures

A wide variety of measures have been used in individual studies, most of which were used one time on one campus. However, many of these are potentially useful; two are described here.

Sorenson and others (1973) showed how a very simple instrument can provide insights into a college's workings when it is backed up with theory. They assessed the degree of influence of five campus segments by using simple five-point ratings, which ranged from "little or no influence" to "a very great deal of influence." The groups were the administration, the faculty, students, the Students for a Democratic Society, and the Black Students Association. The experimenters postulated different models of the operations of the colleges that would be reflected in the response patterns of the students. For example, the authoritarian model would show the administration to have great power, with all other groups having little power. A bureaucratic model would show the degree of power among the groups to decrease as follows: administration, faculty, students, and special student groups. A democratic model would have each group holding approximately the same amount of power.

These investigators asked students at two colleges to describe their actual campus and their ideal campus. At one college, the structure appeared to be between the authoritarian and the bureaucratic models. Interestingly, the students' ideal profile was fairly similar, except that the administration had slightly less power and the faculty and students had slightly more. The actual profile of the second college was more like the democratic model. The ideal profile was fairly similar, except that students preferred to have more power—even more than the administration.

Friedman (1974) simply listed forty-two organizations, movements, and agencies typically found on college campuses and asked students to rate their attitudes toward each on a five-point scale, ranging from "highly positive" to "highly negative." Example groups were the student union, Phi Beta Kappa, sororities, and the administration. In Friedman's University of Texas sample, Ecology Action, Zero Population Growth, and the campus newspaper were rated highest, and fraternities, SDS, and the administration rated lowest. However, various groups of students (such as male and female, "Greek" and independent, and upper classes and lower classes) saw the organizations differently. From a factor analysis, Friedman found some interesting clusters of organizations, such as activist–change-oriented groups and religious groups. Subsequently, Manaster and Friedman (1976) adapted the form for organizations at an English university, where the groups were quite different, and subjected the data to a factor analysis.

# References

American College Testing Program. *The Institutional Self-Study Service Manual.* Parts 1 and 2. Iowa City, Iowa: American College Testing Program, 1970.

Anderson, R. E. *College Closings: Causes and Results.* New York: Institute of Higher Education, Teachers College Press, 1975.

Anderson, R. E. *Strategic Policy Changes at Private Colleges: Educational and Fiscal Implications.* New York: Teachers College Press, 1977.

Astin, A. W. "An Empirical Characterization of Higher Educational Institutions." *Journal of Educational Psychology,* 1962, *53,* 224–229.

Astin, A. W. "Differential Effects on the Motivation of Talented Students to Pursue the Ph.D. Degree." *Journal of Educational Psychology,* 1963a, *54,* 63–71.

Astin, A. W. "Further Validation of the Environmental Assessment Technique." *Journal of Educational Psychology,* 1963b, *54,* 217–226.

Astin, A. W. "Personal and Environmental Factors Associated with College Drop-Outs Among High Aptitude Students." *Journal of Educational Psychology,* 1964, *55,* 219–227.

Astin, A. W. *Who Goes Where to College?* Chicago: Science Research Associates, 1965.

Astin, A. W. *The College Environment.* Washington, D.C.: American Council on Education, 1968a.

Astin, A. W. "Personal and Environmental Determinants of Student Activism." *Measurement and Evaluation in Guidance,* 1968b, *1,* 149–162.

Astin, A. W. "Undergraduate Achievement and Institutional Excellence." *Science,* 1968c, *161,* 661–668.

Astin, A. W. *Manual for the Inventory of College Activities.* Minneapolis, Minn.: National Computer Systems, 1972a.

Astin, A. W. "The Measured Effects of Higher Education." *The Annals of the American Academy of Political and Social Science,* 1972b, *404,* 1–20.

Astin, A. W. *College Dropouts: A National Profile.* ACE Research Report, 7, No. 1. Washington, D.C.: American Council on Education, 1972c.

Astin, A. W. *Preventing Students from Dropping Out.* San Francisco: Jossey-Bass, 1975.

Astin, A. W. *Academic Gamesmanship.* New York: Praeger, 1976.

Astin, A. W. *Four Critical Years.* San Francisco: Jossey-Bass, 1977.

Astin, A. W., and Bayer, A. E. "Antecedents and Consequents of Disruptive Campus Protests." *Measurement and Evaluation in Guidance,* 1971, *4,* 18–30.

Astin, A. W., and Boruch, R. F. "A 'Link' System for Assuring Confidentiality of Research Data in Longitudinal Studies." *American Educational Research Journal,* 1970, *7,* 615–624.

Astin, A. W., and Holland, J. "The Environmental Assessment Technique: A Way to Measure College Environments." *Journal of Educational Psychology,* 1961, *52,* 308–316.

Astin, A. W., and Panos, R. J. *The Educational and Vocational Development of College Students.* Washington, D.C.: American Council on Education, 1969.

Astin, H. S. "Self-Perceptions of College Student Activists." *Journal of College Student Personnel,* 1971, *12,* 263–270.

Baird, L. L. "The Effects of College Residence Groups on Students' Self-Concepts, Goals, and Achievements." *Personnel and Guidance Journal,* 1969, *47,* 1015–1021.

Baird, L. L. "The Functions of College Environmental Measures." *Journal of Educational Measurement,* 1971, *8,* 83–86.

Baird, L. L. "Focusing on Measures of College Environments." *College Board Review,* 1973, *86,* 1–3ff.

Baird, L. L. *Careers and Curricula.* Princeton, N.J.: Educational Testing Service, 1974.

Baird, L. L. "Medical Schools Differ in Important Ways." *Findings,* 1976a, *3,* 5–8.

Baird, L. L. *Using Self-Reports to Predict Student Performance.* College Entrance Examination Board Monograph No. 7. New York: College Entrance Examination Board, 1976b.

Bayer, A. E. "Faculty Composition, Institutional Structure, and Students' College Environment." *Journal of Higher Education,* 1975, *46,* 549–565.

Bayer, A. E., and Astin, A. W. "Violence and Disruption on the U.S. Campus, 1968–69." *Educational Record,* 1969, *50,* 337–350.

Betz, E. L., Klingensmith, J. E., and Menne, J. W. "The Measurement and Analysis of College Student Satisfaction." *Measurement and Evaluation in Guidance,* 1970, *3,* 110–118.

Betz, E. L., and others. "A Dimensional Analysis of College Student Satisfaction." *Measurement and Evaluation in Guidance,* 1971, *4,* 99–106.

Birnbaum, R. "Student Attitudes Toward 2- and 4-year Colleges." *Journal of Educational Research,* 1972, *65,* 369–374.

Blau, P. M. *The Organization of Academic Work.* New York: Wiley, 1973.

Blau, P., and Margulies, R. "The Reputations of American Professional Schools." *Change,* 1974–1975, *6,* 42–47.

Bloom, B. S., Hastings, J. T., and Madaus, G. F. *Handbook on Formative and Summative Evaluation of Student Learning.* New York: McGraw-Hill, 1971.

Brown, F. D. "Manipulation of the Environmental Press in a College Residence Hall." *Personnel and Guidance Journal,* 1968, *46,* 555–560.

Buros, O. K. *Personality Tests and Reviews.* Highland Park, N.J.: Gryphon Press, 1970.

Buros, O. K. (Ed.). *The Seventh Mental Measurements Yearbook.* Highland Park, N.J.: Gryphon Press, 1972.

Buros, O. K. (Ed.). *The Eighth Mental Measurements Yearbook.* Highland Park, N.J.: Gryphon Press, 1978.

Bushnell, D. S. *Organizing for Change: New Priorities for Community Colleges.* New York: McGraw-Hill, 1973.

Cain, G. G., and Watts, H. W. "Problems in Making Policy Inferences from the Coleman Report." *American Sociological Review,* 1970, *35,* 228–241.

Caplow, T., and McGee, R. J. *The Academic Marketplace.* New York: Basic Books, 1958.

Caro, F. G. (Ed.). *Readings in Evaluation Research.* New York: Russell Sage Foundation, 1971.

Caro, F. G. (Ed.). *Readings in Evaluation Research.* (2nd ed). New York: Russell Sage Foundation, 1977.

Cartter, A. M. *An Assessment of Quality in Graduate Education.* Washington, D.C.: American Council on Education, 1966.

Cartter, A. M., and Porter, L. W. "The Cartter Report." *Change,* February, 1977, *9,* 44–48.

Carver, R. P. "Two Dimensions of Tests: Psychometric and Edumetric." *American Psychologist,* 1974, *29,* 512–518.

Centra, J. A. "Student Perceptions of Residence Hall Environments: Living, Learning vs. Conventional Units." Research Memorandum 67–13. Princeton, N.J.: Educational Testing Service, 1967.

Centra, J. A. "Development of the Questionnaire on Student and College Characteristics." Research Memorandum 68–11. Princeton, N.J.: Educational Testing Service, 1968.

Centra, J. A. "The College Environment Revisited: Current Descriptions and a Comparison of Three Methods of Assessment." Research Bulletin 70–44. Princeton, N.J.: Educational Testing Service, 1970.

Centra, J. A. "Comparison of Three Methods of Assessing College Environments." *Journal of Educational Psychology,* 1972, *63,* 56–62.

Centra, J. A., Hartnett, R. T., and Peterson, R. E. "Faculty Views of Institutional Functioning: A New Measure of College Environments." *Educational and Psychological Measurement,* 1970, *30,* 405–416.

Chickering, A. W. *Commuting Versus Resident Students.* San Francisco: Jossey-Bass, 1974.

Chickering, A. W., McDowell, J., and Campagna, D. "Institutional Differences and Student Development." *Journal of Educational Psychology,* 1969, *60,* 315–326.

Clark, B. R., and Trow, M. "The Organizational Context." In T. M. Newcomb and E. K. Wilson (Eds.), *College Peer Groups: Problems and Prospects for Research.* Chicago: Aldine, 1966.

Clark, M. J. "The Meaning of Quality in Graduate and Professional Education." In J. Katz and R. T. Hartnett (Eds.), *Scholars in the Making.* Cambridge, Mass.: Ballinger, 1976.

Clark, M. J., and Hartnett, R. T. *The Assessment of Quality in Graduate Education: Summary of a Multidimensional Approach.* Washington, D.C.: Council of Graduate Schools, 1977.

Clark, M. J., Hartnett, R. T., and Baird, L. L. *Assessing Dimensions of Quality in Doctoral Education.* Princeton, N.J.: Educational Testing Service, 1976.

Cohen, M., and March, J. G. *Leadership and Ambiguity: The American College President.* New York: McGraw-Hill, 1974.

College Entrance Examination Board. *The College Handbook.* New York: College Entrance Examination Board, 1977.

*Consumer Protection in Postsecondary Education: Report of the Second National Conference.* Denver, Colo.: Education Commission of the States, 1975.

Corazzini, J. G., and Wilson, S. "Students, the Environment and Their Interaction: Assessing Student Needs and Planning for Change." *Journal of the National Association for Women Deans, Administrators, and Counselors,* 1977, *40,* 68–72.

Corazzini, J. G., Wilson, S. E., and Huebner, L. "The Environmental Satisfaction Questionnaire." *Journal of College Student Personnel,* 1977, *18,* 169–173.

Corson, J. *The Governance of Colleges and Universities: Modernizing Structure and Process.* (Rev. ed.) New York: McGraw - Hill, 1975.

Creager, J. A. *The American Graduate Student: A Normative Description.* ACE Research Report, *6,* No. 5. Washington, D.C.: American Council on Education, 1971.

Danforth Foundation. "A Report: College Goals and Governance." St. Louis, Mo.: Danforth News and Notes, November 1969.

Darley, J. G. *Promise and Performance*. Berkeley, Calif.: Center for the Study of Higher Education, 1962.

Doman, E. G., and Christensen, M. G. "Effects of a Group Life Seminar on Perceptions of the University Environment." *Journal of College Student Personnel*, 1976, *17,* 66–71.

Donahue, W. R. "Student Perceptions of Their Environment in Two Residence Hall Areas in Unisexual to Coeducational Transition." *The Michigan State University Orient*, 1971, *6,* 2–14.

Donovan, J. D. *The Academic Man in the Catholic College*. New York: Sheed and Ward, 1964.

Dorfman, R. *Prices and Markets*. Englewood Cliffs, N.J.: Prentice-Hall, 1967.

Doucet, J. A. "The Implications of Rank-Ordering on the Clark-Trow Typology." *Journal of College Student Personnel*, 1977, *18* (1), 25–31.

Dressel, P. *Handbook of Academic Evaluation: Assessing Institutional Effectiveness, Student Progress, and Professional Performance for Decision Making in Higher Education*. San Francisco: Jossey-Bass, 1976.

Dressel, P., and others. *The Confidence Crisis*. San Francisco: Jossey-Bass, 1970.

Dugmore, W. O., and Grant, C. W. "Experiments in Cluster Registration of College Freshmen: Effects upon Achievement, Anxiety, and Perceptions of the College Environment." *Journal of Educational Research*, 1970, *63,* 216–218.

Dykes, A. R. *Faculty Participation in Academic Decision Making*. Washington, D.C.: American Council on Education, 1968.

Educational Testing Service. *College Student Questionnaire-2 Comparative Data*. Princeton, N.J.: Educational Testing Service, 1972.

Educational Testing Service. *HELIX: A Program to Link Goals and Outcomes to Management and Planning in Higher Education*. Princeton, N.J.: Educational Testing Service, 1975.

Edwards, A. L. *Techniques of Attitude Scale Construction*. New York: Appleton-Century-Crofts, 1954.

El-Khawas, E. H. *Better Information for Student Choice: Report of a National Task Force*. Washington, D.C.: American Association for Higher Education, 1978.

Elton, C. G., and Rose, H. A. "What Are the Ratings Rating?" *American Psychologist,* 1972, *27,* 197–201.

Engelhart, M. D. *Methods of Educational Research.* Chicago: Rand McNally, 1972.

*The Environmental Satisfaction Questionnaire.* Fort Collins, Colo.: Rocky Mountain Behavioral Sciences Institute, 1976.

Feldman, K. A. "Measuring College Environments: Some Uses of Path Analysis." *American Educational Research Journal,* 1971, *8,* 51–70.

Feldman, K. A. (Ed.). *College and Student.* New York: Pergamon Press, 1972.

Feldman, K. A., and Newcomb, T. M. *The Impact of College on Students.* San Francisco: Jossey-Bass, 1969.

*Final Report of the National Commission on the Financing of Postsecondary Education.* Washington, D.C: Government Printing Office, 1973.

Friedman, S. T. "Students' Assessment of the Components of Campus Life." *Journal of College Student Personnel,* 1974, *15,* 311–316.

Froomkin, J. *The Financial Prospects of the Postsecondary Sector, 1975 to 1990.* Washington, D.C.: Joseph Froomkin, 1972.

Fuller, B. "A Framework for Academic Planning." *Journal of Higher Education,* 1971, *47,* 65–78.

Gerst, M. S., and Moos, R. H. "Social Ecology of University Student Residences." *Journal of Educational Psychology,* 1972, *63,* 513-525.

Gerst, M. S., and Sweetwood, H. "Correlates of Dormitory Social Climate." *Environment and Behavior,* 1973, *5,* 440–464.

Glass, G. V. "The Growth of Evaluation Methodology." *AERA Monograph Series on Curriculum Evaluation,* 1971, No. 7.

Gouldner, A. W. "Cosmopolitans and Locals: Toward an Analysis of Latent Social Roles, I." *Administrative Science Quarterly,* 1957a, *2,* 281–306.

Gouldner, A. W. "Cosmopolitans and Locals: Toward an Analysis of Latent Social Roles, II." *Administrative Science Quarterly,* 1957b, *3,* 444–480.

Gourman, J. *The Gourman Report: A Rating of American and International Universities.* Los Angeles: National Education Standards, 1977.

Grande, P. O., and Loveless, L. J. "Variability in the Measurement of Campus Climate." *College and University,* 1969, *44,* 244–249.

Gross, E., and Grambsch, P. V. *University Goals and Academic Power.* Washington, D.C.: American Council on Education, 1968.

Gross, E., and Grambsch, P. V. *Changes in University Organization, 1964–1971.* New York: McGraw-Hill, 1974.

Hagstrom, W. O. *The Scientific Community.* New York: Basic Books, 1965.

Hagstrom, W. O. "Inputs, Outputs, and the Prestige of University Science Departments." *Sociology of Education,* 1971, *44,* 375–397.

Hartnett, R. T. "Strengthening Institutional Quality Through Institutional Research." In C. Stewart and T. R. Harvey (Eds.), *New Directions for Higher Education: Strategies for Significant Survival,* no. 12. San Francisco: Jossey-Bass, 1975.

Hartnett, R. T., and Centra, J. A. "Attitudes and Secondary School Backgrounds of Catholics Entering College." *Sociology of Education,* 1969, *42,* 188–198.

Hartnett, R. T., and Centra, J. A. "Faculty Views of the Academic Environment: Situational vs. Institutional Perspectives." *Sociology of Education,* 1974, *47,* 159–169.

Hartnett, R. T., and Centra, J. A. "The Effects of Academic Departments on Student Learning." *Journal of Higher Education,* 1977, *48* (5), 491–507.

Hartnett, R. T., Clark, M. J., and Baird, L. L. "Reputational Ratings of Doctoral Programs." *Science,* 1978, *199,* 1310–1314.

Hartnett, R. T., and Katz, J. "The Education of Graduate Students." *Journal of Higher Education,* 1977, *48,* 646–664.

Hearn, J. C., and Moos, R. H. "Social Climate and Major Choice: A Test of Holland's Theory in University Student Living Groups." *Journal of Vocational Behavior,* 1976, *8,* 293–305.

Heist, P., and others. *Omnibus Personality Inventory.* New York: Psychological Corporation, 1968.

Herrscher, B. "Patterns of Attainment and the Environmental Press of UCLA Student Groups." Unpublished doctoral dissertation, University of California, Los Angeles, 1967.

Holland, J. L. "Explorations of a Theory of Vocational Choice: VI—A Longitudinal Study Using a Sample of Typical College

Students." *Journal of Applied Psychology Monographs*, 1968, *52* (1), entire issue.

Holland, J. L. *Making Vocational Choices: A Theory of Careers.* Englewood Cliffs, N.J.: Prentice-Hall, 1973.

Hugstad, P. S. "The Marketing Concept in Higher Education: A Caveat." *Liberal Education*, 1975, *56* (4), 504–512.

Husen, T. (Ed.). *International Study of Achievement in Mathematics.* New York: Wiley, 1967.

*The Institutional Self-Study Service Manual: Research and Planning.* Iowa City, Iowa: American College Testing Program, 1970.

Jencks, C., and Riesman, D. *The Academic Revolution.* New York: Doubleday, 1968.

Jones, J. D., and Finnell, W. S. J. "Relationships Between College Experiences and Attitudes of Students from Economically Deprived Backgrounds." *Journal of College Student Personnel*, 1972, *13*, 314–318.

Kahn, A. J. *Theory and Practice of Social Planning.* New York: Russell Sage Foundation, 1969.

Katz, D., and Kahn, R. L. *The Social Psychology of Organizations.* (2nd ed.) New York: Wiley, 1978.

Kluckhohn, C., and Murray, H. A. *Personality in Nature, Society, and Culture.* New York: Knopf, 1949.

Kojaku, L. "Major Field Transfer: The Self-Matching of University Undergraduates to Student Characteristics." Unpublished doctoral dissertation, University of California, Los Angeles, 1972.

Kornhauser, A. "Constructing Questionnaires and Interview Schedules." In M. Johada, M. Deutsch, and S. W. Cook (Eds.), *Research Methods in Social Relations, with Special Reference to Prejudice.* Part II. New York: Dryden, 1951.

Ladd, E. C., Jr., and Lipset, S. M. *The Divided Academy.* New York: McGraw-Hill, 1975.

Layton, W. L. "Review of Stern Environment Indexes." In O. K. Buros (Ed.), *The Seventh Mental Measurements Yearbook.* Highland Park, N.J.: Gryphon Press, 1972.

Lazarsfeld, P. F., and Thielens, W. *The Academic Mind.* New York: Free Press, 1958.

Lenning, O. T., and Micek, S. S. "Defining and Communicating Institutional Mission/Role/Scope and Priorities: The Needs of

Different Types of Postsecondary Institutions." Paper presented at the American Educational Research Association meetings, San Francisco, 1976. (ED 121376)

Lipset, S. M., and Ladd, E. C., Jr. "And What Professors Think." *Psychology Today,* November 1970, pp. 49–56.

Long, S. "Sociopolitical Ideology as a Determinant of Students' Perceptions of the University." *Higher Education,* 1976, *5,* 423–435.

Long, S. "Dimensions of Student Academic Alienation." *Educational Administration Quarterly,* 1977, *13,* 16–30.

Longino, C. F., and Kart, C. S. "The College Fraternity: An Assessment of Theory and Research." *Journal of College Student Personnel,* 1974, *14,* 118–125.

Lunneborg, C. E. "Review of the Institutional Goals Inventory." In O. K. Buros (Ed.), *The Eighth Mental Measurements Yearbook.* Highland Park, N.J.: Gryphon Press, 1978.

McConnell, T. R., and Mortimer, K. P. *The Faculty in University Governance.* Berkeley, Calif.: Center for Research and Development in Higher Education, 1971.

McFee, A. "The Relation of Students' Needs to Their Perceptions of a College Environment." *Journal of Educational Psychology,* 1961, *52,* 25–29.

Manaster, F. J., and Friedman, S. T. "Student Assessment of Components of Campus Life at an English University." *Journal of College Student Personnel,* 1976, *17,* 469–474.

Margulies, R. Z., and Blau, P. M. "America's Leading Professional Schools." *Change,* 1973, *5,* 21–27.

Martin, W. B. *Conformity: Standards and Change in Higher Education.* San Francisco: Jossey-Bass, 1969.

Micek, S., Service, A., and Lee, Y. *Outcome Measures and Procedures Manual.* Boulder, Colo.: National Center for Higher Education Management Systems at Western Interstate Commission for Higher Education, 1975.

Miller, L. D. "Distinctive Characteristics of Fraternity Members." *Journal of College Student Personnel,* 1973, *14,* 126–129.

Millett, J. D. *Decision Making and Administration in Higher Education.* Kent, Ohio: Kent State University Press, 1968.

Moos, R. *The Social Climate Scales: An Overview.* Palo Alto, Calif.: Consulting Psychologists Press, 1974.

Moos, R. H., and Gerst, M. *The University Residence Environment Scale Manual.* Palo Alto, Calif.: Consulting Psychologists Press, 1974.

Moos, R. H., and others. "A Typology of University Student Living Groups." *Journal of Educational Psychology,* 1975, *67,* 359–367.

Morstain, B. R. "The Relationship Between Students' Personality Characteristics and Educational Attitudes." *Measurement and Evaluation in Guidance,* 1975, *7,* 251–258.

Morstain, B. R. *Student Orientation Survey, Technical Manual.* Newark, Del.: University of Delaware, 1976.

Nash, P. *The Goals of Higher Education: An Empirical Assessment.* New York: Columbia University, Bureau of Applied Social Research, 1968.

National Association of College and University Business Officers. *A College Planning Cycle.* Washington, D.C.: National Association of College and University Business Officers, 1975.

National Center for Education Statistics. *Digest of Educational Statistics, 1973.* Washington, D.C.: U.S. Department of Health, Education, and Welfare, 1974.

National Center for Education Statistics. *Fall Enrollment in Higher Education, 1972.* Washington, D.C.: National Center for Education Statistics, 1974.

National Center for Higher Education Management Systems. *An Introduction to the NCHEMS Costing and Data Management System.* Technical Report 55. Boulder, Colo.: National Center for Higher Education Management Systems at Western Interstate Commission for Higher Education, 1975.

National Commission on the Financing of Postsecondary Education. *Final Report.* Washington, D.C.: U.S. Government Printing Office, 1973.

Nixon, E. "The Mechanics of Questionnaire Construction." *Journal of Educational Research,* 1954, *47,* 481–487.

Noeth, R. J., and Dye, H. A. "Perceptions of a University Environment: Students and Student Personnel Workers." *Journal of College Student Personnel,* 1973, *14,* 527–531.

Pace, C. R. (Ed.). *Self-Survey: Report to the Faculty.* Syracuse, N.Y.: Syracuse University, 1949.

Pace, C. R. *The Influence of Academic and Student Subcultures in College and University Environments.* Final Report of Cooperative Research Project No. 1083. Los Angeles, Calif.: U.S. Office of Education, 1964.

Pace, C. R. "Comparisons of CUES Results from Different Groups of Reporters." College Entrance Examination Board Report No. 1. Los Angeles: University of California, 1966a.

Pace, C. R. "The Use of CUES in the College Admissions Process." College Entrance Examination Board Report No. 2. Los Angeles: University of California, 1966b.

Pace, C. R. "Methods of Describing College Cultures." In K. Yamamoto (Ed.), *The College Student and His Culture: An Analysis.* Boston: Houghton Mifflin, 1968.

Pace, C. R. *College and University Environment Scales: Technical Manual.* (2nd ed.) Princeton, N.J.: Educational Testing Service, 1969.

Pace, C. R. *Education and Evangelism: A Profile of Protestant Colleges.* New York: McGraw-Hill, 1972.

Pace, C. R. *The Demise of Diversity? A Comparative Profile of Eight Types of Institutions.* New York: McGraw-Hill, 1974.

Pace, C. R. *UCLA: Who Goes? What's It Like?* Los Angeles: UCLA Laboratory for Research on Higher Education, 1976.

Pace, C. R., and others. *Higher Education Measurement and Evaluation Kit.* Los Angeles: UCLA Laboratory for Research on Higher Education, 1975.

Pace, C. R., and Baird, L. L. "Attainment Patterns in the Environmental Press of College Subcultures." In T. M. Newcomb and E. K. Wilson (Eds.), *College Peer Groups.* Chicago: Aldine, 1966.

Pace, C. R., and Stern, G. G. "An Approach to the Measurement of Psychological Characteristics of College Environments." *Journal of Educational Psychology,* 1958a, *49,* 269–277.

Pace, C. R., and Stern, G. G. *A Criterion Study of College Environments.* College Entrance Examination Board Report. Syracuse, N.Y.: Syracuse University, 1958b.

Panackal, A. A., and Sockloff, A. L. "Factor Analyses of the College

Student Questionnaires." *Measurement and Evaluation in Guidance*, 1975, *7*, 225–233.

Parekh, S. B. *A Long-Range Planning Model*. New York: Phelps-Stokes Fund, 1975.

Parsons, T., and Platt, G. M. *The American University*. Cambridge, Mass.: Harvard University Press, 1973.

Pascarella, E. T. "Students' Perceptions of the College Environment: How Well Are They Understood by Administrators?" *Journal of College Student Personnel*, 1974, *15*, 370–375.

Pelz, D. C., and Andrews, F. M. *Scientists in Organizations: Productive Climates for Research and Development*. (Rev. ed.) Ann Arbor, Mich.: Institute for Social Research, University of Michigan, 1976.

Pemberton, C. L. "The Relationship Between Student Orientations to College, SAT Scores, and Rotter I-E Scores." *Research in Higher Education*, 1975, *2*, 291–303.

Perkins, J. A. (Ed.). *The University as an Organization*. New York: McGraw-Hill, 1974.

Pervin, L. A. "Satisfaction and Perceived Self-Environment Similarity: A Semantic Differential Study of Student-College Interaction." *Journal of Personality*, 1967a, *35*, 623–634.

Pervin, L. A. "A Twenty-College Study of Student × College Interaction Using TAPE (Transactional Analysis of Personality and Environment): Rationale, Reliability, and Validity." *Journal of Educational Psychology*, 1967b, *58*, 290–302.

Pervin, L. A. "The College as a Social System: Student Perception of Students, Faculty, and Administration." *Journal of Educational Research*, 1968a, *61*, 281–284.

Pervin, L. A. "Performance and Satisfaction as a Function of Individual-Environment Fit." *Psychological Bulletin*, 1968b, *69*, 56–68.

Pervin, L. A., and Rubin, D. B. "Student Dissatisfaction with College and the College Dropout: A Transactional Approach." *Journal of Social Psychology*, 1967, *72*, 285–295.

Pervin, L. A., and Smith, S. H. "Further Test of the Relationship Between Satisfaction and Perceived Self-Environment Similarity." *Perceptual and Motor Skills*, 1968, *26*, 835–838.

Peterson R. E. *Technical Manual: College Student Questionnaires.* Princeton, N.J.: Educational Testing Service, 1965.

Peterson, R. E. *College Student Questionnaire: Technical Manual.* Princeton, N.J.: Educational Testing Service, 1968.

Peterson, R. E. *The Crisis of Purpose.* Washington, D.C.: ERIC Clearinghouse on Higher Education, 1970.

Peterson, R. E. "Toward Institutional Goal Consciousness." In *Proceedings, Western Regional Conference on Testing Problems.* Berkeley, Calif.: Educational Testing Service, 1971.

Peterson, R. E. "Goals for California Higher Education: A Survey of 116 Academic Communities." Report to Joint Committee on the Master Plan for Higher Education, California State Legislature, 1973.

Peterson, R. E., and Bilorusky, J. A. *May 1970: The Campus Aftermath of Cambodia and Kent State.* Berkeley, Calif.: Carnegie Commission on Higher Education, 1971.

Peterson, R. E., and others. *Institutional Functioning Inventory: Preliminary Technical Manual.* Princeton, N.J.: Educational Testing Service, 1970.

Peterson, R. E., and Uhl, N. P. *Institutional Goals Inventory: Comparative Data and Bibliography.* Princeton, N.J.: Educational Testing Service, 1975.

Peterson, R. E., and Uhl, N. P. *Institutional Goals Inventory Manual.* Princeton, N.J.: Educational Testing Service, 1976.

Peterson, R. E., and Uhl, N. P. *Formulating College and University Goals: A Guide for Using the IGI.* Princeton, N.J.: Educational Testing Service, 1977.

Pfeifer, C. M., and Schneider, B. "University Climate Perceptions by Black and White Students." *Journal of Applied Psychology,* 1974, *59,* 660–662.

Richards, J. M., Jr., and Braskamp, L. A. "Who Goes Where to Junior College?" In L. A. Munday (Ed.), *The Two-Year College and Its Students: An Empirical Report.* Iowa City, Iowa: American College Testing Program, 1969.

Richards, J. M., Jr., Rand, L. M., and Rand, L. P. "Description of Junior Colleges." *Journal of Educational Psychology,* 1966, *57,* 207–214.

Richards, J. M., Jr., Rand, L. M., and Rand, L. P. "A Description of

Medical College Environments." *American Educational Research Journal,* 1968, *5,* 647–658.

Richards, J. M., Jr., Seligman, R., and Jones, P. K. "Faculty and Curriculum as Measures of College Environment." *Journal of Educational Psychology,* 1970, *61,* 324–332.

Riesman, D., and Jencks, C. "The Viability of the American College." In N. Sanford (Ed.), *The American College.* New York: Wiley, 1962.

Rock, D. A., Baird, L. L., and Linn, R. L. "Interaction between College Effects and Students' Aptitudes." *American Educational Research Journal,* 1972, *9,* 149–161.

Romine, B. H., David, J. A., and Gehman, W. S. "The Interaction of Learning, Personality Traits, Ability, and Environment: A Preliminary Study." *Educational and Psychological Measurement,* 1970, *30,* 337–347.

Roose, K. S., and Andersen, C. J. *A Rating of Graduate Programs.* Washington, D.C.: American Council on Education, 1970.

Rothman, J. *Planning and Organizing for Social Change: Action Principles from Social Science Research.* New York: Columbia University Press, 1974.

Sarason, S. B. *The Culture of the School and the Problem of Change.* New York: Allyn and Bacon, 1971.

Sarason, S. B. *The Creation of Settings and the Future Societies.* San Francisco: Jossey-Bass, 1972.

Sasajima, M., Davis, J. A., and Peterson, R. E. "Organized Student Protest and Institutional Climate." *American Educational Research Journal,* 1968, *5,* 291–304.

Saunders, D. R. *A Factor-Analytic Study of the AI and the CCI.* New York: College Entrance Examination Board, 1962.

Saunders, D. R., "A Factor Analytic Study of the AI and the CCI." *Multivariate Behavioral Research,* 1969, *4,* 329–346.

Schulberg, H. C., and Baker, F. "Program Evaluation Models and the Implementation of Research Findings." In F. G. Caro (Ed.), *Readings in Evaluation Research.* New York: Russell Sage Foundation, 1971.

Scott, W. A. "Attitude Measurement." In F. Lindzey and E. Aronson (Eds.), *The Handbook of Social Psychology.* Vol. 2. Reading, Mass.: Addison-Wesley, 1968.

Scriven, M. "Evaluating Educational Programs." *The Urban Review,* 1969, *3,* 20–22.

*The Second Newman Report: National Policy and Higher Education.* Cambridge, Mass.: M.I.T. Press, 1973.

Selvin, H. C., and Hagstrom, W. B. "The Classification of Formal Peer Groups." In T. M. Newcomb and E. K. Wilson (Eds.), *College Peer Groups.* Chicago: Aldine, 1966.

Sinder, J. G., and Osgood, C. E. (Eds.). *Semantic Differential Technique: A Sourcebook.* Chicago: Aldine, 1969.

Skager, R. W. "Review of Stern Environment Indexes." In O. K. Buros (Ed.), *The Seventh Mental Measurements Yearbook.* Highland Park, N.J.: Gryphon Press, 1972.

Smail, P. M., DeYong, A. J., and Moos, R. H. "The University Residence Environment Scale: A Method for Describing University Student Living Groups." *Journal of College Student Personnel,* 1974, *15,* 357–365.

Sorenson, P. F., Jr., and others. "Student Perceptions of University Power Structures." *Journal of Educational Research,* 1973, *66,* 195–198.

Southern Regional Education Board. *Fact Book on Higher Education in the South, 1975–1976.* Atlanta, Ga.: Southern Regional Education Board, 1976.

Spaulding, C. B., and Turner, H. A. "Political Orientation and Field of Specialization among College Professors." *Sociology of Education,* 1968, *41,* 245–262.

Stark, J. S. "The Relation of Disparity in Student and Faculty Educational Attitudes to Early Student Transfer from College." *Research in Higher Education,* 1975, *3,* 329–344.

Stark, J. S. *The Many Faces of Educational Consumerism.* Lexington, Mass.: Lexington Books, 1977.

Stark, J. S. *Inside Information: A Handbook on Better Information for Student Choice.* Washington, D.C.: American Association for Higher Education, 1978.

Stern, G. G. "Environments for Learning." In N. Sanford (Ed.), *The American College: A Psychological and Social Interpretation of Higher Learning.* New York: Wiley, 1962.

Stern, G. G. "Characteristics of the Intellectual Climate in College Environments." *Harvard Educational Review,* 1963a, *33,* 5–41.

Stern, G. G. *Scoring Instructions and College Norms: Activities Index and College Characteristics Index.* New York: Syracuse University Psychological Research Center, 1963b.

Stern, G. G. "Student Ecology and the College Environment." *Journal of Medical Education,* 1965, *40,* 132–154.

Stern, G. G. *People in Context.* New York: Wiley, 1970.

Stigler, G. *The Theory of Price.* New York: Macmillan, 1967.

Strong, S. R. "Review of the College Student Satisfaction Questionnaire." In O. K. Buros (Ed.), *The Eighth Mental Measurements Yearbook.* Highland Park, N.J.: Gryphon Press, 1978.

Struening, E. L. "Social Area Analysis as a Method of Evaluation." In E. L. Struening and M. Guttentag (Eds.), *Handbook of Evaluation Research.* Beverly Hills, Calif.: Sage Publications, 1975.

*Student Reactions to College: Manual for Users.* Princeton, N.J.: Educational Testing Service, 1974.

*Student Reactions to College: Preliminary Comparative Data.* Princeton, N.J.: Educational Testing Service, 1978.

Sturtz, S. A. "Age Differences in College Student Satisfaction." *Journal of College Student Personnel,* 1971, *12,* 220–223.

Suchman, E. A. *Evaluative Research.* New York: Russell Sage Foundation, 1967.

Suchman, E. A. "Evaluating Education Programs." *Urban Review,* 1969, *3,* 15–17.

Summers, G. F. (Ed.). *Attitude Measurement.* Chicago: Rand McNally, 1970.

Terenzini, P. T., and Pascarella, E. T. "An Assessment of the Construct Validity of the Clark-Trow Typology of College Student Subcultures." *American Educational Research Journal,* 1977, *14,* 225–248.

Thistlethwaite, D. T. "College Press and Student Achievement." *Journal of Educational Psychology,* 1959, *50,* 183–191.

Thistlethwaite, D. T. "College Press and Changes in Study Plans of Talented Students." *Journal of Educational Psychology,* 1960, *51,* 222–234.

Thistlethwaite, D. T. "Rival Hypotheses for Explaining the Effects of Different Learning Environments." *Journal of Educational Psychology,* 1963, *53,* 310–315.

Thistlethwaite, D. T. "Effects of Teacher and Peer Subcultures

Upon Student Aspiration." *Journal of Educational Psychology*, 1966, *57*, 35–47.

Thistlethwaite, D. T. *The Effects of College Environments on Students' Decisions to Attend Graduate School*. USOE Project Report, Nashville, Tenn.: Vanderbilt University, 1968.

Thistlethwaite, D. T. "Some Ecological Effects of Entering a Field of Study." *Journal of Educational Psychology*, 1969, *60*, 284–293.

Thistlethwaite, D. L., and Wheeler, N. "Effects of Teaching and Peer Subcultures upon Student Aspirations." *Journal of Educational Psychology*, 1966, *57*, 35–47.

Trow, M. "Student Cultures and Administrative Action." In R. L. Sutherland, and others (Eds.), *Personality Factors on the College Campus*. Austin, Tex.: Hogg Foundation for Mental Health, 1962.

Trow, M. (Ed.). *Teachers and Students*. New York: McGraw-Hill, 1975.

Tupes, E. C., and Madden, H. L. "Relationships Between College Characteristics and Later Performance of College Graduates." *Educational and Psychological Measurement*, 1970, *30* (2), 273–282.

Uhl, N. *Identifying Institutional Goals: Encouraging Convergence of Opinion Through the Delphi Technique*. Durham, N.C.: National Laboratory for Higher Education, 1971.

Uhl, N. "Identifying Institutional Goals." In P. Caws, S. D. Ripley, and P. C. Ritterbash (Eds.), *The Bankruptcy of Academic Policy*. Washington, D.C.: Acropolis Books, 1972.

Uhl, N. "A Faculty Evaluation System." Paper presented at the annual meeting of the Southern Conference on Institutional Research, Atlanta, 1976.

University of North Carolina, General Administration, Planning Division. *Statistical Abstract of Higher Education in North Carolina*. Chapel Hill, N.C.: University of North Carolina, 1978.

Vreeland, R., and Bidwell, C. "Organizational Effects on Student Attitudes: A Study of the Harvard Houses." *Sociology of Education*, 1965, *38*, 233–250.

Walsh, W. B. *Theories of Person-Environment Interaction: Implications for the College Student*. Iowa City, Iowa: American College Testing Program, 1973.

Warren, J. R., and Roelfs, P. J. "Student Reactions to College:

The Development of a Questionnaire Through Which Junior College Students Describe Their College Experiences." Research Project Report 72–23. Princeton, N.J.: Educational Testing Service, 1972.

Webb, E. J., and others. *Unobtrusive Measures: Nonreactive Research in the Social Sciences.* Chicago: Rand McNally, 1966.

Weiss, C. H. (Ed.). *Evaluating Action Programs: Readings in Social Action and Education.* Boston: Allyn and Bacon, 1972.

West, E. D., and Andersen, C. J. "Changing Public/Private Ratios in Higher Education." *Educational Record,* 1970, *51,* 347–350.

Wilcox, B. L., and Holahan, C. J. "Social Ecology of the Megadorm in University Student Housing." *Journal of Educational Psychology,* 1976, *68,* 453–458.

Wilson, L. *The Academic Man.* London: Oxford University Press, 1942.

Wilson, R., and others. *College Professors and Their Impact on Students.* New York: Wiley, 1975.

Yale Daily News. *The Insiders' Guide to the Colleges, Compiled and Edited by the Staff of the Yale Daily News.* (6th ed.) New York: Berkley, 1975.

Yankelovich, D. *The New Morality: A Profile of American Youth in the 70s.* New York: McGraw-Hill, 1974.

# Index

A

Academic Alienation Scales, described, 256–257
Academic Development, as institutional goal, 31, 35, 40
Accountability/Efficiency, as institutional goal, 34, 37
Achievement (Ach) scale, for student orientation, 243
Activities Index (AI), and perceptual measures, 17–18, 252

Administrators: attitudes of, 60; and campus surveys, 194; and institutional functioning, 30, 32–33; and institutional goals, 35–37
Advanced Training, as institutional goal, 31, 36, 40, 240
Advancing Knowledge (AK) scale, and institutional functioning, 120, 121, 237
Affiliation (Affl) scale, and student orientation, 244

Meeting Local Needs *(continued)*
236–237; as institutional goal, 31, 36
Menne, J. W., 235
Messiah College, climate at, 229
Micek, S. S., 40, 148
Michigan, University of, graduate department ratings at, 15
Michigan State University, living units climate at, 42–43, 60
Miller, L. D., 234
Millett, J. D., 96
Minnesota, University of: environment of, 91; graduate department ratings at, 15
Mission, changes in, and environment changes, 155–173
Mitchell, J. V., Jr., 232, 250, 254, 256
Moos, R. H., 43, 106, 107, 249, 250
Morstain, B. R., 94, 246
Mortimer, K. P., 114
Murray, H. A., 17, 116, 250–251

**N**

Nash, P., 240
National Association of College and University Business Officers (NACUBO), 133
National Center for Education Statistics, 156
National Center for Higher Education Management Systems, 83, 133, 222
National Commission on the Financing of Postsecondary Education, 52
National Merit Scholarship Corporation, 76, 261
National Task Force for Better Information for Student Choice, 52–53
Newcomb, T. M., 10, 19, 42, 221, 231
Nixon, E., 211

Noeth, R. J., 52, 262
North Carolina, long-range planning in, 138–139, 145

**O**

Off-Campus Learning, as institutional goal, 34, 37, 242
Omnibus Personality Inventory (OPI): correlations with, 231, 245; and subcultures, 94
Oral Roberts University, success of, 157
Osgood, C. E., 258

**P**

Pace, C. R., 14, 17–19, 20$n$, 21, 23, 42, 58, 65, 66, 90–112, 140, 142, 143, 148, 159, 229–230, 246, 250, 253
Panackal, A. A., 234
Panos, R. J., 62–63
Parekh, S. B., 133
Parsons, T., 96
Pascarella, E. T., 30, 60, 234
Pelz, D. C., 114
Pemberton, C. L., 246
Pennsylvania, University of, graduate department ratings at, 15
Perceptual measures: described, 17–41; of graduate and professional schools, 43–49; limitations and strengths of, 58–61; for other purposes, 49, 52; for students as consumers, 52–58; of subenvironments, 41–43
Perkins, J. A., 96
Personal development dimension, of environmental press, 107, 109
Personnel Services scale, at Purdue, 52, 262
Pervin, L. A., 264–265, 266
Peterson, R. E., 19, 21, 23–24, 30–31, 35–37, 40, 94, 97, 120, 121$n$, 214, 217–218, 234, 238, 242
Pfeifer, C. M., 49, 267
Physical sciences, graduate school